THE SACRAMENTS IN A SECULAR AGE

THE SACRAMENTS
in a secular age

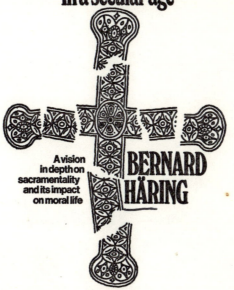

A vision
in depth on
sacramentality
and its impact
on moral life

BERNARD HÄRING

SP St Paul Publications

ST PAUL PUBLICATIONS
SLOUGH   SL3 6BT   ENGLAND

Copyright © B. Häring 1976

Imprimatur: D. Valente
Nihil obstat: + Charles Grant, Bishop of Northampton
                15 March 1976

First published May 1976

Printed in Great Britain by the Society of St Paul, Slough

ISBN 0-85439-122-3

CONTENTS

ACKNOWLEDGEMENTS

Repeatedly I have been teaching a course on the sacraments and Christian life at the Accademia Alfonsiana (the graduate school of moral theology in Rome), and I have taught such a course once at the University of San Francisco and once at the Catholic University of America. Each time I re-worked the course anew. For the outcome I am greatly indebted to the lively and active participation of my students who come from different cultures and traditions. I want to express my gratitude to them.

I thank Sr Gabrielle L. Jean and Mrs Josephine Ryan who at the various stages of the development of this book assisted me generously by typing and in the wording of the English. I also thank Mrs Rijnep Moskey for careful secretarial help.

INTRODUCTORY CHAPTER

The Protestant theologian Langdon Gilkey sees the four essential traits of Catholicism in 'people, tradition, *caritas*, and sacramental presence'. In all-embracing openness to the joys and hopes, the sorrows and anguishes, the experiences of all of mankind and with a strong sense of continuity, Catholic theology, hand in hand with the pastors, has to work for a convincing synthesis that brings the best of tradition home in order to help people to find the integration of faith and life. Gilkey notes, 'a sympathetic observer may well state that *this* is where the hope of revitalized Christianity probably lies'. [1] What he expects from the present renewal is above all that 'the sacraments would bring to explicit expression at appropriate points the divine presence in all of life, as the divine Word would mediate the divine judgement and mercy to all issues of common life'. [2]

It is my conviction that a profound fidelity to the biblical vision of creation and redemption can enable us to present a sacramental model of the Church as well as of Christian life in a way that can overcome the gap between worship and morality. To this end I give great attention here to the sacramentality of all of creation, of the 'signs of the times', and to the sacramentality of the human person as 'image and likeness of God'. The seven sacraments of the Church will be envisaged only after having considered how in Jesus Christ all things and

[1] Langdon Gilkey, *Catholicism Confronts Modernity* (New York: Seabury Press, 1975), p. 22.
[2] *Op. cit.*, p. 198.

1

events, but especially Christ-like persons and communities, are tangible signs of God's loving, creative and redeeming presence.

Such an endeavour goes against the currents of secularism and horizontalism; but equal care must be given to capture the positive challenge of an era of secularization. Only a broader, truly biblical understanding of sacramentality can counteract the dichotomy between religion and common life.

Since the Second Vatican Council, a good part of the Church has made a serious effort to bridge the gap separating worship from daily moral life in both the private and social spheres. Moral theology is duty-bound to serve this effort to which the whole Church is committed if the liturgical and other reforms are to bear the rightly expected fruit.

A primary pre-requisite is that theology be thoroughly conscious of its insertion into the history of salvation. In this awareness the theologian comes to accept the past heritage as an existential response to a historical situation. In a serene re-thinking, he is then better equipped to sift the real possibilities from those features which changing times have made meaningless, and thus to place his own thinking more validly in the present.

A joyful vision of Christian life, centred wholly in Christ whom we meet in the sacraments, is a patrimony of the sacred scriptures and of the various traditions. In the Orient, it has been kept alive until now although with developments varying with the different churches. In the western churches, on the contrary, after St Leo the Great, this central vision fell into second place. Never, however, has it lacked supporters. In the seventeenth and eighteenth centuries, for example, there was the French school of Cardinal Bérulle; in the last century in Germany, Magnus Jocham presented the whole of moral theology in a clearly sacramental perspective centred in Christ. Despite these and other noble efforts, however, the teaching and moral catechesis of the West often remained bound to a certain sacramentalism favouring legalism.

Allow me to explain further. The traditional manuals (Génicot, Noldin, Vermeersch, Marc-Gestermann, Merkelbach, Aertnys-Damen and so on) presented Christian life by taking the decalogue as starting point; the written law was integrated with the natural law which was subsequently set forth almost like a moral code written once and for all. Then were added all the Church laws, without any clear distinction between the permanent values of the law written in man's heart and the norms of moral codes reflecting past historical conditions. Only after this were the sacraments mentioned, with countless reminders of the vast aggregate of regulations, laws and rubrics formulated by Church authorities in view of a becoming celebration. The moralists detailed which rules obliged under pain of mortal sin and which under venial sin, all the while placing the greatest importance on sacred things: stones, places, vestments and the like. 'Validity' became a function of external forms. Little was said relating moral life to the sacraments; a brief hint here and there was about all one could expect. Supposedly, the sacraments conferred grace to observe the norms regulating the moral life as expressed in the various legal formulations.

The Second Vatican Council firmly opposed every form of legalism and sacramentalism. Considering the Church as a sacrament, and experience of the Church as sacramental experience, it sought to reform the liturgy and the whole sacramental vision so that they would bear the fruit of love and justice for the life of the world. If today we wish to present Christian life in a way that will truly help our priests, our educators and the faithful who have been accustomed to a certain sacramental formalism in worship and morality, it is imperative that we set out decisively on the path indicated by the Council.

To this end we need keep foremost in our mind the close interdependence that exists between the manner of sacramental celebration and attitudes towards moral life. If, in celebrating the sacraments, there is no room left for spontaneity or initiative (with serious preparation and a context of order, however), the moral life and the moral theologian's presentation of it will invariably reflect the same lack of vitality.

Confronted as we are by the depersonalizing forces of modern life, both young people and thoughtful adults experience acutely the need for a morality that focuses squarely on the person: a morality that recognizes the pre-eminence of the person who cannot be sacrificed to any institution, organization or cause, a morality that places *things* at the service of the *person* and community of persons.

Theology ought to welcome this desire for a morality that functions for the personal good. The sacraments are then envisaged much more clearly as a personal presence of Christ, as personal encounters, as messages of joy and of life. They attest to the fact that Christ did not come to serve the law but that the law is made to serve the person. Christ himself lived and died for all persons.

Since the sacraments are personal and personalizing encounters, great openness and constant vigilance are essential in pastoral, moral and liturgical theology if sacramental celebrations are to awaken all the responsive energies of the person. They are creative events that generate in the participants the desire and will to grow in the love of Christ, and through Christ in the love of the Father and of the brethren who are created and recreated in the image and likeness of God.

We accept the fact that the hierarchical Church needs to watch over the renewal so that it will not become anarchy; we must also keep in mind that a considerable number of bishops, who have contributed so much towards liturgical reform by approving the decrees of the Council, have been products of a schooling in moral theology which stressed the juridical, the legalistic and the sacramentalistic. In no way do I mention this to arouse aversion towards them; rather, I wish to encourage a mutual understanding, one favouring dialogue which alone can help both parties, the bishops and the faithful. Moral theology, if it wishes to serve the Church, must reconcile *docility to the magisterium* with *openness to the intuitions of charismatic leaders* who help the magisterium to take new steps forward. A sound presentation of the inter-dependence of the liturgy and moral life remains indispensable in working towards a better understanding of the profound significance of the actual reforms, and in preparing for others.

One of the greatest evils in the Church has been what the saintly Rosmini called 'the first wound of the body of Christ': alienation, isolation of the priestly class, and isolation of the liturgy from life. There is still much to be done to eliminate this dichotomy which Karl Marx and others condemned with all the wrath of the old prophets, lacking however their piety and integrating vision. These men accused the Church and religion of distracting man from his real task of building an economic and social system that would serve man and liberate him from all forms of alienation. They have condemned a religion that does not heed the humble ones, the victims of discrimination, or that does not care about better conditions of life. The Marxists viewed religion's promise of future bliss as individualistic in type, weakening the lower classes' capacity to form an enlightened social conscience capable of helping them escape from slavery and servility.

The wrathful prophet Karl Marx remained in the vicious circle of reaction and reductionism. In these days of upheaval, we surely gain much by turning to genuine prophets, those of the great tradition of Israel and the Church, prophets of the last century, like Rosmini and Newman, and prophets of our own days. All their concern and effort sought to bridge the gap between daily life and faith. Whoever follows Christ, the Prophet, desires nothing less than that all life — private, social, cultural, political — be worship of the living, loving God.

Are we disposed to listen to the prophets of our time? Dietrich Bonhoeffer, while he was waiting for his execution, tried to respond to the question: 'How can Christ become the Lord of the religionless as well? Are there religionless Christians?' His response is surprising: 'In that case Christ is no longer an object of religion, but something quite different, really the Lord of the world'. [3] Bonhoeffer opposes life-giving faith to individualistic and evasive religiosity. The conversion he calls for is to 'be caught up into the way of Jesus Christ, caught up into the messianic suffering of God in Jesus Christ'. 'The "religious act", is something partial; "faith" is something whole, involving the whole of one's life'. [4] Bonhoeffer feels that in this perspective has to be raised the fundamental question: 'What is the place of worship and prayer in a religionless situation?'. [5] He really means the situation where faith permeates the whole of life. The sacraments of faith must free us from frozen traditions, from escapism and other forms of alienation.

However, we are not to forget the constant temptation to alienation that arises from the worldly world, in the economic, social, cultural, political realm as long as similiar alienation is found even in religious people and in religious institutions, where lack of faith and of discernment confuses moral and religious questions of all kinds. One of the main purposes of this book is precisely to counteract these dangers in the field of liturgy and moral life.

(1)   The genuine priestly and above all the great prophetic tradition, as well as the deepest experiences of people of our secular era, prove that individual persons and communities are not condemned to become slaves of idols, ideologies and tyrants. People who learn to worship God in all their life with all their being, will find their true self. They will not be enslaved to their own work. But they realize that the danger exists. A genuine renewal, therefore, rejects all forms of alienation, any separation of life and worship. Such is the spirit of the great theology of the sabbath in the first chapters of Genesis. Man is destined to rule the earth but in the image of God and in such a way that he does not become enslaved by the economic structures

[3] Dietrich Bonhoeffer, *Letters and Papers from Prison* (New York: Macmillan, 1967), p. 141.
[4] *Op. cit.,* p. 191.
[5] *Op. cit.,* p. 141.

of his own creation, no matter how beautiful they seem. Only if he finds his centre of gravity and of value in God can he preserve and develop his freedom, become able to subject the earth, every institution and structure to the welfare of persons.

Such is the vision expressed by St Paul: 'Knowing God, they have refused to honour him as God or to render him thanks. Hence all their thinking has ended in futility and their misguided minds are plunged in darkness. They boast of their wisdom but they have made fools of themselves, exchanging the splendour of the immortal God for an image shaped like mortal man, even for images of birds, beasts and creeping things. For this reason God has given them up to the vileness of their own desires and the consequent degradation of their bodies.... Thus, because they have not seen fit to acknowledge God, he has given them up to their own depraved reason' (Rom 1: 21-25, 28). Marxism and modern secularism are two horrifying examples of such gigantic alienation.

(2) Another form of alienation is that of an *ossified cult,* a form of worship so rigid as to be incapable of expressing the freshness and newness of the divine message or of communicating it to the world of human hopes. Christ himself sharply and explicitly protested against all those religious forms which had become, for man, a cause of alienation from God and from his neighbour. Great prophets and many Christian saints, moved by the prophetic spirit, have reacted forcibly against this alienation through religious forms which may have been brimming with life and actuality earlier but which became ossified and meaningless in subsequent historical periods.

The prophets were gifted with a sweeping view of human history, a vision based on the worship of the one God and Creator whose presence they discovered in all events of daily life. They had encountered the living God, and the experience of his holiness drove them to seek the good of all men, to give witness to their brothers of God's love and concern for all who are created in his image and likeness.

The prophetic call to renewal challenges all forms of worship, all formulations of religious truth which are not a living testimony of faith in the one God and do not actively lead to love of the poor and the alien, our neighbour. Renewal is not pitted against what is truly priestly, but against those sterile forms of religion which do not bear the fruit of love for the life of the world, that is, against priestly decadence. The parable of the merciful Samaritan stands as a prophetic protest against a clergy (priests and levites) more preoccupied with rubrics, minutiae and cultural precepts than with the man lying wounded and bathed in his blood.

(3) True adoration and prophetic renewal find their zenith, perfection and full integration in Christ, whose whole life — particularly in his death and resurrection — is at once *adoration* of God in spirit and truth and *full manifestation of love* for the one Father of all men and Creator of all things.

Christ the Prophet likes symbols. He often drastically expresses truth by symbol. When he presents himself at a general baptism in the Jordan (Lk 3:21), he joins miserable sinners, prostitutes, blackmailers, robbers, a 'crowd of bad characters' as the Pharisees would say. By this gesture, Christ inexorably symbolizes how he identifies himself with his brethren, how he bears their burden. He thus goes beyond the symbol to the full reality of baptism: his death, surrounded by those crucifying him, others cursing him, and yet, in that hour, befriending the brigand at his right and praying for those who crucified him.

All of Christ's life symbolizes the full reality of truth and love incarnate. In flesh and blood, in his life and in his death, he fully becomes the martyr (witness), the Sacrament of God's saving presence, and can say 'the one who sees me sees the Father'. Not with words alone but with his whole life and death he points to the Father and draws us to him who is calling all men to be his sons and daughters.

Christ never speaks in the abstractions so common in our artificial theology. He resorts to parables which come close to the experiences and feelings of people in their everyday life. With symbols, gestures and deeds he gives flesh and blood to the gospel he proclaims. With his whole being he communicates to the eyes, ears, heart and mind, to the whole person. 'We have seen the Word of life', exclaims John, 'we have heard him, we have touched him!' (1 Jn 1:1-3).

This is what sacrament means for us: not an abstract ritualism but Christ in all his life and in his death. It is Christ with his arms outstretched on the cross, drawing all men to the love of the Father. The sacraments require true discipleship whereby one makes visible to the world the life-giving love of Christ.

(4) The renewal launched by the Second Vatican Council, a work guided by a truly prophetic spirit, took as its point of departure the reform of the liturgy. It was natural, then, to conclude the Council's work with *The pastoral constitution on the Church in the modern world,* calling for prophetic vigilance for the 'signs of the times' (GS 4). They are also called 'signs of the presence of God' (GS 11). This call leads to new avenues for the understanding of a sacramental spirituality of history and creation. The sacraments of the Church must be so understood and celebrated as to bring us in contact with the historical events that stand as signs of God's presence, a gift and challenge to men.

The Second Vatican Council evinced deep concern about the gap between religion and life and eagerly searched for a synthesis. Use of the vernacular, adaptation of rites to the diverse contemporary cultures, a firm insistence on the centrality of the paschal mystery — all tended to restore the desired unity between everyday life and liturgical celebration. 'It is through the liturgy, specially the divine Eucharistic Sacrifice "that the work of our redemption is expressed". The liturgy is thus the outstanding means by which the faithful can express in their lives and manifest to others the mystery of Christ and the true nature of the Church' (SC 2). The text then goes on to present the nature and mission of the Church, starting from her mission in the world, and it does so in such a way as to reconstitute the lost synthesis.

B

The introductory article of *Lumen gentium*, the dogmatic constitution on the Church, specifies the perspective in which both ecclesiology and sacramental theology are to be considered. Since Christ, 'light of the nations' brightens 'the countenance of the Church', she has come to understand herself above all as 'a kind of sacrament or sign of intimate union with God and of the unity of all mankind' (LG 1). We find here that synthetic vision which was later elaborated more fully in the pastoral constitution *Gaudium et spes*. [6]

The self-understanding of the Church as sacrament requires that she be truly a sign of salvation for all men. Hence, she cannot isolate herself from the world or give in to any form of egotistic introversion. Her members, the 'priestly people', are called *to witness and to serve in the world*, while the ministerial priesthood, in turn, serves the priestly people of God by leading each of them to fulfil his mission in the Church and in the world in increasingly more significant ways. The Church understands herself as the messianic people whose law is the Spirit. She is called and guided by the Spirit to become more and more a royal priesthood, and thus a sign of God's gracious presence. The discrepancy between her vocation and her pilgrim reality will not constitute a credibility gap so long as she humbly confesses her faults and shortcomings, and presents herself as a 'sacrament of continuous conversion'.

The constitutions and decrees of the Council sought a priestly-prophetic synthesis in the whole life of the Church.

(5) It is in this perspective that the following pages will attempt to synthesize, in a sacramental key, the whole of Christian life. Such a synthesis, of necessity, begins with Christ: 'For a change of priesthood must mean a change of law' (Heb 7: 12).

The centre and foundation of Christian life, of the new covenant and the new law, is Christ, priest and prophet, servant

---

[6] Avery Dulles, in his illuminating book *Models of the Church* (Garden City, N.J.: Doubleday, 1974), shows well how essential the sacramental self-understanding of the Church is in the Second Vatican Council.

and king of glory. He is, as the Fathers of the Church called him, the 'law and covenant'. His prophetic message and priesthood culminate on the altar of the cross and continue with the sending of the Spirit, so that his people, sanctified in his sacrifice and the sacraments, are united with him in the challenging signs of his love and life's truth.

What makes Christian morality distinct from every other ethical system is precisely the fact that it has its origin, form, norm and goal in the priesthood of Christ and in the sacraments of the new law. The whole of sacred scripture, particularly Paul and John, and the Fathers of the Church of both the East and West, insist on this sacramental Christocentrism. Medieval theology, still following the patristic tradition, generally concerned itself with life and Christian morality, especially in its treatises on the sacraments of the new law, on creation and redemption. The final purpose of creation is seen in the light of the new creation, the privileged signs of God's presence which we call sacraments.

The liturgical renewal now allows us to return to a similar vision. The reform of the liturgy conditions the renewal of moral theology and vice versa; it brings this about in two rather dissimilar steps.

(a) It seeks first to recover the realism of symbols; the words and the rites are meant to be a sacramental kerygma. 'Grant us, O Lord, to honour the signified reality in your glorious sacraments. . . .' So does the Church invite us to pray, in the final prayer of the Eucharistic celebration commemorating the martyrdom of John the Baptist. In a liturgical celebration, the gestures, rites and words form one message and praise of God by making clear and intelligible that reality which the glorious sacraments signify and bring about.

In times of religious decadence, priests along with pious people generally have considered the rites, rubrics, and even the signs and words, primarily if not exclusively as laws and as conditions for validity. The first question of the moralists was, 'Do they bind under pain of mortal or venial sin?' And from

the obedient sons of the Church came a commitment to a most
scrupulous external observance. If any psychic energy remained,
they tried also to be recollected enough to pray interiorly.

Today's rediscovered liturgical piety venerates 'the signified
reality of the glorious sacraments'. It seeks primarily to understand the full meaning of the sacramental signs and words and
how, through them, the liturgy carries out the essential sacramental message. By perceiving the significance of the sacred
mysteries, we come to a deeper understanding of all the signs
of God's saving presence in the world, and to a greater vigilance
for the present opportunities. The sacramental signs and words
(*sacramenta significata*) then serve to nourish the faith and to
shape the life of believers. Indeed, there is a close relationship
between liturgical action, personal prayer and the transformation
of one's whole life. 'The sacraments of the new law are causes
and signs which, as we commonly say, bring forth that which
they signify.' [7]

Liturgical-sacramental spirituality is based on the unity of
body and mind, signs and words, perception of meaning and
interior piety. In a way, the sacraments are a prolongation of
the mystery of the Incarnation, an extension of the open arms
on the cross. Therefore, liturgical spirituality is essentially
'incarnate'. The symbolic expression of the liturgy turns our
attention and our will to daily life in the light of faith (SC 2).
'Thus, what was visible in our Redeemer has now passed into
the sacraments.' [8] The first and indispensable period of liturgical
renewal found classical expression fifty years ago in a book by
Romano Guardini, *Sacred Signs*. [9]

(b) The second step in rediscovering the unity of life and
the sacramental reality has to do with the moral life which

---

[7] Thomas Aquinas, *Summa theologica,* III : 62 : 1 : 1.

[8] Leo the Great, 'Quod Redemptoris nostri conspicuum fuit, in sacra-
    menta transivit', *Sermons* 74. 2, Migne PL 54, 398.

[9] Romano Guardini, *Sacred Signs* (St Louis: Pio Decimo Press, 1956);
    also by the same author, *The Spirit of the Liturgy* (New York and
    London: Sheed and Ward, 1930).

receives its norm in the gifts of God, signified by the sacraments.
The post-communion cited earlier continues, ' . . . and to rejoice
in the life it brings about in us'. In the opening prayer for the
octave day of Easter, the Church prays, ' . . . help us to put into
action in our lives, the baptism we have received with faith'.
The prayer after Communion for the second Sunday of Easter
is, 'May the Easter sacraments we have received live forever in
our minds and hearts'. The prayer after Communion for the
Wednesday of the second week of Easter, is 'May these
mysteries give us new purpose and bring us to a new life in
you'.

The capacity to understand what a truly Christian life should
be flows from the very meaning of the sacraments. A living
and enlightening celebration reveals to the Christian the reality
signified by the sacraments and, in itself, presents the gentle law
of the 'following of Christ': the law of grace which inspires a
morality of gratitude in response to God's goodness, by the use
of his gifts for the common good. It follows, therefore, that it
is not without outward communication that the sacraments
'bring forth that which they signify'.

It becomes very difficult to arrive at this second and most
urgent stage of synthesis between liturgical piety and life if the
sacramental celebration is not significant, is not performed in
a clear and authentic way, and therefore, does not indicate the
synthesis intended by Christ. An example will clarify this. The
unity of the people of God is, according to classical theology,
the chief grace indicated by the sheer significance (res et
sacramentum) of the Eucharist. In fact, the Church prays in the
offertory prayer on the feast of Corpus Christi, ' . . . may the
bread and cup we offer bring your Church the unity and peace
they signify'.

This unity and solidarity of the people of the new covenant
are not meant to remain invisible, mysterious effects of Eucharistic grace. Symbolically and perceptibly, the sacraments express
God's gift and call to unity and peace. Obviously, then, it is
incongruous for confessors and preachers to insist that the

faithful assist at the Eucharist in parishes where unity and
solidarity are non-existent, where the liturgy fails to invite it in
any visible way. Think of a parish that accepts racial discrimination with no effort of conversion. Christians cannot truly
participate in the Eucharistic celebration unless they perceive
and accept the message and the grace of the sacrament as the
norm of unity and solidarity. If in the whole life of the parish
there is little or practically no concern for fostering these
Christian and human attitudes, the lack becomes, by necessity,
strikingly evident in its way of worshipping. What does it, then,
mean to assert the doctrine that the Eucharist is the sacrament
of unity if there is no visible and effective bond uniting people
and if the cult does not change their life for the better? What
good is the sacramental activity if there does not shine through
in the participants that unity before God that would make
them operators of peace, reconciliation and unity in the world?

Since the main goal I have set for myself in this book is
the integration of worship and life, I should be remiss were I
to begin immediately with the seven sacraments. It is my hope
that we shall better appreciate their significance and spiritual
wealth if we gain that holistic vision that helps us discover God's
saving and loving presence in all of creation and history,
especially in the human persons created in the image and likeness
of God. The sacraments should help us to become for each
other, and even for those who do not yet believe, a kind of
sacrament, a visible sign of Christ's redeeming love.

The reader is invited to join me as we address ourselves to
the Christo-centric dimension of our whole life, as persons and
as communities. In the centre is Christ, the great Sacrament in
whom the Father reveals his design for all men to transform
them into the same image. Then, in the light of Christ we shall
consider the Church which, united with him and subject to him,
is a perpetual sacrament without which we should be unable
to understand and to celebrate the seven sacraments. Since all
things are made by him who is the Word, and for him, the
Word incarnate, as signs of the heavenly Father's love for men,

we shall explore the sacramental significance and dynamics of the entire creation in this light. This will help us to grasp the meaning of the sacraments of the Church for our daily life and for the most decisive events of present history. After exploring the dimensions of the seven sacraments as privileged signs of grace, faith, hope, unity and truthful adoration (second part), I shall try to illustrate, by the sacraments of matrimony and of penance, the main emphasis that gives a constructive response to the critical mind of our culture (third part).

PART ONE

CHRIST, THE GREAT SACRAMENT

THE CHURCH'S MISSION
TO BE A SACRAMENT OF CHRIST

Chapter 1

CHRIST, THE GREAT SACRAMENT

1. *Christ, summit and source of the sacramentality of all creation*

In the beginning, God spoke and 'the spirit of God hovered over the waters' (Gen 1:2). God spoke and made man in his image and likeness. In the fullness of time the Word, in whom all things were made, became flesh and dwelt among us, making visible the full extent of God's love. Through God's Word and life-giving Spirit, then, man can be a sign of God's loving presence.

Even before the coming of the Word Incarnate, all creation had a profoundly sacramental value, not by itself but because of its being the work and a word of God. [1] In the Hebrew language, the word *dabar* means both 'word' and 'work' (event). God's works are a communication, a message, so that even the material world conveys a spiritual message. That is why Teilhard de Chardin could say 'everything is sacred', but sacred only to those who, by the Spirit, perceive the message which the eternal Word of God speaks in creation and in the new creation (redemption). All the words of the Word are 'spirit and truth'.

In the dynamics of God's design, everything pointed to the moment when man, God's image, would appear, able to grasp

[1] A. Schmemann, *Sacraments and Orthodoxy* (New York: Herder and Herder, 1965).

the message, to recognize himself and everything entrusted to him as God's gift, to understand himself, also, as a word, a communication and as one called to listen, to perceive and to respond.

A sacramental vision of the works of God is already found in the Old Testament. The psalms speak of the heavens, the firmament and of all things singing the glory of God (Ps 14, 96, 97, 104). The pious Israelite senses God disclosing himself in history, his saving presence in all events, which bring redemption to those who entrust themselves to God but punishment to those who resist (cf. Ps 105, 107, 114, 135). Everything speaks of God and of his will to communicate, to reveal himself, and all this prepares for the moment of God's fullest self-manifestation in Jesus Christ.

The sacramentality of creation is not a new conception; it appears in the great tradition of the Orthodox Churches since their beginning when they were fully united in the one Christian Church. It was and is cherished by them because they see everything in the light of Christ and the Spirit, the Spirit who has hovered over the waters ever since the creative words of the Word were spoken.

The New Testament admits a distinction but no separation between supernatural revelation and natural events. The disjunction appears when comparing the outlook of the believer with that of the unbeliever or superficial man. For those who know Christ in his mission, the material world is not speechless. The created universe transcends the mere terms of causality and utility. Once the full light of Christ has shone, the believer perceives the whole of creation and the ongoing history of mankind in the perspective of God's self-disclosure, of an unfolding manifestation of God's loving design for man.

It is not a case of man proving the existence of God by his own initiative. The emphasis is absolutely on God's initiative. He truly speaks through all his works and it is he who assists man and renders him capable of sharing with others; he enables man to admire, to discover the One who discloses himself, and to adore him. 'For all that may be known of God by men lies plain before their eyes; indeed God himself has disclosed it to them. His invisible attributes, that is to say, his everlasting power and deity, have been visible ever since the world began, to the eye of reason, in the things he has made' (Rom 1: 19-20).

Paul likewise looks on the 'law inscribed in man's heart' (Rom 2: 15) — what we call 'natural law' — as a manifestation of God's work. It is indeed God's masterwork in which his presence becomes all the more visible the more man becomes sensitive to all that is good and just. It is he who acts as Revealer wherever his love glows in a loving person.

So the Incarnation of the Father's Word and creation in the Word are one great sacramental reality. Not only is the uniqueness of the revelation in Christ God's supreme self-manifestation but it discloses also the wonderful presence of God in the ongoing creation: Emmanuel, God with us. In this clearer vision, the continuing creation becomes an ongoing disclosure of God's presence in the world. 'When all things began, the Word already was. The Word dwelt with God, and what God was, the Word was. The Word, then, was with God at the beginning, and through him all things came to be; no single thing was created without him. All that came to be was alive with his life, and that life was the light of men' (Jn 1: 1-4).

These texts, like so many others, loudly proclaim that all creation is meant to be a visible word, a dynamic revelation, a message, a gift and a call to man. At the very centre is the presence of him who speaks, who gives being and maintains all things in existence. When man probes its depth, creation reveals its content of word, message and gift, the purpose of which was, from the beginning, communication. The key word is man himself, a man of body and spirit, man in community, one who, through the creative message, can appraise himself of the greatest gift of the love of God.

But the gifts cannot be isolated from the Giver. If man dismisses the Giver, he becomes alienated and lost; the gifts deteriorate by their being reduced to bare utility and thus

alienate man. Alienation, frustration, exploitation, utility, perversion come from the fact that man no longer adores, does not
realize that God is present in all of creation and fails to accept
all things and events as communication, a call to listen and to
respond in shared reflection and co-responsibility.

This sacramental vision is a challenging synthesis: through
his dynamic presence God communicates to us his calling; he
manifests to us our task through his gifts; he thus enables us to
respond to the needs of our neighbour. God's active presence
and the oneness of gift and task reach their summit in Christ,
the Word Incarnate. 'He is the visible image of the invisible
God; his is the primacy over all created things. In him everything in heaven and on earth was created, not only things visible
but also the invisible . . . the whole universe has been created
through him and for him' (Col 1: 15-17).

Visibility is understood in this text; if we are able to grasp
the message of the visible world it is due to the coming of the
Word 'in the flesh'. In the epistle to the Colossians, St Paul
takes issue with speculations on invisible angels, undue preoccupation with an invisible world or things that obscure one's
perception of visible reality. In view of creation in the Word of
the Father, in view also of the Word Incarnate, we are entitled
to ascribe to visible reality a sacramental quality, a capacity to
make the presence of God perceptible to the eyes, ears, touch,
reason, will, indeed to the whole man, and to predispose him
to respond. It is not by metaphysical jargon that man can grasp
the marvel of his being made in the image of God, the wonders
of the history of salvation, the deep meaning of the whole of
creation or history as sacrament; this can be achieved only by
turning his whole being to God.

Such a sacramental visibility is emphasized even more in
the first letter of John in relation to fraternal love: a fellowship
with one another in the sharing of the visible experience of
him 'Who is with the Father and has appeared to us' (1 Jn 1: 2).
Christ himself describes the sacramental character of his coming
'in the flesh': 'Who has seen me has seen the Father. Then how

can you say, "Show us the Father?" Do you not believe that
I am in the Father and the Father in me? I am not myself the
source of the words I speak to you: it is the Father who dwells
in me doing his own work' (Jn 14: 9-10).

This is precisely what is meant by sacramentality. We do
not speak abstractly but refer to the reality which, as gift of
God's pressing love, opens the eyes of the created person and
invites him to admire, praise and render thanks. Hominization
progresses as the world around us and especially the person are
no longer seen as things, but as a message reassuring us of God's
creative presence and telling us that if we listen to him, we shall
share in his creative freedom. All this has its *sitz im leben* in the
context of the history of salvation which reaches its apex in the
Incarnation, death and resurrection of Christ. In his hypostatic
union of divinity and humanity he is the visible Covenant, the
incarnate Solidarity with the whole of mankind: the Grace of
God present and perceptible (cf. 1 Jn 1: 1-13), the great
Sacrament of salvation.

In this same perspective we see the 'signs of the times' as
sign of God's loving and life-giving presence, and, therefore, as
a kind of sacrament. [2]

In the book of Revelation the scroll of history is secured
with seven seals, and a mighty angel asks, 'Who is worthy to
open the scroll and and to break its seals?' There is anxious
silence in heaven; for there is no one in heaven or on earth or
elsewhere worthy of opening the scroll. But then there is the
liberating response: 'Do not weep, for the lion of the tribe of
Judah, the scion of David, has won the right to open the scroll
and break its seven seals' (Rev 5: 2-5).

We cannot grasp the full religious sense of creation and of
the history of salvation without turning to him, the Word
Incarnate. Only in his light and by his grace can we understand
the meaning of history, of a person and a human community,

---

[2] Cf. my book *Evangelization Today* (Slough: St Paul Publications
1974), pp. 7-23.

of the whole created universe. On the other hand, we shall not come to a full and vital knowledge of Christ unless we see the manifestation of his loving presence everywhere.

We fail to grasp all the signs of Christ's love if we do not include the seven sacraments, those privileged signs of his ongoing work of redemption. Yet, if we see Christ in the sacraments alone or in the Bible alone, we have not found Christ as the Bible and the sacraments want to present him. They should help us to see Christ in his humility and in his greatness, in all the manifestations of his goodness in the experiences of our own life. If we look into the face of a person, even a face disfigured by sin, we can still see, with Christ's loving eyes, the image of God that can be repaired. If a child has a loving mother and father, if harmony reigns between the parents and in the household, and if the child sees them reaching out to others who need them, then the name of Jesus, our brother, and the words 'Our Father' will ring with vitality and truth for this child.

Everything has meaning for the adorer; even the most agonizing experiences are a signal of God's redemptive plan. The key to everything, particularly to the sacramental vision of life, is Christ in his full humanity, the Emmanuel, the great Sacrament of life: 'It was there from the beginning; we have heard it, we have seen it with our own eyes, we looked upon it and felt it with our hands, and it is of this we tell. Our theme is the word of life. This life was made visible; we have seen it and bear our testimony; we here declare to you the eternal life which dwelt with the Father and was made visible to us. What we have seen and heard we declare to you, so that you and we together may share in a common life' (1 Jn 1: 1-3).

2. Christ, the Sacrament of encounter with God and man

When we speak of Christ as Sacrament, we mean that he is the encounter of God with man and that, in him and through him, man comes to the saving awareness of God reaching out to man. [3]

(a) *Christ is the Emmanuel* (*God with us*)

Christ is the Sacrament of God's nearness to all men. He shows us the Father and, coming from God, he brings us the saving message. In his humanity he responds at once in a redeemed and redeeming way to the Father by embracing the whole human race in a love that truly glorifies the One God and Father of all men.

When Yahweh spoke on Mount Sinai, Moses so felt his blessed presence that he dared to ask, 'Lord, show me your countenance' (Ex 33:18). Moses received a tremendous experience of both God's holiness (*mysterium tremendum*) and God's graciousness (*mysterium fascinosum*). But Moses was alone on the top of the mount; the Israelites were not allowed — or rather were unable — to approach even the foot of the mount. Even to Moses God said, 'My face you cannot see, for no mortal man may see me and live' (Ex 33:20).

With Christ on the mount of the beatitudes it is different. 'Looking to the crowd, Jesus went up the mount and took his seat, and his disciples gathered close around him' (Mt 5:1). Waves of joy and goodness communicate the gospel to the crowd. Jesus is the Emmanuel for all men, 'God with us'. He draws people to himself. 'Jesus came down the mount and took his stand on level ground. There was a large concourse of his disciples and great numbers of people from Jerusalem and Judea and from the seaboard of Tyre and Sidon, who had come to listen to him ... and everyone in the crowd was trying to touch him because a healing power went out from him' (Lk 6:16-19).

---

[3] A classical presentation of this vision is given by E. Schillebeeckx, *Christ the Sacrament of Encounter with God* (New York and London: Sheed & Ward, 1961).

C

(b) *Christis the Sacrament of the covenant.*

In the hypostatic union of his divine and human nature, Christ is *the* Sacrament of the covenant. Throughout his life, which reached its climax in his death, he is one with the Father and one with humankind. He is the great and efficacious sign of the love of the Father who calls all men to unity, by bearing the burden of all men. Christ who died and is risen for us is the Sacrament of hope that all may be one in him. By the love that has become visible in him he is pressing us to be converted to peace, justice, mercy, brotherhood.

God's holiness that calls us to be holy, united in his love, shines forth in Christ who is at the same time the Servant of Yahweh and the servant of all men. He is the call to holiness and reconciliation. 'He is the head of the Church. He is its origin, the first to return from the dead, to be in all things supreme. For in him the complete being of God, by God's own choice, came to dwell. Through him God chose to reconcile the whole universe to himself, making peace through the shedding of his blood upon the cross to reconcile all things, whether on earth or in heaven, through him alone. Formerly you were yourselves estranged from God, you were his enemies in heart and mind, and your deeds were evil. But now by Christ's death in his body of flesh and blood, God has reconciled you to himself so that he may present you before himself as dedicated people, without blemish and innocent in his sight' (Col 1:18-22).

Paul's message of salvation centres on the sacramentality of Christ's death and resurrection. For all men and for all ages he is the visible sign of peace and reconciliation. All those who through faith and the sacraments of faith are configured with Christ can with Paul praise the Father who 'has reconciled us through Christ and has enlisted us in this service of reconciliation' (2 Cor 5:18). Christ is the effective and visible sign both of reconciliation with God and of fraternal reconciliation among men.

3. *Christ, the great Sacrament, and thus our law*

Christ, the Emmanuel and Priest-Prophet, brings to an end the old law which did not sufficiently make visible the saving presence of God. More definitively yet he brings to an end any morality based primarily on an abstract concept of law, a system of laws or even on an abstract concept of love. Christ came to make visible and experiential the saving kindness and justice of God to all humanity. That is why the whole of morality must be grounded in a sacramental vision unequivocally centred in Christ. One's share in the love and law of Christ is essentially sacramental, that is, it takes place whenever a disciple of Christ becomes a witness by word, sign and trust, making conspicuous the grace of the Holy Spirit.

The Christo-centric self-understanding of the Church of the Second Vatican Council would not be incarnate if it did not thoroughly shine through in the scientific teaching of moral theology, especially in moral catechesis. Liturgy and moral teaching together should enable the faithful to 'manifest in their life the mystery of Christ and the true nature of the Church' (SC 1).

(a) *Christ, 'Covenant and Law'*

In his moral life, the believer is not faced with an ideology or an abstract code of laws. The fundamental happening is the encounter with Christ.

In his complete union with the Father and perfect solidarity with the whole human race, Christ is the final Covenant, the visible and effective presence of the covenant and thus of the law of the covenant. It was in this sense that the early fathers of the Church spoke, basing their teaching on the scriptures.

The apologist Justin further developed this theme. 'We place our hope neither in Moses nor in the law. Things are now wholly otherwise; there is one definitive law and one covenant, more stable than all others, which God bids to be observed by all those who want to share in his heritage. . . . To us, Christ is given as the eternal and definitive law and as the faithful guide, outside of which there is no law, no precept, no valid commandment. . . . From his deeds and from the miracles attendant on them, everyone can recognize that he is the new law and the new alliance. . . .' [4]

The law of Moses and circumcision 'yielded to the blood of the Redeemer in which we believe. From Sion came another law and another Covenant, Jesus Christ. . . . Let us then walk in the light of the Lord'. [5]

'Christ, Son of the Father, by the Father's will was born of a virgin, of the descent of Abraham, of the race of Judah, of the family of David, and was announced to the whole world as the eternal law and new covenant.' [6]

Like Justin, Irenaeus applies directly to the person of Christ the words of Psalm 78:5, 'He laid on Jacob a solemn charge and established a law in Israel, which he commanded our fathers to teach their sons'. [7] So is it also with the text of Isaiah 2:3, 'For instruction issues from Zion, and out of Jerusalem comes the word of the Lord'. [8]

Clement of Alexandria expresses the same truth in almost identical terms. 'The law of the Lord is blameless. It guides souls. The same Saviour becomes law and word (*nómos kaì lógos*); thus the *kerygma* of Peter is already found in the prophet Isaiah: "For instruction issues from Zion and out of Jerusalem comes the word of the Lord".' [9] In the *Stromata* it is stated that the resemblance of the spirit of the true gnostic to God

---

[4] Justin, *Dialogue with Tryphon*, 11; in Migne PG 6, 497-499.

[5] *Ibid.*, 24, PG 6, 528.

[6] *Ibid.*, 43, PG 6, 568; see also 51, PG 6, 599; 65, PG 6, 625; 122, PG 6, 760.

[7] Irenaeus, *Against the Heresies*, III, ch. 16, 3; PG 7, 923.

[8] *Ibid.*, IV, ch. 34, 4, PG 7, 1085.

[9] Clement of Alexandria, *Eglogae* 58, PG 9, 728.

arises from dedication and faith in Christ, 'who is truly the law, the commandment and the eternal Word'. [10] 'The great tree which covers the mountain and the valley and all the land is the law of God which has been given to the whole world: this is the Son of God who is preached to the world.' [11]

These few quotations taken from the writings of the most honoured fathers of the Church and uttered in full fidelity to the scriptures, particularly John and Paul, prove how Christocentric was the moral message of the new covenant.

The above-mentioned and other great teachers and catechists present Christ, the Covenant, as the one who personally signifies the loving solidarity with all of mankind whom God loved so much that his only-begotten Son became the brother of all men, even to the point of sharing his blood and bearing the burden of all men. And by doing so, Christ gave his law to us: to bear the burden of one another and thus fulfil the 'law of Christ' (Gal 6:2). It is not a law which Christ explains to us by words alone or that he imposes on us; it is, rather, what Christ himself makes visible, tangible, experiential by his life and death, by his incarnation and by sending us his own Spirit, by loving and accepting us, by drawing us to him so that we too may love each other as he did. It is Christ in us. This is the great message, the gospel of St Paul. All his letters express the good news: Christ lives in us, therefore we can live a new life.

The law of Christ is Christ himself who has fulfilled the great mission entrusted by the Father, of manifesting all his love to all men. For us Christ becomes the 'law of grace' since he lives in us through the power of the Holy Spirit and persuades us to bear 'the fruits of the Spirit' (Gal 5:24). We live in Christ and thus his love dwells within us. Every friend of Christ can say with St Paul that he no longer comes under law but is abiding in Christ and in his love and thus in his 'law' (énnomos Christoû) (1 Cor 9:20). The full surrender to Christ present in

[10] Clement, *Stromata* I, ch. 3, PG 9, 421.
[11] Hermas, *Similitudines*, 8, 3, 2.

us by grace becomes the liberating event. It gives us a new life and is, in this sense, the 'law of liberty'.

With the growth of Christ in us, we gradually find our true name, our authenticity and full freedom as sons of God. But this growth is inseparably bound to that of the whole Church, the sacrament of Christ, 'which is his body and as such holds within it the fullness of him who himself receives the entire fullness of God' (Eph 1:23). The gifts of God, the grace of the Holy Spirit, our tasks in the family of God require that 'we all at last attain to the unity inherent in our faith and our know-ledge of the Son of God — to mature manhood, measured by nothing less than the full stature of Christ' (Eph 4:13).

Christ is the new and eternal Covenant. Just as the Old Testament law was proclaimed 'law of the covenant', so the New Testament law receives meaning and value from the new covenant. Originally and essentially it has form, subsistence and reality in Christ before inviting all men, through the work of the Holy Spirit, to be the people of the covenant. In a special way Christ is himself the new Covenant in his vital and absolute union with the Father and in his boundless solidarity with mankind. In him, humanity and divinity meet in hypostatic union which we can also refer to as hypostatic covenant, the most intimate, most stable and indestructible alliance.

This covenant is the absolute and perfect synthesis of the vertical and the horizontal. Those who are united to Christ and live in him transcend every form of alienation and find the perfect synthesis of faith and life.

(b) *Christ, 'Word and Answer'*

The sacraments of faith express our glad, humble and grateful acceptance of the word of God. They engender the dynamic response to be expressed in our whole life.

Christ, the great Sacrament, is the divine-human synthesis of the word-deed-message, and the life-response. He is the definitive and perfect Covenant, since he is the Word in whom the Father fully expresses himself from all eternity and in whom, in the final revelation, he manifests all his love and his plan of salvation. In the saving mysteries of the Incarnation, passion, death, resurrection and ascension of the Lord, the ultimate word of love has been said. And he who has given the most loving and complete response in the name of all mankind renders by his grace all men capable of responding to the Father in union with him.

The same Christ who, in his person and all his deeds, speaks and gives, commands and suffers, is the Word of God to us; He is not a word scattered ineffectively but a word that remains in eternity, a fully visible and understandable word for the little and humble ones, a word that invites us to an active response. Whatever comes specifically within the domain of Christian morality shines forth in him alone. Separated from him, all is dead and speechless. When he is taken seriously, man is then compelled to ask himself, 'Who is it that calls me? Who communicates this message to me?'

This Christo-centric and personalistic vision applies also to the so-called *natural moral law*. It reaches us as his message, as an appeal, since it has its source and signification in the Word. 'No single thing was created without him' (Jn 1:3). In the Incarnate Word, in Jesus Christ, is expressed the ultimate purpose of creation and of man's nature, and consequently of natural moral law. 'The whole universe has been created through him and for him' (Col 1:16). The persistence of created things points to a continuous dynamic presence of the creative Word who enables man, his image, to listen and to respond at once.

Natural law manifests itself depending on one's ability to listen and to perceive the meaning of reality in terms of the best mode of living for a person in community, listening and responding to the opportunities and present exigencies. Christ alone, the Word of the Father, gives to creation the significance of word and appeal, and grants man the capacity gradually to perceive God's design in human history. All authentic human experiences are inserted in the law of Christ because everything subsists in him and for him. Everything is brought together in him for the final answer of adoring love and fraternal love (cf. GS 22).

That Christ agreed to be, in his whole life and in his death, the wholehearted answer given to the Father in our name is witnessed by the morning and evening prayer of his earthly existence. His human nature, above all its assumption into the hypostatic union, are gifts of the Father who asks for a total answer. Christ answers from the first act of human consciousness and freedom right up to the shedding of his blood: 'Here am I. As it is written of me in the scroll, I have come, O God, to do thy will' (Heb 10:7). He does not respond with a ritual sacrifice but makes himself the perfect response by offering his life for his brethren: 'Father, into thy hands I commit my spirit' (Lk 23:46). All this has a sacramental character since it is a visible acceptance and response in the name of humanity, with the power to save all.

The history of salvation and of Christian life is the history of a similar acceptance and response by those believers who understand their whole existence as 'a vocation in Christ' (OT 16). They unite themselves in their whole being to the answer which Christ has already given in the name of all. There is no question of an arbitrary answer or of one left completely in man's independent power. It is rather the interior dynamics of life created in the Word of God and renewed in Christ, the inborn dynamics of the whole Church, of the whole people of God.

Man will be able to understand himself and to realize his true name and his greatest possibilities only to the extent that he directs himself to Christ, listening and responding to him with all his being. This attitude of attentive listening and vital response frees the human person from all self-sufficiency and alienation. It puts to death the selfish self and allows the birth or rather rebirth of the true self in a life of responsibility and co-responsibility. Man gains his true autonomy and succeeds in becoming himself only in union with Christ.

4. Christ in us

The key to the sacramental understanding of the whole Christian life is the truth so forcibly set forth in the gospel of Saint John and the letters of Saint Paul: 'Christ in us, and we in him'. More than a hundred and sixty times, Saint Paul turns our attention to this message in which he synthesizes his gospel: 'The secret is this: Christ in you, the hope of the glory to come' (Col 1:27). The moral teaching of Saint Paul is a vital translation of Christ's farewell message: 'Dwell in me as I in you. No branch can bear fruit by itself, but only if it remains united with the vine; no more can you bear fruit unless you remain united with me' (Jn 15:4). The life in Christ is our joy, our strength and thus also our law.

In our time, so severely tempted by a new form of Pelagianism, this fundamental truth cannot be too strongly emphasized. Every effort must be made to translate it into the language and experience of modern man. A new brand of 'horizontalism' seduces many people to believe more in their own achievements than in God's life-giving presence. They lose, even if they continue to be believers, the deep consciousness of our union with Christ and our dependence on his grace. The whole Church, in each person and community, should seek, therefore, in the most vital and visible way, to manifest that she places all her hope in her union with Christ and in the life-giving presence of his Spirit. [12]

The Church does not stand in a purely external or superficial relationship with Christ. She lives in him, through him and for him. She does not and must not set her hope in earthly means and expressions of law and authority. She is meant to be a sacrament of unity and of salvation for all mankind by her deep

---

[12] Cf. Heribert Mühlen, *Una Persona mystica* (Paderborn: Schöningh, 1968); Sabbas J. Kilian, 'The Holy Spirit in Christ and in Christians', *American Benedictine Review* 20 (1969), pp. 99-121; Emile Mersch, *The Theology of the Mystical Body* (St Louis: Herder, 1958).

union with Christ. Christ lives in her with his Spirit who is her life-giving breath. She is a saving presence for the world to the extent of this awareness that she receives everything from Christ. It is her gratitude that makes her gracious and generous towards all.

The same holds for the individual believer. He will bear the fruits of the Spirit for the life of the world, 'love, joy, peace, patience, kindness, goodness, fidelity, gentleness and self-control' (Gal 5:22), only when vitally united with Christ. As long as the Christian sees his relationship with Christ as something extrinsic and, as a consequence, limits himself to an external submission and obedience to the written law, he has not truly entered into the 'law of Christ'.

From this fundamental vision flow some very important implications for a deeper understanding of a specifically Christian morality. I mention only the most evident points.

(1) A legalistic approach could seduce a man enjoying special gifts of God when faced with the particular needs of his neighbour; he could ignore this 'kairos' of personal initiative and generous response in so far as there is no general law imposing the action which should follow the appeal of God's grace and the need of his fellowman. But a radical vision of our life in Christ, and of man's vocation to act in such a way as to become more and more an image of Christ, forces us to a quite different judgement. To ignore the call that comes from within for a specific situation is alienation from our true life in Christ. Whoever rejects the present opportunity and the inner call of grace (of the concrete gifts God has bestowed on him) says 'no' to his authenticity. He repudiates the essential dynamics of the history of salvation which tends to make the whole Church a fully visible and efficacious sign of Christ's presence in and through each believer. When this attitude becomes habitual, the believer not only brings on an 'energy crisis' but deprives himself of the liberating power of the 'law of grace' and of the joy of the gospel. By hiding behind a legal screen he blinds himself to the most fundamental realities.

(2)   We have all learned that a sacrament becomes a saving event only in so far as the external sign expresses or encourages faith and a vital giving of self. Without this opening to the gracious presence of God, the reception of a sacrament is not a truthful sign. This needs to be applied to our more fundamental vision of man called to be a truthful sign of Christ's presence in him. It follows, then, that a person who does not live in God's grace, who consciously puts off his conversion to him does not and cannot live authentically according to his vocation in Christ even if, by the standards of the written laws, his deeds are blameless. His life bears witness only to laws and discrete values but not to Christ; he cannot be effectively and truthfully a sign of life in Christ. When redeemed love does not reside and work in us, everything bears the stamp of futility.

Christ's life in us becomes most manifest in a progressive liberation from egotism. We leave behind our petty preoccupation with self-importance, self-reliance, self-determination, self-fulfilment, self-pity and find a new orientation in the mystery and new commandment of the love of God and our neighbour. The love of our fellowman becomes sacramental when experienced in thanksgiving for God's own love, knowing that it is a gift of the Spirit, a dynamic manifestation of the glory of Christ and of God the Father.

Chapter 2

THE CHURCH, THE SACRAMENT OF LOVE

Thus far our attention has focused on Christ. 'Thee, Christ alone, do we know'. We now extend our reflection to the Church whose reason of being and mission is to make known Christ to all men. The perspective is: How does Christ, the light of all nations, continue to reveal the name of the Father and his presence to all men in and through the Church? The Second Vatican Council begins the dogmatic constitution on the Church by insisting that in Christ, the light of the world, 'the Church is a kind of sacrament or sign of intimate union with God and of the unity of all mankind' (LG 1).

Christ alone is the perfected Sacrament. In him alone shines forth all the love of the Father and the power of the Holy Spirit. All other signs of God's love and presence are valid signs, visible and effective for the salvation of the world, only in view of him and in him. [1]

1. *Christ extending his sacramentality to the Church*

There are different models of the Church. [2] The most appropriate is surely the sacramental one. The Church should

---

[1] Cf. René Latourelle, *Christ and the Church: Signs of Salvation* (Staten Island, N.Y.: Alba House, 1972).

[2] A. Dulles, *Models of the Church* (Garden City, N.J.: Doubleday,

consider herself as the extension of the open arms of Christ on the cross. Christ extends to her his sacramentality whenever she renders witness to him, sharing the joys and the hopes, the sorrows and fears of all people. Whenever the Church fully attends to him and directs all her attention to him, when she entrusts herself totally to him who alone is the source of life and the perfect image of the Father, she also becomes more and more a sacrament of salvation, with him, in him and through him.

People who think that the vision and purpose of the Second Vatican Council centres in the Church herself, have been yielding to a superficial impression. The real thrust is to free herself from the temptations to self-importance which in the Constantinian era arose from a one-sided emphasis on the institutional elements. The Church's self-understanding cannot be other than sacramental: drawing all her attention and that of all men to Christ. She comes to know more existentially that she can be a sign of salvation only by following Christ the Servant and seeking his glory and that of the Father alone.

In the constitution *Lumen gentium*, the Church closely examines herself, her inner life and her mission in the light of Christ, the primordial Sacrament, the Prophet, and prophetic High Priest. The theme of the constitution *Dei verbum* is based on the presence of Christ in his word. She puts herself totally under the authority of his word. He himself is the Revelation and it is only by turning totally to him that the Church can receive the saving message and decipher the meaning of the Bible and of history. Christ's redemptive presence in the totality of human life and in all events of history provides the basic orientation for the pastoral constitution on the Church in the modern world (*Gaudium et spes*). Only in him and through him can the Church consider herself 'a kind of sacrament and an

---

1974) considers the sacramental model as the most fruitful. I hope that a sacramental vision of creation and of the history of salvation, and one centred in Christ the Servant, will avoid some of the disadvantages mentioned by Dulles.

instrument of intimate union with God, and of unity with all mankind' (GS 42). Far from monopolizing God's presence, then, the Church has to direct attention to Christ and thus to all signs of God's saving presence in the world.

With Paul, apostle of the Gentiles, the whole Church takes on the great mission of completing the full message of Christ's suffering still be endured in her poor human flesh. She has to present herself truly as his body (Col 1:24) in order to 'deliver his message in full: to announce the secret hidden for long ages and through many generations, but now disclosed to God's people to whom it was his will to make it known: to make known how rich and glorious it is among all nations' (Col 1:26-27).

The self-understanding of the Church must be thoroughly imbued with the sacramental dimension if she is to test not only her liturgical celebrations but also her pastoral ministry, her legislation, her administration of finances as well. [3] It becomes all the more important in view of her mission to make visible Christ, the Saviour of the world, the great Sacrament of the unity of mankind.

This same perspective is needed for constant renewal in Catholic moral theology and catechesis. In the following pages, I shall concentrate mainly on the sacramental self-understanding of the Church, its impact on Christian ethics and the teaching of it.

Early in his pontificate, Pope John XXIII gave a Christocentric vision to the effort of renewal and reform and thus a sacramental and incarnational direction. In his Pentecost message in 1960, he tells us how the Church can come to a full understanding of herself: by starting from her centre, Christ, the

---

[3] A. Dulles is able to show how the institutional aspects of the Church gain their genuine meaning when seen in a sacramental perspective: 'The institutional elements in the Church must ultimately be justified by their capacity to express or strengthen the Church as a community of life, witness, and service, a community that reconciles and unites men in the grace of Christ' (*Models of the Church,* p. 42).

visible love of God, and from her mission to make him loved by all.

'The ideal of life here below for every redeemed man, the highest ideal of every society on earth — family, nation, the whole universe, and above all and eminently the ideal of the holy, Catholic and apostolic Church, to which an ecumenical council can aspire to contribute — is the victory of Christ Jesus. It is the growth of Christ in us, by living truth in mutual love (*veritatem facientes in caritate*) that denotes our true and definitive progress. What words and what inspirations we find in St Paul writing to the Ephesians: "He is the head, and on him the whole body depends. Bonded and knit together by every constituent joint, the whole frame grows through the proper activity of each part, and builds itself up in love" (Eph 4:16).

Through the single phrases of this quotation from St Paul, it is easy to perceive the luminous points which should result from the beauty and splendour of this self-understanding of the Catholic Church articulated in the ecumenical council, always vigilant, as it is meant to be, for the great events of the present and of the future. Truth and charity: Christ as the vertex and head of the Mystical Body.' [4]

In the essentially Christo-centric and therefore sacramental concept of the Church fostered by the Second Vatican Council, the Church can come to understand herself, her mystery and her mission by starting from Christ, looking at his mystery and his witness, and putting all her trust in him. She cannot, therefore, seek her own triumph, nor can she ever be satisfied to remain static. Always and everywhere her mission is the *victory of the love of Christ* in a continuous renewal of all the expressions of her life. She assumes the magnificent task of participating in the mystery of Christ, renouncing herself in the fulfilment

---

[4] *Discorsi, messaggi, colloqui del S. Padre Giovanni XXIII,* vol. 2, (Poliglotta Vaticana, 1961), pp. 396-397.

of her mission, in her service of love, her manner of offering praise to the triune God.

With the same love expressed in his being sent by the Father, Christ commits his Church to make visible throughout the ages that love revealed by his cross and his death. Therefore, the Church can never propose the mystery of salvation in merely rational or abstract categories. She has to communicate by manifesting Christ's own love that shines forth in truth and through the witness of her unity. She must indicate it by her willingness to serve, to provide a living celebration of the sacraments, to accept the challenge of speaking in a language accessible to every people and to all social classes. As Paul VI said at the opening of the second conciliar session, the whole life of the Church and all efforts of renewal and reform must be expressed in 'Christ our beginning, Christ our life and guide, Christ our hope and our goal. . . . There is no light shining on our assembly that is not Christ. . . . With the words of the sacred liturgy let us say, "Thee, Christ alone, do we know".' [5]

2. *The Church as the Sacrament of Christ: the rallying call*

Christ's mission is to call all people to unity, to the glory of the One Father almighty, in the Holy Spirit. He identifies himself with all those who are created in him, the eternal Word, and whom he calls in his humanity to join him in his adoring love for the Father and in his redeeming and unifying love for all his brothers and sisters. Christ is the Sacrament of unity as the rallying call, the New Israel, the true '*qahél*': the one who in self-chosen nothingness is called to be the servant of all and is glorified by the Father as the Lord of the whole world; and thus he is the unfailing promise of the final unity of mankind.

In Christ — to the extent that she is assimilated to him — the Church of the New Testament is the sacrament of unity:

[5] *Acta Apostolicae Sedis,* 55 (1963), p. 846.

a grace and an urgent appeal to all people to be united in one faith, in justice and peace.[6] She is chosen from among the 'non-people' to become God's 'chosen people'. She is meant to be visibly, tangibly and convincingly the body of Christ, the rallying call in which and through which Christ continues his unifying action. This aspect of the sacramental self-understanding of the Church is beautifully expressed in the *Catechismus Romanus*: '*Ecclesia, id est convocatio*' — 'the very meaning of Church is the convocation, the calling together'. The Greek word *Ekklesia* (and the verb *kalein*) have the same root meaning a 'calling', a 'vocation'. The specific character of this vocation is the call to unity.

The Church, in union with Christ, has the vocation to gather mankind in him who is the Word of God for all humanity and for the whole of creation. The Church is called to transmit this Word to all men. She will succeed in her mission and will be faithful to it only to the extent that she lives visibly and sincerely as a witness of Christ, living in that unity which is the essence of her calling and of her loving response. If she succeeds in keeping together, in love and faith, the people of different social classes, cultures, interests, she is truly a sign of God's loving presence.

The consequences of the Church's witness for the moral attitude of believers are obvious. Because Catholic morality is Christo-centric and ecclesial, it is always responsorial, personal and communitarian, social and salvific. Only thus can the Church form Christians able to 'express the mystery of Christ and the real nature of the true Church in their lives and to manifest the same to others' (SC 2). In this sacramental vision, all the diverse

---

[6] Regarding the synthesis of the sacramental model and the community (*koinonia*) model see: Yves Congar, *The Mystery of the Church* (Baltimore: Helicon, 1960); Paul Minear, *Images of the Church in the New Testament* (Philadelphia: Westminster, 1960); Dietrich Bonhoeffer, *The Communion of Saints* (New York: Harper & Row, 1963); Jerome Hamer, *The Church is a Communion* (Westminster, Md.: Newman Press, 1965); John Powell, *The Mystery of the Church* (Milwaukee: Bruce, 1967); Stephen B. Clark, *Building Christian Community* (Notre Dame, Ind.: Ave Maria Press, 1972).

D

parts and the various aspects of Christian life converge and become organically unified in Christ, the point Alpha and Omega, the centre of all creation.

But Catholic morality remains faithful to its sacramental character only by educating the faithful to a humble listening and alertness to the signs of the times, to acceptance of the gifts given by God to persons and communities, to vigilance for the present opportunities and the real needs of neighbour and community. The response cannot be limited to the customary; it must be total, spontaneous and creative, a response in Christ who is the creative and redeeming Word of the Father to all men. The liturgical celebrations are intended to insert all men and women more and more in Christ by means of faith, hope, love, justice and peace, to awaken them gradually to the fullness of their vocation and to the dignity of universal brotherhood. The liturgy cannot be properly understood except as a part of the whole life of the Church in her urgent mission to reconcile and unite all people in love, justice, mutual respect, benevolence and peace, and thus help them to become adorers of the One God and Father.

3. *The whole Church and each member: the sign of Christ's love*

Christ the perfect Sacrament, makes fully visible the love of the Father in his own infinite love for the whole of human-kind, for each and all of his brothers and sisters. In him alone has become tangible the perfect synthesis between the love of God and the love of neighbour, between adoration of the One Father and liberating love, justice and concern for all people and the world in which they live. The mission of Christ whom we call the Prophet, the Sacrament, the Covenant and the High Priest is not isolated from his love and his 'law of love'. In all his roles, in speech and deeds, he embodies the dynamism of God's saving love and he draws all who turn to him into this same dynamic movement. He thus invites all people to join together in honouring the One Father and Creator through their mutual love.

Analogously the same is true of the Church. She is not called into being by a mere commandment, nor does she fulfil her mission merely by preaching the command of love or by adding love to her structure, laws and celebrations. The Church authentically manifests herself as Christian to the extent that in her very life-breath and in her whole life she is a visible and attractive sign of love, a sacrament pointing to the mystery of God's love as revealed in Jesus Christ. Through her, Christ continues his revealing presence — although not in a sense of monopoly; he is also present beyond her structures.

Christ works throughout the whole of history, in all events. However, he has chosen the Church, has abundantly bestowed the Holy Spirit on her and has sent her so that she may be more and more a unique sacrament of union with God and of the unity of mankind in him and through him. The source of her vitality is the Holy Spirit. Through the Spirit, Christ's human nature became the perfect Sacrament of God's love, and in the fullness of his redemptive love Christ bestows on the Church the same Spirit as the sign and token of his infinite love. Through the Spirit, the Church in all her members joins in the love-and-live response which Christ offers to the Father in sacrifice for all men.

The Church receives life from the open heart of Christ. Chosen by his graciousness as his bride, she lives the mystery of his love in glad fulfilment of her witness. Her mission, her ultimate and decisive goal is to be a sign of his heart, of his loving care for men.

The Church cannot live her union with Christ, and her mission, without announcing the mystery to the world in a perceptible and credible manner. In her whole life and in that of her people, in her celebrations, in her concern and responsibility for humane conditions, in her learning and unlearning, in her changes and adaptations, in all that she is, has and does, the final and ultimate criterion is that she grow in love, make Christ's love visible to all men, just as he manifested God's love to us. Obviously, then, the commandment of love is not something added to the juridical structures of the Church; love, as response to God's love to all men, is her very essence. Her structures are valid only in so far as they manifest her specific mission of being an efficacious sacrament of the love of her divine Bridegroom.

Each and everyone of us, and the Church as a whole, must give continuous attention to this essential criterion. Privileges, customs, forms, laws, human traditions, our own preferences, our own desire for change or for greater stability — all are to be judged in terms of whether or not they contribute convincingly to the manifestation of God's love for all men.

The Second Vatican Council made a solemn declaration in this regard. 'The Church stands ready to renounce the exercise of certain legitimately acquired rights if it becomes clear that their use raises doubt about the sincerity of her witness' (GS 76). This one statement stimulated considerable discussion among the bishops to whom the text was submitted. One bishop objected by stating humbly that since bishops are not ready to put the principle into practice, it should not be spelled out. Another bishop queried: 'Can we dare to reduce the gospel to that minimum which we can be happy with or do we have the courage to place ourselves under the judgement of the gospel?' The statement was approved almost unanimously. We put ourselves under the judgement of what God truly wants for the Church, that is, that she be credible as the living gospel of God's love. No sacrifice can be too great for the fulfilment of this sacramental mission.

The Church of the Word Incarnate realizes that she needs juridical structures, administrative bodies, money and many other tangible and transient things for her pilgrim situation. She also needs criticism. However, in all these things she can never do without love. All her structures, administrative bodies and personnel must continually witness to their validity in serving the proclamation of the gospel message of God's love and the redemptive power of unifying love.

The Church's critics, on the other hand, must scrutinize their own behaviour and ask themselves: are we inspiring greater love, better discernment of what constitutes genuine love, or are we creating barriers through bitterness and lovelessness? Are we sacrificing the great reality for a petty goal or are we really making the local Church an incarnate message of the primacy of love?

After stressing how the teaching of morality should proceed in the perspective of the loftiness of 'the vocation of the faithful in Christ and their obligation to bring forth fruit in charity for the life of the world', the Council then applies the same principle to the teaching of canon law. 'In the explanation of canon law and Church history, the mystery of the Church should be kept in mind, as it was set forth in *The dogmatic constitution on the Church*, promulgated by this holy synod' (OT 16). It should be evident that if this is necessary in the programme for the formation of priests, all the more is it mandatory for the ongoing reform and revision of canon law and its application.

Even the administration of finances in the Church comes under the same test. In times past no government was held publicly accountable for its budgetary practices; the Church could follow similar practices. Today, however, when every corporation, city, state, nation gives a detailed public accounting of the handling of moneys, the Church makes herself vulnerable to unjustified suspicions if she continues to maintain secrecy about her possessions and their administration. If she has nothing to conceal, her practices should be such that she is clearly seen as worthy of trust (cf. GS 44).

In final analysis, it all amounts to proper motivation and emphasis. A body ought to be the mirror of its spirit. When the corporeality becomes too massive, it conceals and risks suffocating the spirit. Something similar happens in the life of the Church. Her juridical element, administration, preoccupation with earthly belongings, can assume such importance and be so accentuated that they develop to a point where parts of the Church no longer radiate the spirit of love, the *unum necessarium,* but conceal and may even betray it.

4. *Consequences for the understanding of Christian ethics*

Whoever has studied the history of moral theology in its inter-dependence with the whole life of the Church becomes aware of their mutual influences. The self-understanding of the Church encouraged by the Second Vatican Council flows from scripture and the best tradition; that is why it should permeate the total formation of priests as well as all forms of moral catechesis. It should be reflected in the totality of the life of the Church (OT 9).

There are two tasks that assume great importance for catechesis and for a scientific presentation of morality. They are: synthesis and balance.

(a) *Synthesis*

Moral theology — the theology of Christian life — as much as the dogmatic treatise on the Church has to direct its attention to a synthesized Christo-centric vision. It is Christ who, through the gifts of the Holy Spirit, continues in the Church the revelation of redeeming love which became visible in his earthly life.

It follows, therefore, that it is not sufficient to propose an ancillary treatise, or another discipline in order to teach that the love of God and neighbour is 'the summation of the law' (Rom 3 : 10). It must be abundantly evident that the very core of all Christian doctrine lies in love, the gift of God and centre of all tasks. Every Christian virtue has to be an expression of love as it appears in the countenance of Christ and his true disciples.

We need only look at the great effort and success of the apostolic community in synthesizing the teaching of Christ. In the foreground stands Christ, the loving person who is radiating love, joy and peace, teaching through all that he is and all that he says and does, that great primordial commandment of love of God and neighbour.

It is now a widely accepted thesis that the sermon on the mount was a catechesis; its *sitz im leben* is the sacramental encounter with Christ. It was offered to neophytes before and after their reception of the 'sacraments of initiation'. We see, in the unfolding beatitudes, God's love poured out onto those whose hearts are pure, the peacemakers, the humble, those who thirst for justice. Then, seven times we hear repeated the Lord's 'but I tell you . . .', where he wishes to divert the emphasis and the attention of his disciples from the prohibitive laws of their tradition to the affirmatives of his new law, as he leads them to the summit of Christian morality. 'There must be no limits to your goodness, as your heavenly Father's goodness knows no bounds' (Mt 5:48) or 'Be therefore compassionate as the Father in heaven is compassionate' (Lk 6:36).

The farewell discourse and the high priestly prayer of Jesus (Jn 13-17) also serve as a marvellous apostolic synthesis of Christ's teaching. Here Christ is visibly the Servant, the one who serves his brethren and will die for them. Thus he appeals, 'This is my command, that you love one another as I have loved you' (Jn 15:12). It is not a commandment in the sense of an imposition; the Greek text could be translated better by 'this is my communication'. Through words, but even more through his own love, this is the way of salvation that he communicates and shares with his disciples.

It is impossible to present Christian life, that life of a follower of Christ, as one based on the commandments of Sinai to which are added the thousand and one precepts of the Church, and after which or among which would be inserted the commandment to love God and neighbour. How can 'love of neighbour' be treated as part of a commandment, such as 'Thou shalt not kill?' If one wishes to keep the traditional scheme, all commandments ought to be presented as expressions of love of God and neighbour along the lines of the sermon on the mount and the farewell discourses, with a sweeping vision of the whole of Christian life and of all God's gifts. Love does not truly and effectively touch us through imposition; it reaches us through witness, visibility, experience. The Church is primarily sacrament through the faithful who communicate genuine love and thus reveal Christ.

If one were to present the sacraments as an added set of duties over and beyond those imposed by the ten commandments and by a codified 'natural law', he would be committing another grave error. The sacraments are gifts, gratuities of Christ's love, efficacious signs of salvation through which dignity, grace and commitment to a Christian life come to us. They cannot be understood in the abstract or as bare precepts. Christ is the Word Incarnate, flesh and blood, fully visible and attractive. So must be the Christian message presented to those who wish to follow him.

The proper place and task of the sacraments in a scientific and catechetical presentation of the moral message is to show, in an incarnate way, the expanse and primacy of God's love and the loving response we are expected to give. Christian life has to be presented as infinitely more than an aggregate of 'three adjacent circles of duties' as in many manuals by German moralists of the past decades. The true perspective is the visible and fascinating presence of God's love in Christ Jesus, which manifests itself in the Church and her members through the work of the Holy Spirit. His love is a gratuitous *gift*, and precisely because it is gift, it elicits a more heartfelt, more generous pledge; therefore, the emphasis cannot be on duty. Furthermore, there must be great concern to work out a convincing synthesis between love of God, of neighbour and of self.

(b) *Balance*

When one's whole attention is focused on a loveless juridical casuistry, it is useless to remind incidentally that love is primary and that it ought to be the energy which gives life and substance to the whole of Christian life. Instead, this primacy has to pervade and illumine a total vision in which it is absolutely basic to follow Christ who is Love Incarnate. All Church laws and all formulations of natural law ought to manifest this essential relation, this indispensable goal of all morality, that we should make visible, as disciples of Christ, his love for the Father and for all humanity.

Above all, in arriving at a balance among the various tasks, values and duties, moral theology will have to indicate how, in all principles and applications, morality is for persons, not persons for an abstract code of laws. [7] If the scientific teaching and moral catechesis of this post-conciliar age recognizes the urgency of greater emphasis on the primacy of love, it does not follow that law, duty or obedience are to be ignored or depreciated. However, these will be seen in a different perspective and fulfilled in another spirit.

When the moral formation and instruction of the faithful clearly and decisively follow the path indicated by the Second Vatican Council, the dimensions of a truly Christian life, the loftiness of the Christian vocation will be seen in its beauty and attractiveness. As a consequence, it will be effective in its appeal. Yet, whoever is aware of this cannot deny that much still needs to be done.

[7] See my book *Morality is for Persons* (New York: Farrar, Strauss, Giroux, 1971).

Chapter 3

THE CHURCH: FELLOWSHIP IN
THE HOLY SPIRIT

The life and the mission of the Church must be seen, above all, in the light of Pentecost.[1] Christ calls her into being, keeps her alive and guides her through the Spirit. He continues to reveal himself as the Anointed in the Church. In his life as in his death, in his resurrection, in the Eucharist and in the life of the Church he is the primordial Sacrament of the presence of the Holy Spirit. He attains the summit of the beatitudes when after having given himself totally on the cross and being manifested as the acceptable gift in the resurrection, he ascends to heaven to send the fullness of the Spirit to his disciples.

The farewell blessing of Paul to the Church in Corinth allows us to see the essential mission of the Church in the light of God's gracious gifts: 'The grace of our Lord Jesus Christ, the love of God, and the fellowship of the Holy Spirit be with you all' (2 Cor 13:14). The Church can become more and more, in each of her members, in each family and community as well as in her ministries and offices, a sacrament of love and salvation, to the extent that she understands herself and acts as the fellowship gathered and guided by the Spirit. It is the Holy Spirit who creates community (*koinonia*) and gives life and

---

[1] This aspect of a sacramental self-understanding of the Church — so important for our Orthodox brethren — is brought to the foreground by Heribert Mühlen, *Una Persona mystica* (Paderborn: F. Schöningh, 1968).

direction to the societal, institutional aspects of the Church. By the diversity of his gifts the Spirit unites all in the love of Christ.

The Church adores the Holy Spirit together with the Father and the Son above all by her loving docility to his guidance. The Church grows visibly into a fellowship in the Holy Spirit if each disciple of Christ allows himself to be guided not so much by external laws as by the gifts of the Spirit, serving the community with all the charisms he has received. Thus the life of each person and each community becomes gratitude, an incessant effort to return to the Lord all that he has given them. Thus did Christ return to the Father all his life, dying with arms open to all men. It is in this docility, in trust and gratitude, that the Church can, in her whole life, witness authentically to the mystery of Christ, the Anointed.

1. *A crucial point in an ecumenical ecclesiology*

The focus on the presence of the Holy Spirit was probably the turning point in the Second Vatican Council. It may have been an important experience that the original document on the Church drafted by the conservative preparatory commission ignored almost completely the role of the Holy Spirit in the life of the Church; and where it mentioned the Holy Spirit it stressed particularly the power and the privileges of ecclesiastical authority. During the Council strong objections were raised by many, but especially by the Catholic Melchite Church and by the observers from the Orthodox Churches. For them it was not sufficient to mention somewhere the truth taught by Pius XII, 'If Christ is the head of the Church, the Holy Spirit is her soul'. [2] All the teaching, the life of the faithful, the exercise of authority, the encouragement of spontaneity, even the institutional aspects of the Church, must proclaim the Holy

---

[2] Pius XII, Encyclical Mystici corporis, *Acta Apostolicae Sedis* 10 (1943), p. 220.

Spirit, the giver of life and the Church's total dependence on his grace. The Holy Spirit is not only present in the Church but is her very life-breath. Without him redeemed love is non-existent. Where he is not adored and glorified institutions, laws and the exercise of authority are dead issues. His dynamic presence irradiates and enlivens the whole life of the faithful and of the ministers of the Church, to the extent, however, that, by the same Spirit, they know and confess that 'they are in need of God' (Mt 5 : 3). Through him the Church truly becomes the mystical body of Christ, the messianic people of God, and a sacrament of Christ the Servant.

The manifold gifts of the Spirit unify the people of God, drawing them into fellowship by the very variety of charisms and ministries. Thus they form a community (*koinonia*) in Christ, and not just an institution or organization. 'You are no longer aliens in a foreign land, but fellow citizens with God's people, members of God's household. You are built upon the foundation stone. In him the whole building is bonded together and grows into a holy temple in the Lord. In him you are being built with all the rest into a spiritual dwelling for God' (Eph 2 : 19-22).

The self-understanding of the Church reached by the Second Vatican Council no longer allows her to be considered first and foremost as an external organization. When we speak of the 'Church' we cannot refer solely to the curia in Rome or to the papal and episcopal magisterium, although we do recognize their ministry: but we cannot criticize them as if we were outsiders. Rather we are speaking of all of God's people. *We* are the Church. Of course, this fundamental vision demands an equilibrium. We honour the Holy Spirit in all the ministries that are vivified by him; for he works in all, through all and for all. We give special attention to the saints, canonized or not, who manifest abundantly the harvest of the Spirit for the building up of the whole Church. Authority and obedience in the Church have a liberating quality wherever they are a response to the Spirit. What unites all believers in Christ's authority is docility to the Holy Spirit, openness and respect for all the charisms and operations of the Holy Spirit — not only within the Roman

Catholic Church, but in the whole of Christianity, and even in the whole of humankind.

All that has value in the Church, be it ministry, rank or charism, can be only the work of the Holy Spirit. This is decisively demonstrated in the fourth chapter of Paul's epistle to the Ephesians and in the first letter to the Corinthians, chapter twelve. And since all that the Church receives is the gift of the one Spirit who renews the hearts of men and the face of the earth the proper use of charisms and ministries in the Church is possible only when we are concerned for the good of all humankind. The adoration of the Holy Spirit in the Church calls for an attitude of gratitude and generosity in the service of one's fellowmen, commitment to social justice and peace.

Christ has come to baptize all believers in the Holy Spirit. The diversity of his gifts and promptings make the Church a sacrament of unity for all mankind. 'In their diversity all bear witness to the admirable unity of the body of Christ. This very diversity of graces, ministries and tasks gathers the children of God into one, because "all these gifts are the work of the one and the same Spirit" (1 Cor 12:13)'. [3] The baptism in the Spirit that unites believers to the baptism of Christ becomes visible in a firm commitment to peace and unity in that diversity which allows creative liberty. The building up of the mystical body of Christ, inspired by faith in one God turns the attention of believers to the needs of all men. 'There is one body and one Spirit, as there is one hope held out in God's call to you' (Eph 4:4). The saving solidarity of those baptized by the Spirit knows no limits.

Modern totalitarian regimes tend towards a rigid organizational style that imposes uniformity, levelling and manipulation of minds. The Church, however, wherever she lives as a fellowship united by the Spirit, recognizes diversities in the exploration of truth and in life styles as the work of the Spirit who brings about unity in variety. It is precisely on this spiritual premise

[3] LG 32 (chapter on the laity).

that collegiality on all Church levels is based. At the centre of attention is not a societal organization but the community of faith, hope, love and justice, the *koinonia* understood as fellowship in the Holy Spirit. This unrenounceable model of the Church demands respect for the diversity of cultures, temperaments and capacities and the correlative obligation to welcome, in humility, gratitude and co-responsibility, the fruits of all the operations of the Spirit. Genuine collegiality rests upon the art and grace of appreciation and listening, very much like that of the Servant Messiah announced in the great poems of the Second-Isaiah. 'The Lord God has given me a well-trained tongue, that I might know how to speak to the weary a word that will rouse them. For morning after morning he opens my ears that I may listen' (Isaiah 50:4).

A sign that the Holy Spirit is given and received by the 'teaching Church', the pope, the bishops and theologians, is their willingness and capacity to listen to all and thus to be taught by the Spirit who works in all, through all and for all. Collegiality implies humble collaboration in the search for truth and truthful solutions to the burning problems of life, openness to shared experience and co-reflection, in the community of faith and in the fellowship of all men. A bishop is an outstanding leader and preacher of the gospel to the extent that he is a humble servant, a brother among brethren, a listener who can appreciate the experience and wisdom of priests and lay-people. In time, it may become accepted by all Christian Churches that the successor of Saint Peter enjoys a special assistance of the Holy Spirit in teaching and guiding the Church if it is evident that he honours the charisms, experiences and reflections of all, considering himself the first among brothers ('*primus inter pares*') and not the lord of 'subjects', since he is not called to rule from above or with an insistence of superiority in power. This vision is in keeping with the mystery of authority and leadership taught by the gospel; it expresses our faith in the Holy Spirit, the giver of life who speaks through the prophets and reveals the mysteries of the kingdom of heaven to little ones.

Liturgical renewal, adaptation to the various cultures, sub-cultures and social classes, the search for a more encompassing yet unifying pastoral approach, the encouragement of the specific apostolate of lay-people in the multiplicity of their experience and competences: all this has to be approached in the same sense of fellowship and listening to the Spirit. Through faith and trust in the Holy Spirit the Church can overcome any temptation to seek unity by unhealthy uniformity through narrow juridical ties or exaggerated centralization. There is a strong awareness in the Church of today that such administrative strategies cannot be reconciled with the principle of subsidiarity and even less with faith in the Holy Spirit and gratitude for all his gifts. [4]

By the joy of faith, solidarity in hope and docility to the Holy Spirit the Church can harmoniously maintain unity in multiplicity and pluralism in unity. Not to allow for courageous initiatives, co-responsibility or variety in expressions, points to a sad weakening of faith in the mystery of the Holy Spirit to which the whole life of the Church, including her institutional structures, must bear witness. Those who have faith will never try to manipulate persons or communities to their own advantage or for anything else. The 'ministry of the Spirit' (2 Cor 3:8) enables all believers and especially officeholders to realize that the very diversity of graces, ministries and works can gather the sons and daughters of God, since 'all these things are the work of one and the same Spirit' (1 Cor 12:11).

Every presentation of the moral message, whether scientific, catechetic, kerygmatic or pedagogic, should clearly witness to this 'fellowship in the Holy Spirit'. Our teaching and our life should manifest that the law of Christ is a law of freedom, spontaneity, and creative fidelity and one of profound solidarity. This demands also that in the exercise of authority and in the realm of ecclesiastical law there should shine forth reverence for and trust in 'the law of the Spirit that gives life in Christ Jesus'

[4] Cf. LG 12 and 32.

(Rom 8:2). The Church will thus actively encourage a spiritual understanding and implementation of laws and moral directives that foster initiative and generosity. For those who believe in the Holy Spirit his gifts are accepted as an urgent appeal to a clear commitment to the common good, beyond laws and rules. In itself a charism entails a consecration to the spiritual building up of the community, a service in manifesting the fellowship of the Holy Spirit.

2. Consequences for the understanding of Christian ethics

If we say 'Church' we mean the people of God and the whole Christian life. Therefore, the characteristics of the Church mentioned above must, vivified by the Spirit, permeate morality and moral doctrine. The moral message of the New Testament is one (a) of true freedom in the Spirit and (b) of inspiration and motivation that gives equal attention to the communal and the existential aspect.

(a) True freedom in the Holy Spirit

The desire for increasing freedom is at the very heart of today's human experience. Yet modern man is not always able to discern the path that leads to it. Indeed, he often fails to understand what genuine freedom is. In his teaching on 'the liberty of the children of God' (Rom 8:21) the apostle of the Gentiles opposes to selfishness and arbitrariness 'the law of the Spirit that frees us from the law of sin' (Rom 8:2). Under 'the law of sin' (hamartia) he understands the utter power of individual and collective selfishness that enslaves people, the accumulated and incarnate trends of misused authority, of bitterness, deception, hatred and injustice, structures in the economic, cultural and social realm that are investments of and constant temptations to sinfulness. In a sense, one could say that 'sin' creates its own 'law', a kind of perverted 'sacramentality' with visible, tangible, experiential signs and efficaciousness in contaminating people and their environment and attracting men to evil.

The people of God obtain freedom and become a source of freedom for others under 'the law of the Spirit'. The Spirit of God guides them by his gifts. He opens their eyes and ears to all that is good, to the needs and especially to the good of their fellowmen. Released from 'the law of sin' that chains egotists together in evil, believers make a solidary investment of their freedom in the actual human situation about them. This mission belongs to the visibility of the Church as a sacrament of freedom and liberation. Through her members and communities, the Church joins with all men of good will in creating a humane, healthy environment. In this solidarity, believers engage in an authentic dialogue for what is truthful and good, for the purpose of making the world around us a home of respect, honesty, justice and peace for everyone, regardless of race, colour, social status or religion. Thus does the Church become a visible, tangible, efficacious sign of God's loving presence and care for all people, a 'divine *milieu*'.

A living faith in the Holy Spirit leaves as little room for individual or collective selfishness as for a dehumanizing legalism. In the one Spirit, all who have received and honoured the variety of his gifts are brought together in mutual respect and service. Each person's gifts and capacities are to be used for the common good in gratitude to the one Lord and to the praise of the Anointed who has manifested and incarnated on earth his saving solidarity. Believers implore from the Spirit the gift of discernment, so necessary in order to find out what, in a particular case, is good and just, what truly strengthens saving liberty, what promotes world wide liberation and brotherhood, what fosters that continuity which is, at the same time, openness to progress and change.

Moral theology would go counter to the Spirit if, by favouring one aspect or the other, it attempted to reduce the tension, or better, the contrast-harmony that exists between solidarity and the spirit of initiative and freedom. It seems to me that any

approach to moral theology can be judged by the value it gives
to the virtue of *epikeia*. The word means 'reasonableness',
'equity', 'suitability': it is the virtue of freedom in wisdom and
is mostly used in reference to the application of laws and principles. It takes for granted that the purpose of laws and rules is
to serve the common good, in respect for the freedom and
dignity of all persons, and that, consequently, they cannot be
applied automatically when they do not truly serve the common
good. Today there is an urgent need to rediscover, re-evaluate
and re-instate this virtue in the Church, with the meaning which
the best tradition ascribes to it. It has to be radically separated
from the restrictions to which the individualistic mentality of
the last two centuries has subjected it. It goes beyond a kind
of self-dispensation in view of a disproportionate burden; it is
much more a mature commitment to discernment in view of
the common good. *Epikeia* is the virtue of creative freedom.

Both Aristotle and St Thomas considered *epikeia* an indispensable virtue for legislators and administrators. It keeps them
from making unjust decisions in particular cases, from stifling
spontaneity and the spirit of initiative in individuals, which is so
necessary for the common good. That is why it should be the
distinctive virtue of legislators and ecclesiastical superiors. If
they lack this virtue so direly needed and lacking in civil society,
they betray what is essential to their witness, namely, that the
Church is a fellowship in the Holy Spirit, a community of loyal
and courageous persons consecrated to responsible obedience
and mature initiative by the baptism of the Spirit.

Canonists and moralists who require a servile obedience to
the letter of the laws of the Church not only insult the Church
and its pastors by projecting an image of lovelessness and insensi-
tivity, but they also keep the faithful in a state of immature
dependence, a sort of infantilism. As for the faithful themselves,
they possess *epikeia* when they sincerely try to interpret each
law in the overall perspective of solidarity and charity, acting
for the good of each person and for the common good, in a
spirit of courageous loyalty without yielding to egotism.

Epikeia should not be restricted to cases where a particular law imposes a disproportionate burden. There are situations where courageous initiative, beyond laws and rules, can demand a much more generous response to the common good than slavish observance or an all too literal application of the law. Rightly understood, *epikeia* can liberate us from the great dangers of legalism so strongly condemned by the Lord: 'How well you set aside the commandment of God in favour of your traditions' (Mk 7:9).

The individualism of the last centuries which often reduced religion to an egotistical search for security and personal salvation was somehow compensated for by legal inflexibility. However, it has become evident that the clinging to the letter of the law stifles man's response to the exigencies of that law which God himself has written into man's heart. As a consequence of legalism, man becomes unresponsive to the needs of his fellow-man and to the present opportunities to bring forth a greater good than that which the man-made law allows.

The whole process has an intrinsic logic. The person who thinks individualistically, even as far as the ultimate questions of salvation, cannot be deemed capable of a considerable use of freedom. But whatever may be the risks of allowing the virtue of *epikeia*, it must be said clearly that legalism and paternalism that discourage the initiative of our fellowmen in striving towards discernment and maturity are a sin against liberty and liberation, a sin against 'the law of the Spirit', that alone can set us free from sin.

If the spirit of Christian freedom and the courage to assume tasks in responsibility and creativity are not to be suffocated with petty and mistrustful barriers, all the more must the whole of Christian life be based on 'the law of the Spirit who gives us life in Christ Jesus' (Rom 8:2). Adherence to this liberating law implies courageous initiatives in a firm decision to free oneself of selfishness and to oppose group egotism or domineering tendencies. It then becomes possible to actualize true freedom and genuinely to exercise co-responsibility in the fellowship

granted by the Spirit and to withstand the enormous dangers
of manipulation. [5] A Christian can never forget that all this
constitutes an undeserved gift of God. He will therefore perse-
vere in humble prayer of petition and thanksgiving. Only thus
can his freedom be on the 'wave-length' of the Spirit. Any
attempt to inspire Church legislation on this matter, or to
encourage a mature attitude towards law by obedience to the
Spirit, will remain ineffective, if we do not withstand the
tendencies of those who assume that even the least of the
Church's law requires or allows a metaphysical, or a-historical
justification.

It is imperative that the abiding exigencies of the law
written in man's heart be clearly distinguished from written
laws. The laws of the Church are truly 'spiritual' (inspired by
the Spirit) if they are based on vigilance for 'the signs of the
times'. They must never be in contradiction to the dynamic,
historical nature of man; in their flexibility they ought to be
faithful to the continuing work of God throughout history.
Hence laws must reflect sensitivity to the events and needs of
today and be in tune with them.

Immobilism in any form contradicts 'the law of the Spirit'
and the Church's witness. In a period of great historical upheaval
such as ours, the Church ought to adapt her legislation fearlessly
and not to regulate life by law where this is not necessary. In
order to avoid acting unwisely she will avail herself of all the
human means at her disposal, including the new forms of
knowledge offered by divine providence to modern man. She
will then come to a better understanding of the signs of the
times and not tempt the Spirit.

The Church is not only a 'fellowship gathered by the Spirit',
she is also the Church of the Word Incarnate and as a pilgrim
a sign of God's presence. When she treats of the salvation of
mankind, therefore, she constantly has to learn and unlearn, to

[5] Cf. my book *Manipulation. Ethical boundaries of medical, behavioural and genetic manipulation* (Slough: St Paul Publications,
1975).

listen, see and feel through her leaders and her members. She cannot disregard any appropriate means. A moral theology decisively centred on 'the law of the Spirit' will not be likely to fall into an unhealthy 'spiritualism'; instead, it will integrate, prudently and courageously, all that the Holy Spirit has led man to discover about himself through shared experience and reflection, anthropology, psychology, sociology and other disciplines and sciences. [6]

(b) *An inspiring morality: communal and existential*

Early in the last century, the moral theology of men like Johann Michael Sailer, Johann Baptist Hirscher, Magnus Jocham and Franz Xaver Linsenman brought about a profound renewal of Catholic moral theology in the perspective of 'the law of the Spirit', 'the law of freedom'. However, in the second half of the century, this was superseded by the legalistic type of manuals which became so familiar to us. A juridical theology evidently seemed more 'churchly' than that which these great theologians had attempted to outline in the *spiritual* sense of the great tradition of the East and West. The First Vatican Council seemed to canonize both a neo-scholastic, stereotyped dogmatic theology and a juridical moral theology.

In the wake of the Second Vatican Council, it seems clear now that the 'churchliness' of the canonical-juridical types of moral theology was bound to an over extrinsic and centralistic ecclesiology and did not focus sufficiently on 'fellowship in the Spirit'. As a result, this theology eventually became almost completely reduced to the categories of external obedience and legal submission.

The revitalized and deepened ecclesiology of the Second Vatican Council justifies the efforts of those earlier moralists and thereby returns to the great oriental and western tradition of the Church classically expressed by St Augustine, St Leo

[6] Cf. GS 44.

the Great and St Thomas. The ecclesial character of Christian morality arises from the saving mystery of the Church. It takes shape in accordance with the self-understanding which the Church attains, and in turn fosters a certain type of ecclesiology.

The signs of the times have forced us to wrestle with collectivism, Marxism and many other ideologies. Our human dignity is threatened by overpowering organization, collective prejudices, concealed pressures and insidious manipulation. As a result, we have acquired a keen sensitivity to the uniqueness of every human person and to existential values. However, the existentialist spirit of our time, good and necessary as it is, in opposing collectivism, runs the risk of going to the opposite extreme of arbitrariness, of blind, violent global protest against all institutions and laws, against social and ecclesiastical order. This threat becomes even greater when Church authorities, administrators, canonists and moralists react in a purely negative way in defence of the *status quo* and of the existing discipline and distribution of power.

A genuine ecclesial sense will not only express itself in a mature obedience to just laws but also in all kinds of creativity and generous initiatives. The Holy Spirit pours forth his gifts and charisms on everyone so that, with whatever a person is and has, he can contribute to the building up of the mystical body of Christ, making the freedom of the sons and daughters of God visible and incarnate in the world.

One of the most urgent problems in theology and in moral teaching today is the search for an organic and internal synthesis between the roles and realms of community and those of the individual. The perspectives of *collegiality* and *subsidiarity* bring sharply to light the pastoral need for stronger unification but with more explicit respect for plurality, diversity, and personal and local initiatives. Our time calls for a great effort towards communitarian and well-organized apostolates; this is indispensable in an epoch of socialization like ours. It also calls for creativity and a spirit of initiative, respectful always of each individual and of the new possibilities offered by Providence for the service of God's kingdom. The true synthesis arises from a just perception of the Church and of the Christian life as a 'fellowship in the Holy Spirit'.

It follows that an understanding and inspiring renewal of the liturgy and of prayer-life are indispensable. A renewed liturgy is as important as the presentation of a morality in which Christians sincerely confront themselves with Christ the Anointed, with the Church as the fellowship of the Holy Spirit, and with the community of Christians baptized in the same Holy Spirit.

Chapter 4

THE CHURCH:
THE SACRAMENT OF PILGRIMAGE

1. *The Church of the Word Incarnate*

The ecclesiology of the Second Vatican Council turns our attention to 'the law of the Spirit' while, at the same time, disallowing any form of spiritualism that seeks salvation for souls alone and as a reality cut off from human experience. We believe with the Council in the Church of the Word Incarnate and therefore are called to be attentive to 'the signs of the times'. *The pastoral constitution on the Church in the modern world* especially calls our attention to the humanity of Christ and urges us to honour him by all our life as the Lord of history. We cannot proclaim the gospel unless we take into consideration the thinking of modern man; we are expected to listen before we speak. This is true for office-holders as well as for other believers. The Church listens with discernment in order to consolidate whatever is good, honest, valid and vital, to purify what is open to progress, and to reject what is unworthy of man.

Already the popes preceding the Vatican Council had emphasized the Church's duty to announce the mystery of Incarnation not only as a saving event which took place in a concrete historical moment of the past but also as an ongoing dynamics and orientation. The norms of action for the Church therefore embrace both levels, that of the abiding truth of the gospel and that of the insertion of the saving truth into today's world. [1]

2. Consequences for the understanding of Christian ethics

The teaching of morality, the pastoral and juridical reforms called for by the Second Vatican Council should consistently make these norms evident in all of their planning and action. In this context, it seems useful to consider three aspects:

(a) moral teaching in a perspective of the history of salvation;

(b) credible forms of the presence of the Church in all sectors of life;

(c) natural law in the law of Christ, with a dynamic understanding of the history of salvation.

(a) Moral teaching in a perspective of the history of salvation

One can easily state that moral theology has always seriously taken into account the social and historical context of man's life, since it has always sought a prudential outlook on the total reality and has always worked to bring truth and goodness into the real world. Nevertheless one can ask if it has fully appreciated what comes into play by virtue of the Incarnation, that fundamental event of Christ's insertion into humanity's pilgrimage in

---

[1] I have given attention to these problems in everything that I have published but especially in the chapter 'Tradition and Adaptation in the light of the mystery of the Incarnation', in my book *This Time of Salvation* (New York: Herder and Herder, 1966). The vision of the Church as a pilgrim and as a sacrament of Christ the Servant comes strongly through in Karl Rahner, *The Shape of the Church to Come* (New York: Seabury Press, 1974); see also: Richard P. McBrien, *The Church: The Continuing Quest* (New York: Newman, 1970), and Eugene Bianchi, *Reconciliation: The Function of the Church* (New York: Sheed & Ward, 1969).

the history of salvation. It is this vision that ought to permeate the whole Christian outlook on human existence.

The Church of the Word Incarnate is a pilgrim Church. Her pilgrim condition is foretold by the great mission of Abraham who left his family and culture and set out facing an unknown future. It is prefigured also by the twelve tribes, migrant workers who became pilgrims in the desert. It is in that uncertain situation that they were made the people of the covenant. The Church is always on pilgrimage, sharing man's journey, the whole having been prepared in God's design by aeons of evolution, change, and constant challenge in the face of an unknown future.

It follows that the teaching of Christian life, that is, moral theology, is to be elaborated in the light of the mystery of salvation, in the light of the Church who wants to be faithful to the Word Incarnate. Centred in Christ, it is to be presented in a way that clearly indicates the historical and social dimensions of salvation. The judgement of Christian action rests on the humility and courage to respond to the *present opportunities* that God, Lord of the history of salvation, offers in the midst of the ongoing journey in human history. [2]

This Christian vision imposes a thoroughgoing consideration of the existential context, including historical continuity and the environmental situation. It thus becomes evident that, for Christians, an 'existential ethics' does not imply arbitrariness, a dangerous discontinuity or improvization; rather, it requires an understanding of the unique possibilities of the historical moment and of the concrete situation, in fidelity to the task of salvation. Such an ethics and such a moral teaching is marked by the eschatological virtues of vigilance and hope. [3]

---

[2] I gave a fuller treatment to these questions in the introductory chapter of my book *Marriage in the Modern World* (Westminster, Md.: Newman Press, 1966).

[3] I refrain here from going into a detailed discussion of this important aspect of Christian ethics, since I have elaborated on it in my book *Hope is the Remedy* (Slough: St Paul Publications, 1971).

(b) *The presence of the Church in all sectors of life*

The Church enjoys many forms of being present. In the first century there was little organization, no church buildings; yet the Church was visibly and effectively present through individual Christians rooted in lively communities. Their outstanding family life, the integrity of their young people, their credibility and trustworthiness in everyday human relations, their mutual love, all made the Church present to the world around them. They were 'leaven in the dough'.

In the medieval system, the Church's presence was almost ubiquitous, and particularly so in the cultural and political fields. It was for the most part a paternalistic presence, as somehow befitted an epoch marked by lack of scholarship in the masses and a consequent paternalism among the *élite* and powerful. When the Church-state came into being, it was a service in a time of chaos, but gradually it led to the alienating situation that the pope was 'present' in a political concert of powers both as head of the Church-state and as head of the Church. In time, these two forms of presence ceased to be differentiated; they became confused by all, including the popes themselves and the curia. Cardinals, 'princes of the Church', were characterized more by power and privilege than by spiritual charisms, and many of them found their glory in building ostentatious palaces for themselves and equally pretentious churches.

In our day, such a mode of presence would be both ineffective and unacceptable if not offensive. For a long time, it did conceal the authentic mission of the Church to preach the gospel, to be witness to the humility and kindness of Christ and to the kingdom of God.

The Church of the Second Vatican Council defines itself as the people of God present in all of life, like the leaven in the dough, the salt which dissolves to savour the food, or the light which consumes itself to enlighten. The concept is one of a servant Church. To actualize this concept of presence, there is an increasing number of bishops today who are leaving inherited palaces and even less pretentious episcopal residences to live in humble surroundings close to the poor and disadvantaged among their people. Along with all the members of the Church, who, with courage and foresight, are opening new horizons and bringing hope and love into the world around them, they are giving to our modern world effective witness to the presence of the Word Incarnate. Every loving and generous activity of the people of God continues in some way the Incarnation of the Word who 'made himself nothing, assuming the nature of a slave. Bearing the human likeness, he humbled himself' (Phil 2 : 7-8).

The Church is present to the world whenever she perceives and appreciates all forms in which God, Creator and Redeemer, is present in human history. The people of God truly become a sacrament, the visible and effective presence of the paschal mystery when, in their concrete environment, their lives witness to the mystery of the Incarnation. This is the thematic key expressed in the very first article of *The pastoral constitution on the Church in the modern world*: 'The joys and hopes, the griefs and the anxieties of the men of this age, especially those who are poor or in any way afflicted, these are also the joys and hopes, the griefs and anxieties of the followers of Christ. Indeed, nothing genuinely human fails to raise an echo in their hearts. . . . That is why this community realizes that it is truly and intimately linked with mankind and its history' (GS 1).

In the first part of *Gaudium et spes* the fundamental lines of a theology of earthly well-being are developed. The fourth chapter concerns the presence of the people of God in earthly realities, with emphasis on the necessary interaction, the close inter-dependence of Church and world. 'The Church, at once a visible assembly and a spiritual community, goes forward together with humanity and experiences the same earthly lot which the world does. She serves as a leaven and as a kind of soul for human society as it is to be renewed in Christ and transformed into God's family. That the earthly and the heavenly cities penetrate each other is a fact accessible to faith alone' (GS 40).

'For the force which the Church can inject into the modern society of man consists in that faith and charity put into vital practice, not in any external dominion exercised by merely human means' (GS 42).

Today more than ever, the Church's visibility and sacramentality depends on its members who participate in the daily effort to bring reconciliation, peace, freedom, non-violence, brotherhood, humane progress to the city of man. The dogmatic constitution *Lumen gentium* gives expression to the irreplaceable role of the laity: 'Each individual layman must stand before the world as a witness to the resurrection and life of the Lord Jesus Christ and as a sign that God lives. As a body and individually, the laity must do their part to nourish the world with spiritual fruits (Gal 5: 22), and to spread abroad in it that spirit by which are animated those poor, meek and peacemaking men whom the Lord in the gospel calls blessed (Mt 5: 3-9). In one word, "What the soul is to the body, let Christians be to the world" ' (GS 38).

In all ages the Church has been present to the world, but the forms of her presence in any age determine her efficacy as sign and sacrament. Today the question of presence has special urgency: how can we best work to unite all men in making visible to our world the gentleness, the kindness, the love of Christ and of the Father, for which it is longing? Many books, meditations, courses, and the concentrated energies of the Council have contributed towards some definite and many tentative answers. In this perspective, the best commentaries on the two constitutions *Gaudium et spes* and *Lumen gentium* constitute an important effort towards a theology of the secular world in the light of the mystery of the Incarnate Word. [4]

---

[4] Various commentaries on *Gaudium et spes* give great attention to this task. See *Studia moralia* (Rome: Accademia Alfonsiana), IV, 1966. One of the first theologians who worked on a theology of the secular reality was G. Thils, *Théologie des réalités terrestres*, 2 vols. (Paris: Desclée et Brouwer, 1946-1949). *Transcendence et incarnation: deux psychologies spirituelles* (Louvain, 1950).

(c) *Natural law in the Law of Christ*

Why bring up such a remote question in a book on the sacraments? The answer is that it is not remote or irrelevant; it follows coherently from our vision of the sacramental value of the whole of creation and history. Once we have grasped the concept of this sacramentality as envisaged in the great oriental churches, namely, that of God making visible his presence and revelation in the ongoing creation with man as co-creator and co-revealer, then we can see the intimate connection between the two. [5]

Our natural law teaching is a tremendous heritage with much wisdom in it, but it can also be a great handicap. As long as its theories stand unrelated to the mystery of faith, or even reveal a thought-structure alien to the sacraments of salvation, the life of the Church cannot be fully incarnate in the important realm of human experience and reflection. If the sacramental outlook is to contribute substantially to bridging the gap between religion and life, then the past and present experiences and co-reflections of mankind must be brought together into the vision of faith and the sacraments of faith.

Natural law is the historically accessible synthesis of those dynamic orientations which are inscribed in man's innermost being and have gradually been brought to consciousness in an exchange of experiences and co-reflection. It plays a most important role in view of the co-existence and growing co-operation between Christians and other men of good will in working towards a more and more humane world.

The process of secularization and desacralization no longer allows us to cling to past natural law formulations as if they were sacred. Moreover, authoritarian imposition is unacceptable;

[5] I have treated the problems of the relationship between natural law and revelation in an earlier work, *Morality is for Persons* (New York: Farrar-Straus-Giroux, 1971). I here pursue the same and similar arguments but explicitly in view of a broader vision of what I consider a sacramental reality, indeed, in view of a sacramental vision of the whole of life including 'natural law' which, in the traditional manuals, surely had nothing to do with the sacraments.

this is a sphere where the autonomy of modern man is not only strongly felt but is necessary for a sincere search for truth. However, since it is a field in which we see the promptings of the Spirit and the signs of the ongoing presence of the Lord of history, a sacramental vision of human relationships and human history should constitute sound footing for the Christian in a secular age. A fitting presentation of it can constitute a valid basis for dialogue, whereas an erroneous, formalistic or authoritarian imposition or presentation can destroy every possibility of encounter. Our first concern here remains an integrated outlook for believers themselves.

Man discovers the law written in his heart when he actively searches for the good and the true, according to his social and historical nature. 'In fidelity to conscience, Christians are joined with the rest of men in the search for truth and for the genuine solution to the numerous problems which arise in the life of individuals and from social relationships' (GS 16).

The task of seeing natural moral law as a bridge for the dialogue with all men ought not to weaken Christians' consciousness of their own particular gift. Theology must exert every effort to make specific what is unique in 'the law of Christ', 'the law of faith', and at the same time indicate how natural law can be seen as an integrating part of the total 'law of grace and faith'.

Since we do not renounce dialogue with the humanists and scientists of today, we have to explore first how they address that reality which we call traditionally 'natural law'. My own approach to the problem, in so far as it is not a matter of final integration, is very similar to that of men like Erich Fromm, [6]

---

[6] Among the many books of Fromm see: *Man for Himself. An Inquiry into the Psychology of Ethics* (New York: Rinehart, 1974); *The Sane Society* (New York: Rinehart, 1955); *The Art of Loving* (New York: Harper, 1956); *The Heart of Man. Its Genius for Good and Evil* (New York: Harper & Row, 1964); *The Revolution of Hope. Toward a Humanized Technology* (New York: Harper & Row, 1968); *The Anatomy of Human Destructiveness* (New York: Rinehart and Winston, 1973).

Gordon Allport, [7] Viktor Frankl, [8] and especially Abraham Maslow. [9] I should like to point to Maslow's characteristics of what is human, in the sense that in every normal person there are inner needs to respond to, an inner need to realize values. Maslow insists that what is human in the best sense is accessible to what is scientific, through shared experience and reflection. The best of humanness manifests itself not so much in philosophical theories as in persons who embody attractive qualities and human peak-experiences. 'It has been sufficiently demonstrated that the human being has, as part of his intrinsic construction, not only physiological needs, but also psychological ones'. [10] 'Human beings strive perpetually towards ultimate humanness which is itself anyway a different kind of Becoming

[7] See Gordon W. Allport, *Personality and Social Encounter* (Boston: Beacon Press, 1960); *The Individual and His Religion* (New York: Macmillan, 1950); *Becoming: Basic Considerations for a Psychology of Personality* (New Haven: Yale Univ. Press, 1955).

[8] See above all Viktor Frankl, *The Doctor of the Soul* (New York: Knopf, 1965) and *Man's Search for Meaning. An Introduction to Logotherapy* (London: Hodder & Stoughton, 1964). My book *Medical Ethics* (revised ed., Slough: St Paul Publications, 1974) often follows the insights of Frankl, e.g. pp. 167-180.

[9] The best known of Abraham H. Maslow's writings are probably *Motivation and Personality* (New York: Harper, 1954); *Religions, Values and Peak Experiences* (Columbus, Ohio: Ohio State Univ. Press, 1964); *The Farther Reaches of Human Nature* (New York: Viking Press, 1971); the following section quotes from Maslow's 'Psychological Data and Value Theory' in A.H. Maslow (ed.), *New Knowledge in Human Values* (Chicago: Henry Regnery, 1970), where Maslow expresses his conviction (p. 126) that the results of his research are in agreement with the views of Erich Fromm, Kurt Goldstein, C. Buhler, Carl G. Jung, Joseph Nuttin and others. Regarding the question how to integrate all this 'natural' knowledge about man's inborn dynamics towards the good, I refer to the Protestant writer Langdon Gilkey, *Catholicism confronts Modernity* (New York: Seabury Press, 1975), p. 152: 'My suggestion is, that this translation of natural law should be interpreted, not in terms of either the original creation or of present social experience, but rather re-interpreted theologically and eschatologically...'; a theological vision of natural law envisages a 'human being and a human world directed towards their own natural fulfilment in the Kingdom of God'.

[10] Maslow, *New Knowledge,* p. 123.

and growing'. 'We are again and again rewarded for good Becoming by transient states of absolute Being, which I summarized as peak-experiences'. [11]

Maslow thinks that there is scientific proof for 'all the evidence that forces us in the direction of a concept of healthy growth or of self-actualizing tendencies. This is partly deductive evidence in the sense of pointing out that, unless we postulate such a concept, much of human behaviour makes no sense'. [12] Maslow is not blind with respect to the paramount importance of the human *milieu*, but he rightly insists more on the inborn drive towards growth. 'The role of the environment is ultimately to permit him or help him to actualize *his own* potentialities not *its* potentialities. The environment does not give him potentialities and capacities; he *has* them in inchoate or embryonic form, just as he has embryonic arms and legs. And creativeness, spontaneity, selfhood, authenticity, caring for others, being able to love, yearning for truth are embryonic potentialities belonging to his species-membership just as his arms and legs and brain'.[13]

Just as good traditional natural law theory repeated that it does not point to duties imposed from without but rather to what is 'inborn' ('natural' from the Latin '*nasci — natus*'), similarly Maslow insists that his study of fully humane people does not point to laws imposed as 'ought', while unfulfilled people are rather 'under law'. 'I do not say, "he ought to choose this or that", but only, "healthy people, permitted to choose, are observed to choose this or that". This is like asking, "What are the values of the best human beings" rather than "what should be their values?" ' [14] Thus he points out that the point of departure is the experience of spontaneity in doing what is good.

Although following a strictly scientific, empirical method in his research of fully human health he refers frequently to the

[11] *Ibid.*, p. 124.
[12] *Ibid.*, p. 125.
[13] *Ibid.*, p. 131.
[14] *Ibid.*, p. 128.

F

similar visions of great philosophical and religious traditions. 'Our description of actual characteristics of self-actualizing people parallels at many points the ideal urged by the religions, for example, the transcendence of self, the fusion of the true, the good and beautiful, contribution to others, wisdom, honesty and naturalness, the transcendence of selfish motivation, the giving up of "lower" desires in favour of "higher" ones, the differentiation between ends (tranquility, serenity, peace) and means (money, power, status), the decrease of hostility, cruelty and destructiveness, and the increase of friendliness, gentleness and kindness, etc.' [15]

Certainly Maslow does not approach religions with a perspective of religious faith, but as an observer along with believers of what can be observed, seen and made the object of common study and reflection. Maslow's writings as those of the other authors mentioned above do not speak (generally) of such a religious idea as 'man created in the image and likeness of God', but they always have as basis the values which are made *visible and accessible* by those who in a convincing way embody genuine humanness. This is a central point in the broader sacramental vision which I advocate: man who lives according to the law written in his very being is a main sacrament; he makes visible in an attractive manner what is good and beautiful.

As our first concern when speaking of natural law for the sake of dialogue with all the humanists of today is to know what we are speaking about and what our partners speak about — fundamentally we can mean the same phenomenon — so it is our second not lesser concern to preserve our own identity as Christians by expressing how we look at natural law in respect to our total outlook which is determined by faith. It is my conviction that we have as Christians to oppose every horizontalism and verticalism that is oblivious of the specific character of Christian faith. I therefore try to elaborate a theology of 'natural law' within 'the law of Christ', because 'in him everything in

[15] *Ibid.*

heaven and on earth was created . . . and all things are held together in him' (Col 1:16-17).

In the past few years the emphasis on the autonomy of the secular sphere and of the ethics concerning it has led in several countries to a strong tendency among Catholic moralists to assert that the moral message of revelation does not add anything specific to mere natural law ethics (the autonomous ethics of the secular man) but only inspires and dynamizes it by a new intentionality, by new motives. [16] Their conscious concern is the just affirmation that there exists only one order of salvation and they hope that their approach fosters a respectful and meaningful dialogue with all men of good will. But unconsciously their appeal seems to be directed to the magisterium that it cease to monopolize knowledge about natural law and stop asserting in the name of God-given authority what should be the outgrowth of a better knowledge of man (through shared experience and reflection and in a spirit of faith).

But I want to state honestly that I consider this trend as a dangerous reductionism. Christ has wrought and revealed a new creation, not only pious motives. The 'vocation of the faithful in Christ' [17] goes far beyond what reason can think out and prove. Christ is 'the way and the life'. The morality of the beatitudes is based on the new life and the new power of love he grants us by his death and resurrection and by the mission of the Holy Spirit. Some of the modern proposals are more pernicious than the moral doctrine of Pelagius whom St Augustine has so vigorously opposed. Pelagius never negated the uniqueness of the moral message of Christ; on the contrary he called for a radical imitation of Christ. Pelagius failed *only* to speak about the necessity of the grace of the Holy Spirit; he did not elaborate a synthesis between 'the law of faith' and 'the

[16] In order not to be misunderstood I want to stress the importance of motives, and above all the energizing and all-embracing motives of the gospel. On the renewing power of motives see the already mentioned book of Maslow, *Motivation and Personality.*

[17] Cf. OT 16.

law of grace'. *Only* the uniqueness of 'the law of the Spirit' is
obscured in his thought; the Christo-centric character of the
morality of the New Testament remains in his over-all view
strongly asserted, above all in its contents: to live according
to 'the new Adam' as sons and daughters of God.

In the new 'naturalism' on the other hand, the motivation
seems to be taken from a disembodied supernaturalism, and its
content does not at all reflect one's being a new creature in
Christ. Most of the proponents of this view were schooled in
a static morality, a morality of limits; in a certain sense the new
position is a natural heir to the legalistic concept of moral
theology which intended only to specify the minimal require-
ments of external norms, neglecting the dynamics of growth
according to the new commandment, 'Love one another as I
have loved you' (Jn 15:12). Since we are created in the image
of God, the norm and the motive are identical with the rule,
'love your neighbour as yourself'. Christ adds, 'as I have loved
you'. This is more than a motive; it is an orientation which is
an expression of our being in Christ, of the presence of his word
in us, of the fullness of revelation.

My position does not obscure the 'sacramentality' of creation,
of man created in the image and likeness of God, of God's
saving presence throughout history. The point is, however, that
everything receives its final value, orientation and correction
through Christ's coming.

The starting point and the goal, the beginning and end of
New Testament morality is *being in Christ* in whom dwells
the fullness of being. This is new not only with respect to a
hypothetical pure nature but also with respect to all that mankind can derive from its experiences and from its reflections
without the unique revelation in Christ. The 'new being in
Christ' penetrates the whole man and so determines his mission
in the world: *to be its light.*

So we have to be careful, in working out a synthesis, to see
how natural law — all that has been made visible and accessible
in humanity's constant searching, its treasuring up of a living

tradition, sharing of reflections throughout history and its gradual acquisition of what is best in human beings who have lived and reflected on their experiences — to see how all this fits into the law of Christ who is the primordial sacrament.

I see the possibility of a synthesis along the following lines.

(1) *Both the natural law and the law of Christ derive their ultimate and definitive value by being a revelation of the Father's loving design.*

This is very important. If we insist that the heathen and non-Christians can be saved, they will be saved not only through their own reasoning or initiative, but through whatever they found through God's own revelation of his presence in history, his presence in men who are good, holy, just. Whatever we find in human experience that is valid, good, true, beautiful, is a gift from God, that makes manifest his love and his creative and redemptive presence; and by making it manifest he urges men from within to seek him. In searching for God they are searching for self-transcending love; and whenever man truly transcends himself in unselfish love, there is God's presence revealing his own love.

The revelation of God is not fulfilled simply on a verbal level; his economy of salvation is based on the intimate union of word and event. Every event, every reality, all that is made is God's gift and a word that reveals him. Such is the great vision which Paul traces in his first chapter of his letter to the Romans.

(2) *This total revelation is made for man and in view of man. It invites man to participate in the communion of divine love, in Christ, and through the Spirit, for the glory of the Father.*

The reality is made for man. All that is before our eyes reveals love directed to man and accessible to him who is image of God and capable of love. Man is the summit of creation, not only because he can perceive the various 'words' of God but above all because he can understand himself as a word that abides and can unfold its message. As a person, in all that he is and has, and especially in dialogue with others, man is a fundamental 'word' of God, in whose light all others are revealed in their full meaning as words of God. But only in an existential readiness to respond with all his being does he gradually understand himself.

(3) *Between the natural law and the morality revealed in its fullness by Christ, is a difference not merely quantitative but also qualitative.*

It is a tremendous happening after millions of years of human groping, learning, inter-communicating, developing, when the Word Incarnate, the Way and the Light, the Son of God himself, prepared by the prophets, comes into the history of man. That is unique. It is not only a quantitative leap; it is absolutely a qualitative one.

The domain of natural law is what is revealed through the created world and all the events of history accessible to shared human experience and reflection. The special domain of the law of Christ is all that transcends human experience and reason, all that exceeds the human capacity of discovering by reason. The specific character of Christian morality is given by the mystery of Christ, God's design for making all mankind his sons and daughters in his only Son. All human history, however, is directed by God to this event. Christ comes and reveals that in him we are brothers and sisters, called to eternal con-celebration of the Father's love; this totally undeserved revelation is not merely added to the other forms of divine manifestation; it encompasses them and carries them all to fullness. We see then that from the very beginning, in God's design, this is the summit and goal of all creation and history. It is a totally new perspective, a qualitative leap.

We must see, however, the unity of history: that all the moral and religious experiences and reflections of thinking man before Christ and outside of the Judeo-Christian tradition are never purely 'natural'; there is always in them the gracious presence and merciful intervention of God, the Spirit of God renewing the face of the earth. The Spirit acts everywhere. In all ages there are spiritual men and women, prophets, saints in whom the presence of the Spirit is particularly intense. These do not necessarily belong to the people of Israel or to the Church; they are found also outside of both. The difference between the Judeo-Christian prophets and the others is, in fact, difficult to specify. This can be seen by the use which the primitive Church made of the books of the wise men and philosophers who lived before the coming of Christ. Even the books of wisdom of the Old Testament tell us about holy persons not belonging to Israel. However, the absolute uniqueness of Christ sheds a particular light on the religious history of Israel. But this must not be understood to the detriment of God's presence to all men of all ages. We can at the same time say: God has favoured Israel above all nations, and yet 'God has no favourites' (Rom 2:11).

(4) *Christ enters human history as the fullness of revelation, the definitive Word of the Father.*

Christ inserts himself into human history, carrying to completion man's long and difficult search for full understanding of himself and of the gifts and calling of God. He is the final answer, the perfect man because he is God-man. Through faith in his divinity and his humanity, man finds in him his true salvation in the way willed by God.

The historical reality of Christ, his example and his words, are a shared patrimony of mankind even for individuals and communities that have not yet come to explicit faith. All men of good will, although they may not yet have arrived at full knowledge of Christ as the Son of God, are enriched in their moral experience, in their aspirations, reflections and co-reflections because of Christ, sacrament of unity, goodness and justice, somehow made known by his Church.

Not only has the world gained through the great investment of goodness inspired by Christ's coming; there is also the continuing attractiveness of his teachings. Think, for instance, of the almost three million adults who, in the last census in Japan, declared themselves as Christians although only seven hundred thousand adults and children together are enrolled members of Japan's Christian churches. These people feel themselves to be, in their own way, followers of Christ's teachings. And take India. Christians there number only about two per cent. But Gandhi, having learned from the gentleness of Christ, had influence throughout the world. Repeatedly he said, 'We have to preserve the holy books of Hinduism; however, if all were lost, the sermon on the mount would suffice'. And Krishna, who was also a great reformer, said, 'While we have to be faithful to Hindu tradition, we have to correct it by the doctrine of the divine master'. He meant Christ. His presence, then, once entered into history, has been and is effective in countless ways and countless channels. However, it is infinitely more a reality for Christians who fully recognize him as the Divine Master, and direct their lives by what he said and did and brings to life by the mission of the Holy Spirit.

(5) *The law of Christ as well as the natural law comes to be understood only gradually and slowly.*

It was a long time, before Jesus could ask his apostles, 'Whom do you say the Son of Man is?', and Peter and the others recognized him both as the Son of God and the servant of all men. Only after his resurrection did they come to understand more clearly what Christ had told them. Only gradually, too, the primitive community deepened its understanding of Christ's message and came to realize that the gospel must not be kept in the captivity of the Jewish tradition and law.

Our Church goes through a similar spiritual journey today to come to a better understanding of the law of Christ and better discernment of what his example is in his docility towards the Spirit. The Spirit is sent to the Church to guide her to full understanding of the truth. Her sacramentality is that of a pilgrim in her readiness to learn, to listen, to take counsel with others. No man will succeed, with words or with his life, to express the full truth of Christ. The Church, to the extent that she *is* Church — that is, to the extent that she is the fellowship of all her members in the Spirit — grows in her knowledge of truth.

Similarly, man's comprehension of natural law is not readily available to the isolated individual but only to humanity. Through communion and interaction of persons, the human community perceives it gradually. It becomes perceptible to man's observation and reasoning, far more through those who make it visible in their whole life than through any abstract theories. The magisterium of the Church cannot teach natural law without participating humbly in the learning process. It needs a special openness to the Spirit and his promptings in the saints.

(6) *The same God writes in the heart of man both the natural law and that of Christ.*

The natural law is not a well-defined code. Its content can never be defined once for ever because it is all the great reality of God's presence in the history of man, his urging and dynamic presence shaping man in his image and likeness in an on-going creation. It is God's word inscribed in man's heart which man discovers gradually through experience and co-reflection.

Natural law is always a matter of the existential man, man with the tremendous wealth and burden of past history on his long journey in community with others. When a formulation of natural law loses contact with existing reality, turns to the abstract and is externally imposed without constant searching to know man better, its character is changed, just as a dogmatic formulation is changed when words have changed their meaning in the course of time and in another context do not mean what they originally meant. We have constantly to be open to new insights. If the Church should say that she has now all the solutions forever, she would no longer be a saving sign of humanity's journey and God's presence because she would not fit into the human pattern and into the on-going history of God with man.

The starting point of all formulations of natural law ought to be a phenomenology of the best experiences of mankind, gathered in constant contact with men and integrated with past history, tradition, and all new insights. Natural law represents co-reflection in time and in space; consequently diversity in its expressions is not only possible but legitimate and indispensable: as legitimate and indispensable as is the diversity of expressions of the law of Christ in the many diverse cultures and subcultures.

(7)   *Ultimately, the content of natural law unfolds this insight: 'Do to others as you would have them do to you; do not do to others what you would not want them to do to you'.*

This has to do with our 'neighbour'. Mankind travelled a long and difficult road before clarifying the concept of neighbour. Even Israel, in spite of the impetus given under the inspiration of prophets, maintained a restricted vision of the neighbour. This restrictiveness still lingered in the primitive Jewish Christian community to some extent. The position of St James and of the community of Jerusalem in the discussions on the Mosaic law can be explained by the influence of a sacralized racial concept of neighbour, a characteristic trend in Israel. But Christ reveals in a perfect way who is our neighbour: all men, whoever needs our love and our help. He gives us the norm of love for one's neighbour — his own unlimited love. Thus a synthetic vision of the natural law and of the law of Christ can be found only in the fullness of love revealed in Christ and made fully visible in his life and death and by his teaching. He came to tear down all the barriers between Jews and Gentiles.

(8)   *Natural law has a certain resemblance or analogy to faith (an 'analogia fidei') at least as to the attitude it requires of man.*

Karl Barth, one of the great Protestant theologians, has given us the finest perspective of an integrated natural law in his famous expression 'analogia fidei'. The best in natural law is an openness, a search in solidarity and in an existential readiness to love and serve our neighbour, and a creative fidelity. It is characteristic of the best experiences of mankind to have the will to participate, to communicate, to search and to enrich one another mutually, and to put moral insights into practice.

This is also, and even more so, the characteristic mark of faith. Wherever there is genuine hope, absolute readiness to search for truth and to act on the recognized truth, faith knows that all this can only be through the grace of the Holy Spirit: that this is God revealing himself, renewing the face of the earth and the hearts of men. The mark of saving faith is not in saying, 'I believe everything that is taught'; it is much more in constant openness, constant search to know God better, to know Christ better, and also to know man and serve him better. Faith is a journey that is never satisfied until it yields to the vision face-to-face.

So natural law has an analogy to faith. In authentic human experience and true co-reflection, there are many expressions of openness, acceptance, of absolute sincerity in the search for the good and in the readiness to respond to the dignity of the Thou. There is thus a power of salvation in natural law, an implicit presence of the dynamic of faith and a foreshadowing of a community of faith. The wisdom and goodness of non-Christians are 'seeds of the Word' (Clement of Alexandria). If a Christian community manifests this attitude not only in matters of faith but in the common search for justice and goodness, this becomes a pre-evangelization, a kind of prelude to the coming of Christ to all in explicit faith.

(9) *The knowledge of natural law alone exists nowhere in its purity; it is always somehow confused by the sinfulness of the world. Therefore, it always needs to be redeemed by Christ. If it closes itself to Christ it becomes a dead law.*

If a natural law theory closes itself to Christ, it does not manifest humanity on the right journey. There is always in man's yearning for truth and goodness an element of salvation (grace), a presence of Christ and his Spirit. However, there is also present man's collective sinfulness as long as redemption by Christ does not permeate everything.

The natural law is no longer the expression of the true nature of man and it is deprived of every value when man sets himself up as the centre, using his concepts as an instrument for oppressing others and to defend the egotistical interests of individuals and of groups, or when he considers his own personal experiences and reflections sufficient for discovering the whole truth. To be a Christian means to accept in an explicit way the revelation of God which comes to us in the person of Christ and in the community of faith gathered in him. It includes a constant longing for a better knowledge of God and of his will. It means, therefore, also reflecting and co-reflecting on all human experiences in the light of Christ. All this is a redemptive process that regains the authentic and full meaning of all that is true and valid. It tends to eliminate all prejudices, superficiality and forms of idolatry which are found in the doctrines of various cultures and human religions. A static and self-sufficient concept of natural law cannot be integrated into the vision and life of faith.

(10) *The reciprocal relationships between the natural law and the community of faith guided by the magisterium are very complex.*

The magisterium does not invent faith but receives it. It is subjected to divine revelation and is, in a very special way, obliged to be an embodiment of constant readiness to learn: to be a part of the learning Church (*Ecclesia discens*). Its task is to muster the fullness of the faith not only from theologians but also from the lived and incarnate faith of the saints and of all believers: *sensus fidei fidelium*. We should not forget that besides the magisterium of the successors of Peter and of the bishops, God has given us also the most valuable magisterium of the saints who, in their lives were visible images of the pilgrim Church in their total openness and their gigantic strivings. He has given us besides the magisterium of learned men, the magisterium of fathers and mothers who live faith and communicate it to their children. Nobody embodies the whole magisterium, because nobody monopolizes the Holy Spirit. But if there is docility of all to the Spirit, there is no doubt about the ministry of the Church. The magisterium of Peter and his successors is then greatly honoured.

Regarding natural law, the role of the official magisterium is analogous to its role regarding faith. Aided by theologians and by those among the faithful who are expert in the diverse anthropological sciences, its task is to gather the experiences of all the cultures, of tradition, and all the new knowledge of men, so that mankind may share in this wealth. The magisterium's very first task, therefore, is to encourage dialogue and then to bring all the experiences and assertions of human wisdom into light of the gospel. It is rightly a task of integration and discernment.

3. The Church, the Sacrament of the end of times

With the bodily coming of Christ, his resurrection and the overflowing of his Spirit, the fullness of the times is given. Not only with his words but in his whole existence and, above all, in his paschal mystery, Christ proclaims that 'the time of favour has come and the kingdom of God is close at hand' (Mk 1: 15). His coming, and especially his death and resurrection mark the *kairos,* the time of salvation.

Christ forever abides in the midst of his people. His presence is dynamic even though concealed from earthly man. The time of the Church is the intermediate period between Christ's first coming and his return: a time of hope and vigilance. The first coming of Christ is already the sign of the greatest hope, that of his final coming in glory. In all that he has done and made, and particularly in his Church, Christ continues to be a sacrament that urges us to 'look forward to the happy fulfilment of our hopes when the splendour of our great God and Saviour Jesus Christ will appear' (Tit 2: 13).

In this interval the Church is truly the sacrament of Christ in so far as she celebrates in gratitude the greater hope in such a way that all men can experience it.[18] She is the fruitful and efficacious sacrament of the end of times and of the intermediate period to the extent that her visible life manifests vigilance for the good use of the present moment (the *kairos*), and to the extent that her dynamism and fecundity are commensurate with her thanksgiving for the first coming and the awaited *parousia* of Christ.

True vigilance and the best use of the present time require detachment from all superficial clinging to traditions, written laws and customs, all covetousness and desire for earthly prestige. Only if the Church lives this freedom in affirmation that 'the whole frame of the world is passing away' (1 Cor 7:31) can she properly exploit the richness of the present hour. In her renunciation of every form of domination, and in her patience in the ever-present task of humanizing and christianizing all sectors of the life of the faithful, she professes her faith in the power, already present, of the kingdom of God. Thus she expresses her hope in the new heaven and the new earth which will become a full and manifest reality only at the Lord's return.

The Church has the mission to be a sacrament of hope not only in the celebration of her sacraments but in all her being, in all her structures and above all in her faithful. The Church of the end of times knows she is already united to the heavenly Jerusalem in the praise of her Lord and Bridegroom. All this guards her against any form of triumphalism. She is united to that choir only as a pilgrim, a Church of the intervening period of the times which call for patience and repentance. These im pressions of her image are of paramount importance for dialogue with the separated brethren and for overcoming any temptation to secularism and horizontalism, which do not grasp the true dimensions of human history.

---

[18] Cf. LG 48. On the important theme, 'The Church and her sacraments as signs of hope and of vigilance', see my book *Hope is the Remedy* (Slough: St Paul Publications, 1971).

4. *The eschatological hope determining the whole presentation of moral theology*

To the extent that Christian life expresses and witnesses to the eschatological dimension of the Church and thus to the mystery of Christ 'who was, who is and who will come', it has sacramental value and the character of hope. This is the secret for overcoming the *embourgeoisement* of Christianity and the self-sufficiency of all forms of materialism. It also guards against the discontinuities of a false existentialism.

The treatise on the ultimate end (*de fine ultimo*), used as introduction in so many manuals of moral theology, ought to be re-thought thoroughly in this vision of the Church as sacrament of the greater hope: a hope that does not at all alienate one from the present hour or the realities of life, yet does not allow one to lose oneself in the superficiality of a worldly mentality.

But more than this is necessary. Throughout the whole of scientific moral theology and moral pedagogy, the sacramental dynamism of Christian life has to be projected and illumined by this sacramental vision of Christ, the great Sacrament of the end of times, of the intermediate period and of the Church as a sacrament of hope.

(a) *The law of continuing conversion*

Like the Church, the life of every Christian also finds itself energized in the tension between the *already* and the *not yet*, since that which is promised to the Christian in the new creation keeps him from being self-satisfied in the present. When we realize that everything we have received is an undeserved gift, this dynamically prompts us to focus our attention on the final goal and, at the same time, on the step which here and now we can take to attain it.

Both the phenomenon which we call triumphalism and pharisaism which is analogous to it stem from lack of proper attention to the fruitful tension between that which is already

manifest and that which is promised us by God. Without this
tension, people and institutions lapse into a sterile self-satisfaction
or into despair or into violence.

The aspirations of the Christian ought to be both magnanimous and humble. Christian life, if it is to be truly Christian,
is a glad and grateful 'yes' to the whole law of Christ, an ever-
renewed commitment to the unfinished task. It is always submitted to the judgement of Christ, a judgement which never
oppresses those who, with humility and courage, aspire to
higher and higher goals.

The treatise on continuing conversion ought therefore to
synthesize the renewal of structures with the law of continued
purification and growth; valid for every person, every group,
and for the whole Church. [19]

(b) *Commandments, both goal-oriented and prohibitive*

Because its perspective and basic nature is characterized by
the law of continual conversion, moral theology ought to centre
on the universal vocation to sanctity, in the same vision of
growth. It ought, therefore, to emphasize the New Testament
commandments which Christ expressed so decisively in the
sermon on the mount, concluding with the expression, 'There
must be no limit to your goodness, as your heavenly Father's
goodness knows no bounds' (Mt 5:48).

This attitude is expressed classically in Paul. The whole of
his life is a constant and more and more profound effort to know
Christ and the efficacy of his resurrection, and to live more
fully in communion with his sufferings and with the expectation
of the resurrection of the dead in union with him. 'It is not to
be thought that I have already achieved all this. I have not yet
reached perfection but I press on, hoping to take hold of that
for which Christ once took hold of me. My friends, I do not
reckon myself to have got hold of it yet. All I can say is this:
forgetting what is behind me, and reaching out for that which

---

[19] Cf. LG 8; UR 4.

lies ahead, I press towards the goal to win the prize which is God's call to the life above, in Christ Jesus' (Phil 3:12-14).

A presentation of the Church as *sacrament of the end of times and of the intervening period* sets in relief the eschatological virtues: hope, vigilance, gratitude, a spirit of poverty, serenity and discernment.

Emphasis on the sacraments, in so far as they indicate 'the sublimity of the vocation of the faithful in Christ', [20] inspires optimism, endurance and dynamism. At the same time, however, the consciousness of the 'not yet', of the intermediate period between the first and the definitive coming of Christ, leads us humbly to accept the necessity of delimiting, prohibitive precepts. However, in the final analysis, the great commandments of love of God and of our neighbour, which initiate the direction and the dynamic of Christian life, ought to prevail.

Christians, individuals and communities whose life is thus shaped by the energizing tension between the 'already' and the 'not yet' are not threatened by the 'future shock' and will also help others to keep or to regain their mental and spiritual health in this era of rapid changes.

[20] OT 16.

G

PART TWO

THE SEVEN SACRAMENTS TEACH US THE LAW OF CHRIST

PRELIMINARIES

In the first part I insisted on the fact that in Christ the sacramental economy brings to a climax the full visibility of God's love, and that in Christ and for him, the Church is the great sign and sacrament of salvation. At the same time we have seen how the sacramentality of all creation and of history, of all the works of the Word, is also revealed in Christ.

In the following pages I shall speak of the seven sacraments in so far as they 'teach' the fundamental character of Christian morality. However, we should keep constantly in mind the broader sacramental vision outlined earlier.

To avoid any misunderstanding, it seems well to state the following premises.

1. Even in speaking of the seven sacraments, the point of view remains always the *unique sacramentality of Christ,* the Word Incarnate, in his dynamic presence in the Church as sign of his presence among us and symbol of his love. The sacraments will be considered in their *capacity to open us to a broader view of the saving presence of Christ in history and in the daily events of our lives and of our times.*

2. The sacraments are privileged and efficacious signs of grace. They are true symbols of God's gracious presence instituted by Christ and dispensed by the Church in obedience to him. This does not mean, however, that the sacraments hold a *monopoly* of grace.

It is true that man has to submit himself humbly to the will of Christ who gave his Church some visible signs of grace; but the fact that Christ has given these special signs in which he manifests his graciousness and invites man to open himself visibly to this grace, cannot be interpreted to mean that Christ himself or the Holy Spirit is bound to these signs in such a way as to be unable or unwilling to operate salvation in other ways. The opposite is true. As privileged signs of salvation, the sacraments open us and direct our attention to all the other ways in which God shows men his graciousness. The sacraments do not allow any form of evasion or alienation, but demand vigilance for 'the signs of the times' and great respect and reverence for the wonderful ways in which God works and manifests himself outside of the sacramental life of the Church.

3.   It may not be easy to find the happy medium which, on the one hand, considers the sacraments of the Church as the *privileged key* opening the door to an understanding of the economy of salvation, and, on the other hand, does *not assert that the sacraments have a monopoly* of God's grace. I think, however, that a theology of the world, centred on the sacramental character of creation in the light of redemption, will be able to grasp the dynamics and vitality of the seven sacraments. The broader vision of sacramentality will also help to overcome any tendency towards sacramentalism.

4.   We must not forget that for many centuries the Church stood as the sacrament of salvation and celebrated the sacraments without exactly determining their number.

Keenly concerned as I am not to diminish the value of any of the seven sacraments, I shall seek to avoid in our discussion a too technical concept of them. The direction set by the Second Vatican Council in the theology and in the life of the Church is reflected also in its vision of the sacraments. One cannot forget that in the sacramental theology of the last centuries, an over-emphasis on the role of the minister and great stress on ritual and rubrics resulted in a certain degree of under-development in the doctrine of the universal priesthood of the people. The authoritarian aspect found expression in a variety of forms. The Church of today is more conscious of her freedom with respect to the way she proclaims salvation by means of the actions, words and symbols through which she realizes it. There is much more attention today to the active participation of the faithful.

5. In speaking of the sacraments and of a sacramental vision of life, we must be mindful of the modern phenomena of secularization, desacralization and 'desacerdotalization'. [1]

While many think that the theology of a secularized age can no longer say anything of importance about the sacraments, my thought goes in the opposite direction. It would seem chiefly a matter of emphasizing *the prophetic, the personalistic and the communitarian element of the sacraments*. Past over-emphasis on stones, places and other 'sacred things' was concealing to a considerable extent the real sacramental message. 'Desacralization', then, should generate a more authentic concentration on the sacraments and a deeper, more serious understanding of their sanctifying effect.

It is clear, therefore, that we must learn a new language free from all false sacralization, yet free also from any tendency towards secularism. Accepting the challenge of secularization, we shall not stress so much ritual and rubrics but ask, 'Does the sacrament really become a visible sign, does it truly communicate to men and women of this culture the appealing, challenging, gladdening news of God's love, mercy and fidelity?'

6. Given that those who believe in the Church and celebrate the sacraments of the Church are becoming more and more a minority, we have to ask how others are to have access to salvation; we still have to place in a sacramental perspective the problem of the salvation of all people.

The theological tradition can be of assistance here. St Thomas, for example, speaks of the necessity of 'sacraments' (in the broad sense) even before the promulgation of the old

---

[1] Cf. my book *Faith and Morality in a Secular Age* (Slough: St Paul Publications, 1973).

law and before the coming of Christ. [2] Wherever and whenever
God gives signs of love and mercy, with the grace of the Holy
Spirit and in view of the salvation prepared in Christ, they can
generate a living faith in him who is the source of salvation. All
the signs of mercy, of goodness, of solidarity which quicken
human life can have a sacramental character; not, of course, as
purely human elements but in so far as there is discernible in
them the dynamic presence of Christ. In saying this, however,
let us not forget the privileged role of the sacramental signs
instituted by Christ and entrusted to the Church.

[2] *Summa Theol.* 3:6:3.

Chapter 1

THE SIGNS OF GRACE

1. *The primacy of grace*

Theology ought to be aware of the particular danger which threatens humanity at this time of history. Although man has achieved great powers, is capable of regulating things, of planning and of submitting nature to himself, he frequently remains under-developed in the field of human relationships.

As long as we continue to speak of the sacraments and of grace in a language of causality or of 'means', we fail in two respects. First, we should instead meet modern man's hunger and thirst for personal meaning, for more humane and persona-lized relationships; and secondly, in speaking of grace, we should stress the divine initiative so that today's man will understand that only in openness to the divine creativity can he find his own spontaneity and a real spirit of initiative. The sacraments should be presented as signs by which God himself, through his own initiative, provokes in us initiatives of authentic love, of true mercy, and of a new dimension in personal relationships.

In any teaching about divine grace, it is necessary to return to the biblical vision of what grace is. It is not simply a 'thing'; nor is it to be presented as a metaphysical quality; it is this wonderful event of God graciously turning his face to us. We experience it joyfully, gratefully, and this creates for us a more intimate personal relationship with him and with our fellowmen.

Grace (*charis*) means the graciousness of God in turning his countenance to man. It is a sign of God's nearness, a word of love which arouses in us the answer of love. Grace means gentleness, the attractive energy of true love; it means alliance, a reciprocal relationship which, however, remains wholly the gift of God. On man's part it is received with the awareness that it is an undeserved gift and this awareness energizes us, teaches us, disciplines us, gives orientation to our whole life.

The scholastic doctrine expresses the primacy of grace in the sacraments by the phrase *opus operatum*: the sacrament is the work of God himself. However, it is impossible for us to express this 'work of God' within the Aristotelian categories of causality.

The work of God always has the character of word, of message. If we speak of *opus operatum,* therefore, we speak of the Word in whom all things are created, and of the new creation in the Word Incarnate who, by all that he does, speaks to our minds and hearts.

Along the same line of thought, St Thomas introduces his treatise on the sacraments: 'After that which refers to the mysteries of the Word Incarnate, it is necessary to study the sacraments of the Church which derive their efficacy from the same Word Incarnate'. [1]

We sinners are unworthy of God's grace. The sacramental economy continually reminds us that it is only because we are *redeemed by the passion, death and resurrection of Christ* that we have access to God and receive the signs of his graciousness and his goodness. The passion of Christ is always recalled. 'The sacrament is properly said to be what is ordained to signify our sanctification, in which three elements can be taken into consideration: first, that which brought us sanctification, namely, the passion of Christ. . . .' [2]

[1] *Summa Theol.* 3:60, introd.
[2] *Summa Theol.* 3:60:3.

'From the side of Christ dying on the cross sprang the sacraments through which the Church is saved. Thus it appears that the sacraments derive their virtue from the passion of Christ.'[3]

In the mystery of the Word Incarnate, in his passion, resurrection and ascension, and in the mission of the Holy Spirit, God has revealed his love for man who because of his sin is unworthy of it. In the same mystery, God makes visible to the Church, conscious of her need to be redeemed, the reign of his grace which saves her and all those who unite themselves with her as servant Church. The sacraments, precisely because they make us aware of the gratuitousness of redemption, transform us and constitute us as a sign of the kingdom of God.

A full understanding of the sacraments teaches us to accept all things, principally the love which gives life, with a spirit of gratitude for the goodness of God. Through the sacraments, Christ reminds us continually 'You did not choose me; I chose you. I appointed you to go out and bear fruit, fruit that will last' (Jn 15:16).

When we become fully conscious of being redeemed and chosen by divine mercy, then we bear the fruits of mercy, of goodness, of thanksgiving and all the rest. The farewell discourses teach this sacramental reality which is continued in the Church: 'I am the real vine and my Father is the gardener. Every barren branch of mine he cuts away, and every fruiting branch he cleans to make it more fruitful still. Dwell in me as I in you. No branch can bear fruit by itself, but only if it remains united with the vine; no more can you bear fruit unless you remain united with me' (Jn 15:1-4).

Authentic catechesis and the sacramental celebration itself transform us precisely because they make us all the more conscious that God has predestined us for adoption as sons and daughters 'through Jesus Christ, so that the glory of his grace bestowed on us in his beloved Son might be praised. For

[3] *Summa Theol.* 3:62:5.

in Christ we have redemption and our sins are forgiven through
the shedding of his blood, according to the riches of his grace,
lavished upon us, imparting wisdom and prudence.... He has
made known to us his hidden purpose ... to be effected when
the time is ripe: to re-establish all things in heaven and earth
into a unity in Christ' (Eph 1: 5-10).

In grateful celebration of the wonders of divine grace,
redeemed man becomes more and more aware of his status as
a miserable sinner being called to holiness. In his letter to the
Ephesians (2: 4-10) Paul reminds us that 'God, rich in mercy,
for the great love he bore us, brought us to life with Christ even
when we were dead in our sins; it is by his grace you are saved.
And in union with Christ Jesus he raised us up and enthroned
us with him in the heavenly realms, so that he might display in
the ages to come how immense are the resources of his grace
and how great his kindness to us in Christ Jesus. For it is by
his grace you are saved, through trusting him; it is not your
own doing. It is God's gift, not a reward for work done. There
is nothing for anyone to boast of. For we are God's handiwork,
created in Christ Jesus to devote ourselves to the good deeds
for which God has designed us' (Eph 2: 4-10).

In one of the following chapters the matter of *praise of the
glory of God* will be treated more in depth. Here I mention only
that man, when he is fully conscious of the primacy of grace,
knows also that God glorifies his name of Father through his
gracious love, and that man cannot vitally receive grace without
a new, more sincere and more profound intention to glorify
God and to seek first, in gratitude and service, the coming of
his kingdom.

2. *The kingdom of God*

The celebration, the sacramental catechesis, and the biblical
doctrine of the kingdom of God illumine one another. I should
like therefore to direct attention here to how, in the biblical

vision of God's kingdom, all the signs of his grace are made visible and understandable.

'Blessed are the poor in spirit'. The kingdom of God becomes visible only in his servants, his handmaids, in all who, in full awareness and gratitude, draw their life from the primacy of grace. Only those who, in a spirit renewed by the Holy Spirit, acknowledge themselves as poor, as beggars before God, succeed in recognizing and accepting the kingdom of God. 'The kingdom of heaven is theirs' (Mt 5:3).

The scriptures speak of 'the mystery of the kingdom of God'. Through the economy of salvation, that is, by means of his grace and of the full manifestion of his mercy and goodness, God makes his kingdom visible. It is a *mysterium,* a sacrament revealed to the faithful ones. 'The kingdom of God is a reality of the supernatural order, analogous to the Pauline mystery (Christ in us). It points to a deep intervention of God, who communicates to us a participation in his nature. . . . We consider the objective significance: an economy of divine grace which is open to those who are privileged. . . . A divine economy is essentially a work of God, of the God of Jesus Christ'. [4]

All the parables on the kingdom of God express before all else the primacy of grace and a corresponding attitude of gratitude, of receptivity, of praise of God, humility, and surrender of oneself to God: all this in such faith and trust that the redeemed person radiates a new spontaneity, and takes new initiatives as he becomes, in fact, a sharer in God's creative, renewing love. In other words, the man who gives himself to the kingdom of grace bears fruit abundantly.

All energies and capacities of commitment, of indefatigable work, of firm decision have their source in the gratuitousness of the gift of the kingdom. 'Set your mind upon his kingdom and all the rest will come to you as well. Have no fear, little flock,

---

[4] L. Bonsirven, *La règne de Dieu* (Paris, 1957), p. 201. Cf. R. Schnackenburg, *God's Rule and Kingdom* (New York: Herder and Herder, 1963).

for your Father has chosen to give you the kingdom' (Lk 12: 31-32).

The words of the pastoral constitution *Gaudium et spes* can be considered a commentary on the preceding verses: 'Whoever in obedience to Christ seeks first the kingdom of God will, as a consequence, receive a stronger and purer love for helping all his brothers and for perfecting the work of justice under the inspiration of charity'. [5]

From awareness and thankfulness for the undeserved gifts of God springs vigilance, the readiness for the coming of the Lord: 'Hold yourselves ready, therefore, because the Son of Man will come at the time you least expect him' (Mt 24: 44). 'When that day comes, the kingdom of heaven will be like ten virgins who took their lamps and went out to meet the bridegroom' (Mt 25: 1).

The promise of the kingdom of God and the celebration of sacraments urge us to make God's gracious action in us visible through our own generous action in the service of our fellowmen, so that we too may become a sacrament of his kingdom. 'We urge you to respond to this appeal: you have received the grace of God; do not let it go for nothing. God's own words are, "In my time of favour I have heard you and in the day of salvation I helped you". The hour of favour has now come; now is the day of salvation' (2 Cor 6: 1-2).

God's gracious initiative in manifesting his kingdom is a call for man to be humble: 'I tell you this: unless you turn and become like children, you will not enter the kingdom of heaven. Whoever humbles himself like this child, he will be the greatest in the kingdom of heaven' (Mt 18: 3-4).

Christ, the Servant, totally dedicated to the glory of the Father and to the welfare of his brethren, is the full manifestation of the kingdom: 'Here is my Servant whom I have chosen, my beloved on whom my favour rests; I will send my Spirit

---

[5] GS 72.

upon him and he will proclaim judgement among the nations'
(Mt 12: 18).

Christ rejoices in the mystery of the kingdom: 'I thank thee,
Father, Lord of heaven and earth, for hiding these things from
the learned and wise and revealing them to the simple. Yes,
Father, such was thy choice' (Mt 11: 25-26). But from this
assent to the grace of God there arises a more pressing invitation
to follow Christ, the Servant of God. 'Bend your necks to my
yoke and learn from me, for I am gentle and humble-hearted,
and your souls will find rest' (Mt 11: 29).

Whoever really recognizes the gratuitousness of grace and
the gift of the kingdom will be willing to *sacrifice everything for
the one precious pearl* (Mt 13: 45-46). The kingdom of heaven,
the offer of eternal life, firmly and decisively impose a task on
sinful man. The acceptance of the kingdom of God requires
generosity and a spirit of sacrifice. 'If your hand or your foot
is your undoing, cut it off and fling it away; it is better to enter
life maimed or lame than to keep two hands or two feet and be
thrown into the eternal fire' (Mt 18: 18, Mk 9: 43-45).

Many parables on the kingdom of God speak of its dynamism,
its potentiality for growth; this aspect particularly needs emphasis
today so that modern man will understand that the primacy of
grace, the kingdom of God, does not allow a passive attitude, that
it provides the most dynamic motive and energy available to
man for the good of mankind. There is no greater spontaneity
or more authentic spirit of initiative for gathering everything in
true fraternity than is found in the humble and grateful awareness of having received the grace of God.

The biblical message of the kingdom of God and the sacramental economy, in their teaching about the primacy of grace,
lead us to focus our attention on the mystery of the Holy Trinity
as it is dynamically revealed to all men. In the paschal mystery,
the Word Incarnate reveals to the experience of faith the dynamism of divine life. In the Holy Trinity, the Father gives
himself, with all his wisdom, power and love, to his Word, his

Son. The Word is grace, the revelation of the luminous countenance of the Father. He receives himself from the Father and
responds with the gift of himself. The divine life is the life of
uncreated grace, an eternal exchange of love in the gift of
oneself.

Anointed by the fullness of the Holy Spirit, the human
nature of Christ also becomes gift, uniquely graced by the union
with the Eternal Word. The whole life of Christ to his death
itself expresses gratitude for this unique gift: 'Sacrifice and
offering thou didst not desire, but thou hast prepared a body
for me. . . . Then I said, "Here am I; as it is written of me in
the scroll, I have come, O God, to do thy will" ' (Heb 10:5-7).
And Christ's last breath again expresses gratitude in the gift of
himself: 'Father, into thy hands I commit my spirit' (Lk 23:46).

Christ reveals the mystery of uncreated grace reflected in
his life and death; he insists that his words are not his but the
Father's, that he has not come to do his will but the will of him
who sent him and that he has not come to seek his own glory but
the glory of the Father, confident that the Father, in turn,
will glorify him. In the resurrection the Father makes visible his
full acceptance of Christ's gratitude and trust.

The seven sacraments introduce us with growing consciousness to this fundamental meaning of the paschal mystery: of
grace made visible in the grateful acceptance of and response to
God's gifts. If we consider everything as gift and want to return
to God all the fruits of his gifts, we are already living, here on
this earth, the divine life, sharing in the mystery of the true
God. When we say the sacraments are signs of faith and of grace,
we mean that Christ continues his work through the faith and
graciousness of those who proclaim the gospel, who live the
gospel and thus share the faith with others and encourage the
following of Christ.

3. *The mystery of the kingdom of God and the mystery of the Church*

In gratitude and in praise of his grace, *Christ gives himself to the Father and sacrifices himself for the human race.* His answer to the gratuitous predestination of his human nature to the hypostatic union is an undivided love which, in self-bestowal for the whole of mankind, manifests the grace, the attractive love of the Father. From this love and this grace the Church is born.

The Church manifests the mystery and sacramentality of her life in a synthesis of praise of God for all his gifts, continually received, and her humble service to mankind. The mystery of the Church is that of grace freely received and of the unceasing manifestation of its fruitfulness in love and service which is properly hers. She lives in a tangible way the mystery of the kingdom, in her solidarity with all of humanity and that love for all men, which 'is not selfish' (1 Cor 13:5).

The praise of the grace of God keeps the Church looking outwards, saves her from anguished introversion. For her, grace is mission, an urgent task of making actual and visible in the world the kindness, the humaneness, the self-givingness of the Lord. Where she fails to make the magnetic energy of God's love visible, the talents with which she has been graced remain sterile, unproductively buried. Only in that dynamism which bears fruit in love for the life of the world are the mystery of the kingdom and the primacy of grace revealed.

Thus the pilgrim Church joins with the heavenly Jerusalem in a worship from which flows the more and more attractive power of love, goodness, mercy and gentleness. If catechesis and the celebration of the seven sacraments make perceptible the magnetism and the rallying power of the kingdom of God and the fruitfulness of gratitude in the service of others, the man of our secular age will be drawn once again, in fascination, to the sacraments, to the signs of God's graciousness which makes those who use them creative, spontaneous, gentle, gracious.

4. *Reflections on moral teaching*

(a) Just as man's part in the celebration of the sacraments consists primarily of a humble acceptance and grateful response to the action of God, so in the whole of Christian morality, *every obligation is inherent in the gift and springs from it*. There is no commandment or obligation for Christians in which the gift is not the first and most visible reality. By his gifts God attracts us and gives us the capacity and task of making our life a response to him. Christian life, therefore, is marked by spontaneity and generosity.

An authentic sacramental vision does not lock us in the seven sacraments but rather gives us that indispensable openness that *receives as the gift of God all events and all opportunities*. When one enters fully into the sacramental perspective, all the gifts of God become graces in a certain sense, but that is as an energy, an appeal and an invitation coming from God and making us more fully aware of his gracious presence.

When a system of morality emphasizes first the commandments or the human virtues, it ends by obstructing the fruitfulness of divine grace. A morality that does not fully recognize the attraction and power of God's love for man (divine grace) is sterile, or becomes even an obstacle to redemption. Every presentation of the commandments and of the tasks of men in the world ought to be in the perspective of praise for the glory and the grace of God.

One ought, therefore, to speak of God's gifts and divine grace in a way that calls attention to their dynamism which transforms and vivifies man's heart and inner being and the world around him. It is this that creates in him a spontaneity capable of bearing abundant fruit. The gifts of God, because they are free, ought not to become dead capital.

(b) The whole sacramental economy proclaims the truth, 'He came for us men and for our salvation'. In grace, God comes down to man to manifest his love and draw man to himself. The dynamism of grace yields abundant fruit of 'graced' love for a true brotherhood among men and for the salvation of the world. Gentleness and non-violent action have to be presented in this perspective.

One ought not to forget, however, that we are speaking here always of a morality that has its source in the dynamism of *grace*, which is God himself guiding us by his gracious and merciful love. One cannot equate it at all with a morality based on an anthropocentric horizontalism which is oblivious of the source of life.

The primacy of grace highlights the necessity of a *synthesis between theocentrism and concern for man in his integrity, wholeness and solidarity*. Man will not find his true self unless he recognizes the gratuitous love of God, nor can he express himself authentically except in a morality centred in praise for the glory of God's grace. Every moral effort that does not begin explicitly or at least implicitly with the gifts of God, and does not intend to praise his grace, becomes frustrating to man. Since all salvation comes from grace, it is impossible to find true fraternity, solidarity, wholeness and integrity except in the explicit recognition of God's gifts to us.

(c) It is from the primacy of grace and the nature of God's kingdom that the gospel gives meaning to morality (*gospel and law*, and not vice-versa). The economy of 'the new law' draws its strength and true value from the visible signs of God's graciousness. The primacy of grace demands that the sacramental celebration and the whole *kerygma* be, above all, an *effective evangelization*. Grace is the revelation of the attractive countenance of God, in gentleness, peace and joy which inspire new life. Whoever says 'the law of grace' also means the primacy of the gladdening news. In the communication of the message of joy, in the proclamation of God's gifts, grace is always the saving and energizing event.

(d)   The economy of the new law, in so far as it is a sacramental economy or a distribution of grace, has its *vital centre in the covenant*. Every catechesis and sacramental celebration, then, as well as every scientific presentation of the sacraments, should turn our attention to the covenant between Christ and the Church, between God and mankind: an alliance which is a gratuitous gift and, in its gratuitousness, calls for a total commitment of man to God and to his design to gather all men in a covenant of gracious, gentle and generous love. God's total commitment to the world calls us to confirm our commitment to him, to adore and praise him with our lives. Man cannot know the true norms of the law if he does not recognize the gifts of God in gratitude and in commitment to the covenant.

5. *Infant baptism*

For many centuries the baptism of infants seemed a marvellous expression of the primacy of grace: God, who creates us without asking us, offers predestination and grace to infants who are as yet incapable of making a personal decision. Their baptism expresses very well the need that all men born under 'the law of sin' (Rom 8:2) have to be redeemed and saved by that grace of God which is at the beginning of all redeemed initiatives.

Today, however, in view of a changed mentality and a new cultural context, infant baptism gives rise to some apparent difficulties with regard to the understanding of the whole sacramental economy, the nature of grace itself, and the matter of justification by faith in Christ. During the last decades, discussion has gone on in Protestant circles, although not among the Orthodox. Very great was the influence of Karl Barth, who, in his *Church Dogmatic,* cast doubt on the practice of baptizing infants. [6] In many parts of the Catholic Church there is a new searching.

[6] K. Barth, *Kirchliche Dogmatik* IV, 13 (Zollikon-Zürich, 1959), pp. 595 and 1000.

Ultimately, one of the most authoritative Lutheran theologians, Edmund Schlinck, in a study in depth of the scriptures, has taken a contrary position in favour of the traditional practice and with discernment of the actual situation. [7] A good coverage of the recent discussions, research, and the position of the Catholic Church is given by A. Winklhofer. [8]

The difficulties arise chiefly from the new situation of increased pluralism and secularization which is a sharp challenge of ritualism.

(a)   While the baptism of infants makes evident the need of all men for redemption, it is not easy for modern man to see how infants can be *justified by means of faith*. Grace is a gift that proceeds from divine freedom and invites a free response from man. But the infant, deprived of the use of reason, cannot personally accept the grace nor respond with faith.

(b)   In an era of 'the Church of the people', that is, in centuries when there was a compact Christianity, one could justify the baptism of infants on the basis of the covenant and the people of the covenant, who accepted neophytes and provided for them a sure ground of faith.

Zwingli and other reformers followed the traditional line when they took their position in favour of infant baptism, based on the following argument: as the sons of Abraham have received circumcision as the sign of belonging to the people of the covenant, so all the children of Christian people rightly receive baptism, the sign of the new covenant, soon after their birth. It was evident in that epoch that baptism effectively inserted infants into the community and into a people for whom faith was the normal and common condition.

Today, on the contrary, there no longer exists 'a Church of the people' to guarantee the child's post-baptismal catechumenate. Many who have been baptized before 'the use of reason'

[7]   E. Schlink, *The Doctrine of Baptism* (St Louis: Concordia Publishing House, 1969).

[8]   A. Winklhofer, *Kirche in den Sakramenten* (Frankfurt: Verlag Knecht, 1969), pp. 113-131. (Bibliography, p. 302-308).

have never experienced their belonging to the community of
faith, to the new covenant; the meaning of this sign of God's
gracious love has never been communicated to them in any
living way. Thus they could never personally ratify their baptism.

(c)   In medieval theology, the explanation of the necessity for
infant baptism was confused with the '*theologoumenon*' of limbo.
In this concept, while the necessity of grace, of redemption and
of divine initiative were well expressed, the dogma of the universal salvific will of God was imperilled. Besides, the primacy
of grace was absolutely tied with and monopolized by the
baptismal rite, so that infants who died in the mother's womb
or before being baptized seemed excluded from salvation.
Practically, this left unbaptized infants excluded from the saving
solidarity of Christ but bound in the pernicious solidarity of
Adam. Yet Christ is born and has died for all. 'Where sin was
multiplied, grace immeasurably exceeded it in order that, as sin
has reigned even to death, so also God's grace may reign in
righteousness even to life everlasting through Jesus Christ our
Lord' (Rom 5:20-21).

As the discussions in the preparatory commissions of the
Second Vatican Council have demonstrated, a great many
theologians and bishops no longer accept the idea of 'limbo', the
'*poena damni*' (loss of salvation) for billions of innocent infants
who, through no fault of their own, have not been able to receive
baptism. It has always seemed to me, from my earliest youth,
one of the strangest concepts of theologians. In the Bible there
is not the slightest indication of the existence of any such limbo.
When Christ speaks of the need of faith and baptism as conditions of salvation, he addresses himself to the adult who has
received the good news.

In my opinion one can maintain the necessity or usefulness
of baptizing infants without denying the possibility of salvation
for those who, without fault of their own, do not receive baptism.
It is not the task of theology to find which other way or means
God can use, because the ways of God are inscrutable.

Some theologians have proposed a theory according to which

each person, at the moment of his death, encounters Christ and can make a free choice and receive in gratitude the grace of God. Others have excluded the necessity of baptism, at least for the countless infants who die before leaving the mother's womb, because they cannot be 'reborn' by water and the Spirit since they are not actually 'born'. Still others believe that at least infants of believing parents can be saved through solidarity with the parents' faith. It is my firm conviction that all innocent children are offered the real chance of salvation.

The profound change in mentality, desacralization and secularization, and the emphasis on the character of personal encounter with Christ in the sacraments, do not seem necessarily to justify a radical relinquishing of infant baptism as practised since the second century. However, the manner of celebration of baptism, and the conditions of observance ought to help modern man to perceive its true significance.

(a)   Normally, the celebration of the sacrament of baptism ought to be a *community celebration of the people of God* for the praise of the glory of his grace. It should be a celebration of the covenant and of the active belonging to it, which sustains the faith of all the members. It ought also *to express the renewed commitment of all the faithful* to the vocation which they received in their own baptism, and their pledge to be, for the infants to be baptized, an effective community of faith.

(b)   The communitarian celebration of the baptism of infants ought to be *recognized as a privileged sign of grace* and of justification by grace, without asserting, however, that it is the exclusive way of salvation. *Praise for the sacramental sign of grace ought not to diminish praise for God's will to save all men, and for Christ who wanted to die for all.* The assurance of salvation which the sacramental sign gives ought to be appreciated but not in a way that would cast doubt on the universality of God's salvific will and work.

(c)   A child's baptism *ought never to be considered as an isolated moment* but rather as an intense and privileged moment in a whole series of developments in which the baptized gradually receives and responds to the good news of God's graciousness. All of education ought to be conceived in the perspective and in the light of baptism, as a post-baptismal catechumenate which makes clear that baptism is the initial point of development and not the point of arrival.

This catechumenate should be particularly intensified and deepened in preparation for the sacraments of confirmation and matrimony which in no way can be *sacraments of 'infants'*. There is particular need that this be done in such a way that the sacrament of matrimony can no longer be only an element of social tradition devoid of commitment. Serious preparation for matrimony is indispensable today. Those baptized as infants, but later not evangelized, cannot or at least should not be submitted to a Church-celebration under sanction of the invalidity of their marriage. Confirmation, too, should be celebrated only by those who are ready for a genuine personal commitment.

(d)   Except in the case of imminent danger of death, there should be firm refusal to baptize those infants who are not in any way really inserted into the community of faith. Official Church legislation forbids one to be baptized if there is no hope of a post-baptismal catechumenate. Pastoral decisions should make clear that the baptismal celebration expresses the fact and event of a community of faith receiving the neophyte and guaranteeing him the necessary future evangelization and the attendant commitment.

The faith of the parents and of the family is a fundamental criterion but not the only one. Even if the parents are undependable as heralds of faith if there is a community of lively faith into which the child can be integrated, it is possible that this community guarantees the *evangelization of the child* when he or she reaches the age of reason. The weaker the solidarity of salvation in a community, the less lively will be the liturgy and expression of faith and of praise of God, and the less justified can be the baptism of infants whose parents are not disposed to commit themselves effectively to the children's Christian education.

Chapter 2

THE SIGNS OF FAITH

A discourse on the sacraments as real and efficacious signs of faith has to avoid two dangers: it can either under-estimate the privileged role of the sacraments in the economy of grace or over-value it in such a way as to make God's work and man's faith seem to be a monopoly of the sacraments.

The authentic listening to God in the scriptures and in the liturgy opens our eyes, heart and intelligence, and thus allows us to perceive him who speaks through all his works. The whole of creation and of redemption, all the forms of God's active presence in history have the character of word. They are revelation and communication of God to man who can understand and respond in faith.

1. *The words of the Word, the inspiration of our word*

Christ, himself, is the great Sacrament of redemption. In him the love, the mercy and the wisdom of the Father is fully visible; through him the Father speaks to our hearts and minds. Through the grace of the Holy Spirit we are enabled to understand and also to associate ourselves with him in his perfect response to the Father in the name of humanity.

The seven sacraments tend to open us to the mystery of Christ in an ever-growing faith, so that our life becomes more and more a listening and response to God in all events, in all his works. 'In the liturgy God speaks to his people and Christ is still proclaiming his gospel. And the people reply to God both by song and by prayer'. [1]

In the sacraments we sense the nearness of God; we are listening to his assuring word, and this leads us to listen also to all the other words of him in whom all things are made and restored. Increasingly, then, we understand that wonderful message inscribed in our innermost being, in our whole existence, by the Holy Spirit. As the sacraments help us to find and to understand our true self, we gradually grasp the message communicated to us by the whole created universe and especially by the love and needs of our fellowmen.

The sacraments are a marvellous message of joy, a communion. They are gospel, gladdening news, a message of love, and thus an effective challenge and commandment to treasure in our hearts this message and give thanks for the gift they bestow. By his gifts God communicates his loving will, and by his word he gives us the joyous incentive to a new life.

Christian life is fundamentally 'a responsive word' which springs from a faith that hears and responds, receives and gives back in gratitude. The whole liturgy has the character of listening to God's word and responding to it as wholeheartedly as possible in our individual and communal life. The 'gracious' word of the sacraments wants to make us mature hearers of God's word as it reaches us in the sacramental celebration, in holy scripture, in all creation and history, and in all the events of life.

The liturgy frees men from an empty monologue. Bringing us together in Christ, it speaks its intended message in relation to personal and communal concerns and goals. It teaches us to consider all things and all events in the light of the word of God when he speaks to us through his gifts, and to bring our personal concerns home into the serenity of the liturgical response. Only

[1] SC 33.

one who learns to listen with an attentive and ready heart can truly celebrate with the Church the liturgical response to God's gifts and words.

The Christian whose heart and mind have been formed in liturgical piety carries the celebration over into his whole moral life. As he learns to listen to the voice of God in a way that helps him to recognize his *kairos*, the plan of divine providence taking as point of departure always God's gifts and the present needs of his neighbour, he becomes less tempted to carry out arbitrarily his own human proposals.

One whose mind has been formed by a living liturgy has no taste for formalistic schemes or for any blind application of abstract principles which fail to take into account the opportunities and needs of the present moment. He avoids, too, a superficial existentialistic ethics, since he has learned to consider every particular situation in the light of that fundamental vision written in his mind and heart by the gifts of the sacraments.

2. *A bilateral covenant*

In the sacraments we celebrate a pact of love (the new covenant) between Christ and the Church and deepen our own participation in it.

The New Testament is not a unilateral bequest on the part of God. It is necessary to recall this today when certain Protestant exegetes who, while rightly trying to eliminate all false concepts of a 'commercial contract' from an understanding of the covenant, also tend to eliminate from it true bilaterality. Behm, for instance, writes that *diatheke* is the free gift of God, the declaration of his saving will, the revelation of grace, in relation to which Israel can be only a recipient; *diatheke*, 'disposition', 'declaration of the divine will'; 'the divine will self-revealed in history and establishing religion' — this, he says, is the religious concept of *diatheke* in the Septuagint. [2] 'In the

---

[2] J. Behm, *Diatheke* in *Theological Dictionary of the New Testament* edited by B. Kittel, vol. II (1964), pp. 104-134; *op. cit.*, p. 127.

New Testament, *diatheke* is from first to last the disposition of God, the declaration of the sovereign will of God in history, by which God orders the relation between himself and men according to his own good saving purpose and which carries with it the authoritative ordering, the one order of things which is in accordance with it'. [3] However, he arrives at such an affirmation only by accusing a considerable portion of the scriptures of magical aberration or of a false commercial spirit. He is not willing to pay serious attention to those biblical texts that emphasize the necessity of accepting the proffered covenant in freedom and firm commitment to it.

Certainly every idea of commutative justice, in the existing pattern of commercial activity, is radically excluded by the biblical concept of covenant or testament. The covenant is a gratuitous gift. God, however, prepares it in such a way that it is consummated in a supreme sacrifice of man, the gift received and returned by redeemed humanity. The Father has given us his greatest gift of love in Christ, his only-begotten Son as sacrifice of expiation. And, in return, Christ, as head of humanity, offers himself to the Father in the name of mankind awaiting redemption.

The blood of the alliance does not, therefore, designate only the arrangement coming from the divine will but a *true communion between the two parties* who, although infinitely different, nevertheless come to be united in Christ, true God and true man. God, in his infinite graciousness, does not impose a servile order but rather seals a pact of friendship. In his person, Christ, the Word Incarnate, is the hypostatic Covenant, the loving bond of alliance for all men.

The blood of the covenant not only leads us to accept with a humble heart the order established by God, but also unveils a new order arising from the alliance; an order of mutual love which allows us to give a free and adequate response in the Word.

[3] *Op. cit.,* p. 134.

God gave to the dialogue between himself and man the character of a covenant of mutual agreement. This, in fact, is the form which he gave to the whole order of salvation in the Old Testament, of which the new covenant cannot be other than the supreme fulfilment.

In every Eucharistic celebration we realize anew that we have entered into this covenant between God and his people, sealed by the sacrifice of the body and blood of the Lord which is given here in the form of bread and wine as food to all who manifest their intention of entering into this alliance by eating this sacrificial meal. By means of this alliance they also become partners of the benefits of the covenant. [4]

All the sacraments, as signs and gifts which have their meaning and force only through their intimate relation to Christ's sacrifice and that of the Church, are *signs of the covenant*. Christ's sacrifice is, *par excellence*, the *sign and seal of the covenant*. In the mysteries of the Word Incarnate, God reveals and gives testimony to the love he bears us and appeals for our response. In every sacrament this universal meaning, valid for all mankind, is actualized and communicated to this specific community, this particular individual. To receive a sacrament is to respond with a solemn 'Yes' to the covenant as it applies to our life.

In the sacraments, therefore, God speaks to us with words, with signs and with his gracious gifts of the pact which he offers to us. In receiving the signs of the covenant with the Church, we respond, enabled and authorized by them, with the Church and through the Church, to Christ and with him. Thus we accept in gratitude the grace and the law of the covenant as direction for our whole life. Faith, therefore, includes ortho-praxis as much as orthodoxy.

In that which is their essence, the sacraments *signify* the new and eternal covenant, given us through no merit of our own, and the response of those who, in faith, recognize the

---

[4] Cf. J. Alfrink, in *Irish Quarterly*, 26 (1959), p. 293f.

grace of the covenant. This response is united with that of Jesus Christ.

The liturgy effectively introduces us to the dialogic exchange between God and man by a progressive education in living faith. The celebration of the sacraments and the Eucharistic sacrifice can be likened to the stairs of the patriarch Jacob on which the angels descended and ascended. The Word of the Father *comes to us* in the covenant of love, to bring back to the Father the response of our whole life, in justice, reconciliation, peace, all-embracing solidarity.

The Church and every single member of it celebrate in the sacraments the wonderful bilaterality of the covenant. The sign becomes all the more effective the more we all become ready to accept the grace (the sign-word of love) and to respond with all our heart. And the greater the attractiveness and glory of the word of grace, the more intense can be the response of our life in openness, in listening, in praise of God and thanksgiving.

Every power and capacity of Christian life, therefore, originates from the dialogue of the covenant, from a faith which keeps us in vital contact with God, with all his words and, above all, with the people of the covenant within the community of faith.

3. *Communitarian and personal dialogue*

The biblical idea of *covenant,* and the continuous living experience which the liturgy gives, instruct the faithful in the nature of Christian life. As expressed by the signs of the covenant, Christian life is a dialogue which is fully personal and at the same time fully communitarian.

Every believer receives the grace of faith in the community of faith. The sacraments do not consign us to some secluded spot for souls to be alone with God, separated from the community. Instead, they turn the whole person to God in a community of faith, of hope and of love. The covenant in which we all participate and to which we respond individually is the covenant of God with the community of the redeemed, of Christ with his Church.

The sign-words of the covenant call us together in the ecclesial community, which is meant to be a kind of 'sacrament of unity for the whole of mankind', [5] and our response is valid and just only in the community and in view of the community. From a true liturgical *concelebration* arises the acute consciousness that even the silent prayer in the depths of our heart, in the privacy of our home, and then our whole life as well, is in profound communion with all men already saved or to be saved.

The dialogue of prayer and the dialogue of life, if they are authentic, arise from the covenant and tend always *to unite* men not only with God but also among themselves. We pray truthfully only when we say 'Our Father' in our fraternal love and reverence for all men. We can say 'I believe in one God' only if we are working for peace and brotherhood in the world. We can claim to 'believe in one holy, Catholic, apostolic Church' only in so far as we are trying, in solidarity and co-operation, to make the Church a visible sign of the oneness of humanity.

Cyprian Vagaggini rightly noted, 'The characteristic of a liturgical spirituality that strikes one in the first place and from the very beginning, is probably the strong emphasis placed on the communitarian, ecclesial aspect of salvation. Every Catholic spirituality is necessarily at the same time communitarian and existential-personalistic. But since in a sacramental spirituality it is properly the liturgical action which determines the quality of the special balance and dynamics, the liturgical action itself must visibly manifest this communitarian direction not only in its essence, which is, so to speak, hidden, but in its whole structure, its extrinsic expression and its most intimate psychology. The communitarian aspect in liturgical spirituality necessarily takes first place'. [6]

[5] LG 1.
[6] C. Vagaggini, *Il senso teologico della liturgia*, 2nd ed. (Rome: Edizioni Paoline, 1958), p. 518.

The liturgy, by its very essence, teaches us that *there is no opposition between the fundamental social-communitarian aspect of salvation and the true personalism of faith.*

There certainly exists the greatest opposition between collectivism which expects everything from an imposed uniformity, and the individualistic personalism which views the person not in dialogue but rather in a monologue which would like to make instruments of all others for his own perfection and self-aggrandisement.

Liturgical personalism, however, sees the centrality of the person in his or her capacity to listen and to respond in Christ and in his Church. Man's self-fulfilment is seen as a gift which, in keeping with the blessedness of the gift, leads us to give ourselves back in the covenant. The liturgical dialogue, being a dialogue of faith and adoring love, is therefore most personal. The personalism of each member, however, is authentically deepened as the love and unity increase in all members of the community to which God addresses himself and who, together, respond with their lives.

The true *we-thou-I-personalism* of the liturgy differs radically, then, from the individualistic brand. It is no wonder that those who confuse individualism and personalism would oppose the liturgical renewal with the pretext of defending the personalistic mark of religion. They are mistaken, however, as are the liturgists who expect everything from a simple external organisation of the liturgy. A purely external co-ordination of 'sacred actions', with no synchronization of hearts in the covenant of faith, hope and charity, is wholly against the dialogical character of the sacraments.

The same conclusions are arrived at by starting from the great commandment of love. *To love God with one's whole heart is essentially a dialogical life.* God first assures us of his love for us, but this love can transform us only if we answer truly. It is obvious, however, that no one can love God sincerely and vitally *if he is not united to his brethren in love* (1 Jn 4:20).

The personal dialogue of faith and love with God is the source and basis of fraternal love and unity, as it was with Christ. His whole life is praise, thanksgiving and adoration of the Father, but he adores God by his life of self-bestowal and finally with his life's blood in total giving for his brethren. As his followers, then, we must unite reciprocally with our brethren if we wish to remain and to grow in the dialogue of faith and love. A personal life and a truly communitarian life thus become one in our adoring response to God's love. One cannot be obtained without the other.

The liturgy is one of the privileged schools of this truth. If we neglect it we have little hope of learning the fundamental components of Christian life, since in Christ's intention the Eucharist and the other sacraments are the favoured sources of growth in faith and in undivided love, justice and peace. The intrinsic unity of the love of God and of our neighbour requires, therefore, that truly communitarian celebration of the liturgy which the very nature of the sacraments calls for. They call for truth of life, and this reveals what the manner of celebration should be.

No one, then, can accept the objection that 'if, in the celebration of Mass, my mind and heart are to be concerned for the neighbour, my piety and devotion will be diminished'. It is urgent to transcend the brand of piety that is fearful of the neighbour; otherwise one cannot truly realize a genuine Christian encounter with God in the covenant of faith.

Among the numerous testimonies of tradition there is a marvellous text of Saint Augustine in which the saint certainly does not express himself in accordance with his previous neoplatonic and stoic schooling, but speaks as a witness of tradition: ' ... *and the bread which I will give you is my flesh for the life of the world*: the faithful recognize the body of Christ if they do not neglect to be the body of Christ. They become the body of Christ if they want to live in the spirit of Christ. It is the body of Christ that draws life from his Spirit. My body certainly draws life from my spirit. Do you too want to draw life from the spirit of Christ? Be the body of Christ.... Therefore the apostle Paul, in presenting this bread to us, says, "there is one loaf; we, many as we are, are one body; for it is one loaf of which we all partake" (1 Cor 10:17). O sacrament of piety! O sign of unity! O bond of love! Whoever wants to live has where to live, has the source from which to draw his life. So draw near — believe; so become incorporated in Christ's body and you will be vivified. Do not move away from the other members, do not be a gangrenous member deserving of amputation, do not be a deformed or disgraceful member, but a fitting, a well-formed and healthy member; do not detach yourself from the body'. [7]

4. *The mystery of faith: salvation through faith and through the sacraments*

The reformed communities have often in the past accused the Catholic Church of a sacramentalism destructive of the pre-eminence of faith. The Second Vatican Council, following the authentic Catholic tradition, excludes, through a reformed liturgy of the signs of faith, any teaching of a false sacramentalism.

We are saved through faith. Saint Thomas, true to the authentic tradition, asserts, 'We are saved by means of faith in Christ who was born and has suffered; the sacraments, then, are signs which attest to the faith through which man comes to justification'. [8]

The constitution on divine revelation and that on the sacred liturgy give a central place to faith founded on the word and the grace of God. The sacraments are to be seen thoroughly in a perspective of faith: 'They not only presuppose faith but by words and signs they also nourish, strengthen and express it; that is why they are called "sacraments of faith" '. [9] Christ is

---

[7] Augustine, *In Joannis Evangelium*, tr. XXVI, 13, Migne PL 35, 1612/3.

[8] *Summa Theol.* 3:61:4; cf. T. Gaillard, 'Les sacraments de la foi', *Revue Thomiste* 59, pp. 5-31, 270-309.

[9] SC 59.

present in his word, since it is he himself who speaks when the
holy scriptures are read in church. [10]

The sacraments are to be considered as efficacious signs of
faith through Christ and the Holy Spirit and thus in and with
the faith of the Church. Faith is itself a sacramental reality;
never should it be misinterpreted as only intellectual adherence
to a catalogue of beliefs. Its saving efficacy comes from Christ,
the great Sacrament. In the words and the sacramental rites,
Christ himself is the faithful witness who reassures us that he
came for us, died and is risen for us. By his sacraments in the
community of faith, and by the light of his grace, God gives
to our perception and our intelligence proof that the mysteries
of salvation save us, gather us, if we loyally open ourselves to
them in faith.

The sacraments are saving events only for those who believe
and long for an increase of faith. The one who does not believe
and does not want to believe receives the sacraments *'ficte'*,
insincerely. He makes the sacramental signs 'sacred lies' and
disparages the faith which has God as witness. Unless a person
wants to draw his life from faith and live according to faith,
he receives the sacraments *'infructuose'*, fruitlessly. He scorns
the fecundity of faith which is that experience of God's gracious
love that engenders a creative, gracious and generous response
in his whole life.

The sacramental celebration signifies that the Church —
actual here and now in the celebrating assembly — listens and
responds to the action of God with humble confession and a
glad profession of faith. Those who receive the sacrament in a
spirit of faith and in a desire for increase of faith are *justified by
that faith* which God himself awakens and brings to fuller life
through these sacred signs and symbols. The awakened faith is
the dynamic answer of the Church and of each of her members
in the celebration of the sacraments. The result will be a life
of thanksgiving to God for his work, his word, his grace.

[10] SC 7, 21 and 33.

Through the sacraments of faith it becomes clear not only that faith is essentially dialogical but also that the believer's personal dialogue with God finds a privileged place in the community of believers, the ecclesial community. [11]

The more fervently the ecclesial community celebrates the signs of faith, the more fervent can be expected to be each individual participant's profession of faith. On the other hand, the individual believer's profession of faith, in the liturgy as well as in daily life, will not be fruitful or pleasing to God if he does not want to be united with that of the whole Church.

In the sacraments God reveals to us the power of the mysteries of salvation and thus glorifies his fidelity and love. The only adequate answer of the Church and of each member is a response of faith, of hope, of love that truly honours God. Of itself and essentially, the Church's sacramental profession of faith is that of a faith that adores, hopes and loves since it is the response to the revelation of God's own love in Christ. The sacraments of faith tend to lead the faithful to associate themselves increasingly with the living testimony of faith in the Church.

The authentic disposition for genuine sacramental dialogue with Christ is an attitude expressed in the prophet's words, 'Here am I, Lord; call me', an attitude of eagerness to hear the words of the Word and to act on them in response to the gifts of God and to all the testimony and revelation of his faithful love. God's signs are deeds, events; they are active, alive; and so should be our response.

The Church honours God by a profession of faith informed by love. Living by the life-giving words of the Incarnate Word, the community itself and every one of its members are destined to a *Eucharistic* faith that is full of love and gratitude. Normally, therefore, the sacraments will be all the more fruitful the more the ecclesial community joyfully and gratefully communicates its faith to every member.

[11] LG 11.

The universal Church is actualized in the local Church which arouses and sustains the faith of the individual members. Although she cannot dispose of the grace of God, and although he distributes it when and wherever he wishes, nevertheless the Church, both universal and local, contributes to *the disposition* of every person according to her degree of faith. It can happen often enough, then, that local Protestant communities, although they might be deprived of ministers endowed with juridical validity, can dispose the participants in the sacramental cele-brations to a live faith more than some Catholic parishes that certainly have validly ordained ministers but are deprived of a vital and fervent expression of faith and love.

I am reminded of an incident many years ago in Germany where I directed some research into the sociology of religion: the interdependence and mutual influences of forms of religion, the structure of a parish, the structure of liturgy, of pastoral approach, and so on, and the life of the community, its environ-ment, public opinion, and so forth. Several priests and about two hundred lay-people co-operated in house and street inter-views. In one of my first interviews a young lady who was in love with a fine Protestant told me that she had invited him to Mass on the Christmas vigil. Having always been very moved herself by the Christmas hymns, she thought this experience might encourage him to have their marriage celebrated in the Catholic Church. When they met after Mass (men and women sat separately) her friend said: 'I will not go again to a Catholic Church. The way these men behaved showed that there is no faith in them. Moreover, I could not understand what the pastor was talking about'.

Participation in sacramental celebrations which are rather manifestations of sloth, of formalism or of a frightening lack of faith, hope and charity, can become a main cause of defections and of *embourgeoisement* of faith, even if all the rubrics are scrupulously 'observed'. As Romano Guardini said three decades ago at a national liturgical congress, the great sharing of faith in the sacraments of faith celebrated by true believers is the main source of the conversion of nations, but a dead liturgy is the greatest source of perversion and defection.

God, in all his sacraments and in all signs of his might and goodness, testifies to his unfailing love. Magnificent is his goodness; holy is his name! The answer of the Church, therefore, cannot be confined to a mere cultic profession of faith. In an immediate and vivid way the liturgy teaches us the truth contained in the biblical themes relative to the virtue of religion: *kabod, kadosh, shem Yahweh* (glory, holiness, the name of God)— true religion springs from, centres itself on, and tends always to glorify the divine initiative in the whole of life.

Wherever God reveals his *glory* (the visible splendour of his love and his holiness), he at the same time enables man to open himself to this word-event-revelation so that he can respond in freedom, joy, fidelity and reverence. God's glory is visibly acknowledged wherever man adores him 'in spirit and in truth', wherever our adoration, our prayer, our words and works are truthful. When God manifests his *holiness*, making holy (dedicated) all men for his service, the people of God are enabled to sanctify his holy name in a spirit of faith and love. Where God reveals and proclaims his *name*, Father and Lord, and calls each man personally by his unique name, the human person becomes capable of glorifying the name of the Father and Lord of all men in the community of faith and love where everyone is honoured as a child of God.

From all these biblical and liturgical elements it is clear that a true dialogue of faith is possible only when there is full acceptance of the gifts of God on the part of the community and of every single member of it. That the sacraments of faith be considered in this vision is of paramount importance for ecumenical dialogue in the broadest sense. We shall then realize that whatever is good comes from the one Father, through his Son, as gift of the one Spirit, and will therefore have an open eye for all the signs of faith and love which we find in other Churches and even in non-Christian religions.

With equal insistence the gospels teach the regenerating

power of both faith and sacraments. Of baptism and the Eucharist it is said, 'In truth, I tell you, no one can enter the kingdom of God without being born of water and the Spirit' (Jn 3:5), and 'Whoever eats my flesh and drinks my blood dwells continually in me and I dwell in him' (Jn 6:56).

The same saving power is recognized for faith: 'To those who received him, to those who put their faith in his name, he gave the right to become children of God' (Jn 1:12-13). '... so that everyone who has faith in him may possess eternal life' (Jn 3:15).

These two lines of thought, namely, of faith that saves and of the sacraments that bring salvation, ought never to be separated. 'The problem is easily resolved provided that the two masterly lines of the theology of John are distinguished, *that of gift and that of acceptance.* The perspective of gift extends to all providential dispositions through which the Spirit is given to the world, and encompasses the mysteries of the Incarnation and redemption. The sacrament of baptism is inscribed in their prolongation. But confronted by the gift, man remains free in his decision. To *accept* the gift, he needs to believe in the Donor, in virtue of an interior grace which is already certainly a gift, but an initial gift ordained to a yet greater one'. [12]

As in the intimacy of friendship, the love which is given and that which is received form a unified reality. Thus in a certain way, in the sacraments of faith the action of God that reveals and offers his gifts tends to become one with the acceptance of these gifts by man, who responds with a living, active faith. 'In fact, when man believes in God who justifies him, he opens himself humbly to his justifying action and thus receives the effect'. [13]

Through faith, understood in its full sense, man submits his intelligence, his will and his heart to the Word of God. 'When

[12] F.M. Braun, 'La vie d'en haut', *Revue de sciences phil. et theologiques* 40 (1956), p. 19.

[13] Thomas Aquinas, *Commentary on the Epistle to the Romans* 4:5, lecture I.

the Word pronounces the gift of grace in the form of a sacramental act, the obedience of faith is acceptance of the gracious
gift which becomes visible in the sacraments.' 'Through faith
and the sacraments of faith', [14] justification, the intimate spiritual
contact between Christ and man, comes into being or more fully
into being and more visibly in life. 'By means of faith and the
sacraments of faith, human generations come into real and
spiritual contact with the Lord, actually living and glorified at
the right hand of the Father and with the mysteries by which he
has accomplished the salvation of the world, especially with his
passion and his resurrection. The sacraments are privileged means
of this spiritual contact, in necessary connection with faith, of
which they are signs.' [15]

From all that has been said up to now, it follows that our
whole moral and religious life depends on and subsists in the
words of the Word. It arises from the covenant of love and
develops in dialogue with a faith informed by — or at least
tending to express itself in — redeemed love. It follows also that
the gifts common to the whole people of the covenant, as well
as those given to individual persons, are always accepted and
understood in view of the community. They are in a strict sense
gifts and messages which oblige the members of the new
covenant to a greater dedication in co-responsibility for the good
of all.

Only then, when sacramental spirituality leads us to a
sacramental vision of all the works of God, the signs of the
times and the concrete opportunity of the *kairos*, and when all
of creation is for us, in the light of the Word Incarnate, truly a
word and an appeal, does sacramental morality dynamically open
to us new and radiant horizons.

Karl Barth has overcome the theory of 'scripture alone' by
finding in faith a broader horizon, that of the *answer to the
Word of God, Creator and Redeemer*, without, however,

[14] *Summa Theol.* 3:48:2.
[15] T. Gaillard, *Op. cit.*, p. 290f.

renouncing the light of the sacred scriptures. His famous expression '*analogia fidei*' — analogy of faith — means that in the light of Christ all creation and everything in it becomes a sign inspiring a more vivid and vital gratitude and obedience of faith. Openness and dedication to others can come only from God. They are a sign, as it were, a sacrament of faith.[16]

I intend this same outlook when I emphasize a 'morality of responsibility', which is understood as a morality of unceasing listening and deciphering of the signs of God's presence, as co-responsibility in his work and co-responsibility in an effort to make one's whole personal and social life a genuine and vital response to him who, in all things, reveals to us his design of love for all people.

[16] Cf. my book *Faith and Morality in a Secular Age* (Slough: St Paul Publications, 1973).

Chapter 3

THE SIGNS OF HOPE

1. *Christian hope and other eschatological virtues*

The sacraments, as we have considered them, are 'efficacious signs of the reign of God'. The kingdom of God is, however, essentially an eschatological reality, which means 'a reality of the future world and a reality already present'. [1] So the sacraments too have an eschatological significance.

'The sacraments are not only *commemorative* signs of that which has already occurred, namely, the passion of Christ, and demonstrative signs of that which, by the passion of Christ, is produced in us now (grace); they are also prognostic signs, prophetic of the glory to come.' [2]

St Thomas Aquinas considers the sacraments as signs which characterize our present condition in the economy of salvation and also remind us at every moment of the dynamic tension between the 'already' and the 'not yet'; 'Salvation has already been accomplished' and 'it is not yet fully manifest'. The condition of 'the new law is in between that of the old law, the images of which have become reality in the new law, and that of glory in which the whole truth will be manifest perfectly, without veil. At the time of the final glory there will be no

---

[1] A. Feuillet, *Introduction à la Bible* (Tournai: Desclée, 1959), vol. II, p. 774.
[2] *Summa Theol.* 2 : 60 : 3.

sacrament. Now, on the contrary, since we know only puzzling reflections in a mirror (1 Cor 13:12), we need the tangible reality to arrive at the spiritual realities; and this is the proper function of the sacraments'. [3]

What specifically belongs to Christian eschatology (the redeemed are already effectively initiated into the *eschata* and looking forward to the final coming of the Lord) is posed clearly in the light of the sacraments. Christian life is directed to the perfect state of glory, not chiefly by a relation of desire or of merit but more by grateful awareness of what God has already prepared and by vigilance towards the present opportunities, by that hope which arises from the experience of faith in the on-going presence of God and makes us ready for his coming. [4]

'For we have been saved, though only in hope' (Rom 8:24). The sacraments, as they are mysteries of faith, are also *mysteries and efficacious signs of hope*. Through them the present moment of grace and present decisions move into the perspective of the history of salvation. For the faithful who make use of the immediate opportunities, the sacraments are signs of 'this time of salvation' which has been manifested ever since the first coming of Christ, and a pledge of hope that the fruitfulness of grace will be fully manifested in the *parousia* (cf. Eph 5:16). The celebration of the sacraments of hope opens on to broad horizons of a genuine vision of history.

An understanding of the sacraments cannot be authentic if they are limited to mere remembrance of past events or to the consolation that arises from an expectation of future bliss. The sacramental memorial is not merely a narration of past events but is a vital insertion into Christ, Lord of the history of salvation. The intention of the sacraments is to make us actors of hope in the history of the redemption and liberation of the whole world.

---

[3] *Summa Theol.* 3:61:4:1.
[4] Cf. K. Rahner, 'Eschatology', *Sacramentum Mundi* (New York: Herder and Herder, 1968), vol. II, pp. 242-246; Oscar Cullmann, *Salvation History* (New York: Harper and Row, 1967).

In the celebration of the pledges of hope, the redemption of the present moment becomes urgent and possible; thus the vision of the here-and-now and of the use of present opportunities becomes freed from arbitrariness, superficiality and discontinuity. He who, in the community of hope, celebrates the mysteries of hope perceives the tremendous love of the Redeemer in all that he has done and all that he has promised us. In recognizing the present gift, we see our present possibilities to love our neighbour, and to insert ourselves better into the community of redeeming love.

In this way, with a serenity that flows from trust and gratitude and with that efficient dynamism that discovers the precious pearl of the kingdom of God in the vast field of history, man is on his way to 'the city of the living God, the heavenly Jerusalem' (Heb 12:22). In his celebration of gratitude in hope he will profit by the warning, 'See that you do not refuse to hear him who speaks' (Heb 12:25).

There follows *the unequalled importance of gratitude in Christian life*. Hope and Christian commitment are not founded simply on the sanction of reward or punishment or on the justified desire to attain one's goal. The purposeful dynamism of Christian life arises from the salvific presence of the Lord of history and from the grace already received and responded to by gratitude.

True and effective hope is bound to both present opportunities and the promised reality *with a Eucharistic spirit* that 'renders thanks always and everywhere' for the harvest of grace and the abundant salvation already made manifest.

But the gifts already received, whose purpose we can recognize gratefully because of the dynamic presence of Christ and the Spirit — which he sent us so that we could not remain idle — direct all our energies and all the present opportunities to the final goal: 'I have not yet reached perfection, but I press on, hoping to take hold of that for which Christ once took hold of me.... I press towards the goal to win the prize which is God's call to the life above, in Christ Jesus' (Phil 3:12-14).

By the vivifying Spirit given to us through the sacraments, which are prognostic signs, we recognize, in the humbleness of our time, *the time of grace,* in the heart of which beat the strengths and virtues of the death, resurrection, and the promise of the *parousia* of the Lord. Thus appears the *importance of vigilance* (readiness) which occupies a central place among the eschatological virtues.

For the right understanding and celebration of liturgy and prayer, the decisive test is their fruitfulness in *vigilance* for the potentiality of the here-and-now. Vigilance for present opportunities and unfailing courage to resist the temptations of evasion are marks of Christ's pressing love working in us. The disciple is vigilant if he recognizes the coming of the Lord in the talents that are entrusted to him and in the needs of his fellowmen and of the community that cry to him for help.

The fruitfulness of the liturgy grows when we learn in this privileged 'school of hope' to translate the expression of our hope into living witness of the One who was, who is and who will come. This is only possible if, in its expressions, liturgy never loses contact with real life.

In vigilance, the last decision is prepared (cf. Mt 24:42; 25:13; Mk 13:35; Lk 21:36). Whoever neglects the grace offered at the present moment lives, until the second coming of Christ, in terror and futility according to his indifference (Mt 23:39, Lk 13:35).

The eschatological expectation ought to stimulate in us intense zeal for a more humane world, a zeal which has to be rooted and nourished in a spirit of faith and prayer. 'Why do you stand there looking up into the sky?' (Acts 1:11). The ultimate tension of Christian life, enlivened by sacramental spirituality, will not be misguided by any apocalyptic calculation of the day or hour of the *parousia.* Its dynamic teaches us rather to look to the fertility of the here-and-now in the light of our last moments and final expectations.

A true eschatological perspective on one's life, the fruit of a sacramental spirituality, knows how to reconcile true *respect for human traditions* with a courageous openness to new forms of customs and cultures. The fidelity and continuity which are the living expressions of all the eschatological virtues, leave no room for either an immobile clinging to traditions or a restless discontinuity and sensationalism.

Joy is a characteristic virtue of the sacramental person, in the original meaning of virtue — strength and dynamism. We have seen how the sacraments, signs of grace, reflect the attractive countenance of God. Therefore, they transform men into a visible sign of grace by means of goodness, joy, serenity, graciousness and gentleness. That kind of sadness, sorrow and solemnity that stifles our real humanity has nothing to do with Christian hope, since it veils the gracious presence of God in us.

The sacraments are visible signs of hope for the whole world only through the joy with which the believer and the whole community of faith receive the happy tidings which they symbolize. Where there is no joy, there is no testimony to the strength of faith.

In the celebration of the sacraments of faith, Christian hope is nurtured and deepened in joy. 'For joy in the Lord is your strength' (Neh 8:10). Although the eschatological times to which the sacraments commit us are marked by struggle and final separation, nevertheless Christian hope becomes, by the same sacraments, a source of *mirth and of serenity*. The sacramental man is at the same time serious and gifted with humour. [5]

Eschatological hope embraces and transforms the critical sense and also all the hopes of the secular city. The eschatological dimension develops in the Christian *the prophetic sense of constructive criticism and of discernment*.

The Christian who learns in the school of the sacraments of hope will avoid a vain, superficial, bitter or arrogant criticism, as well as any form of self-sufficiency, or an idle acceptance of

[5] Cf. my book *Celebrating Joy* (New York: Herder and Herder, 1967).

evils. The virtue of criticism, of veritable discernment, springs from a live celebration of the great events of salvation history, where all men are drawn into one hope, and search together for a more and more effective witness to this one hope. He who, in the sacraments of hope, experiences the saving justice and compassion of the Lord, and sees present decisions in the perspective of the final judgment, will exercise criticism only with a compassionate love for all men.

2. *The social purposefulness and dynamism of hope*

The sacraments are signs of hope, signifying that covenant in which God 'gathers the scattered sons into one'. [6] The grace of the covenant urges believers to carry on to the end, *together*, on the road which Christ travelled to the end, in his most radical expression of solidarity with all people.

All the sacraments proclaim that the source of our hope is in the 'one baptism' which Christ took upon himself on the altar of the cross. Ritually and sacramentally it was prefigured by his baptism in the Jordan 'during a general baptism of the people' (Lk 3 : 21). In his baptism he is side by side with all the sinners who, by the Spirit, learn that they are poor: he bears the burden of all so that all may learn the same law (cf. Gal 6 : 2). When we celebrate in the sacraments the 'one baptism' which is the source of all hope, we learn 'to become of one heart in love. . . . The renewal in the Eucharist of the covenant between the Lord and man draws the faithful into the compelling love of Christ and sets them afire'. [7] The celebration is fruitful if we, in turn, become signs and witnesses of hope in a firm commitment to unity and solidarity. It is as Saint Augustine reminded his faithful: 'You, my beloved, you are sacraments of salvation, if all your life makes visible what Christ in the sacraments has made visible to us'. [8]

[6] SC 2.

[7] SC 10.

[8] Augustine, *Ennarrationes in Psalmum CIII*, Migne PL 37, 1348.

The Church is the ark of salvation and the pledge of hope in her charity and unity. Liturgical celebrations are celebrations of the Church which is the sacrament of unity. The whole sacramental *kerygma* makes us conscious of this urgency: 'one body and one Spirit, as there is also one hope held out in God's call to you; one Lord, one faith, one baptism' (Eph 4:4).

Whenever the Lord speaks of the kingdom of God and of the hope of salvation, the perspective is eschatological and communitarian. The same perspective prevails in the whole of the liturgy. Without it the hope of each person would be destroyed. It is therefore necessary to free it courageously from various individualistic contaminations.

The salvation and dignity of the individual person reside *in the hope of salvation of the people of God,* and are thus authentic and safe. The sacramental signs, as prognostic signs that envisage the blessed communion of the saints, are at the same time signs of communitarian hope that lead the faithful to a common commitment.

This truth becomes somewhat veiled if, while recognizing the social nature of the sacraments, we are too little concerned with *making it visible*. It is not enough, at the time of the celebration of the sacraments, to inculcate the meaning and the social motives of Christian hope; the whole celebration ought to become a clear and perceptible sign of it. 'It is to be stressed that whenever rites, according to their specific nature, make provision for communal celebration involving the presence and active participation of the faithful, this way of celebrating them is to be preferred, as far as possible, to a celebration that is individual and quasi-private'. [9]

A Mass celebrated with only one other person can truly express this communitarian meaning if it is the best possible way of celebrating it in a concrete situation where gathering or joining a larger community is not possible. When, on the contrary, the isolation of the celebration is positively sought,

[9] SC 27.

then the social aspect of salvation becomes hidden and the communitarian motives which the celebration should have aroused are diminished or disowned on the level of the visible sign. Thus the sacraments of hope in solidarity are falsified.

It would be equally dangerous to think that an external communitarian celebration of the sacraments would suffice without an internal commitment. The celebration makes sense only in view of the expression of the unique hope which makes us one throughout our daily lives.

3. *The sacraments and the yearning of the created universe*

Eschatological hope, as signified and proclaimed in the sacraments, cannot be restricted to the soul and the resurrection of the body, nor even to the whole community. It has also a cosmic aspect in that it includes the *cosmos,* the world which is entrusted to man and is involved in his failures and achievements. Redemption and hope extend to the whole created universe, particularly to the environmental world which will shape man dangerously unless he himself shapes it in a liberating way.

This aspect of hope and commitment is signified by the use of precious elements of the earth — 'the fruit of human hands', water, bread, wine, oil — in the liturgy. All these signs speak to us of the consecration of the world and of life. However, it would be a terrible distortion of the concept of 'the consecration of the world' to think that blessings and sacramental symbols alone suffice. These symbols are only to turn our attention to that broader concept of the sacramentality of all creation and all history: they indicate and make mandatory a new perspective and a firm commitment to justice and holiness in all our life.

In the liturgy we look forward, with increasing desire and hope, to 'the new heaven and the new earth' (Rev 21:1). 'The

J

created universe waits with eager expectation for God's children to be revealed' (Rom 8:19). To believers this means grace and a mandate to commit themselves individually and in solidarity, with all their strength, to the humanization and redemption of the whole of economic, social and cultural life: to work for liberation and reconciliation on all levels. The awareness, however, that the full liberty of the sons and daughters of God and the full redemption of the world will be granted only in the *parousia,* will prevent wrong messianic hopes as well as acts of violence. The Christian who is shaped by the sacraments of hope will work with patience and *non-violence,* but untiringly.

Through all the sacramental signs, especially the rites for the blessing of things which the liturgy uses for the sacraments, we are reminded of what we have already become aware of through the remission of sins and by our sanctification: that sin tends to break the salvific solidarity of man with the cosmos and with all the other creatures of God.

The sacraments make us *conscious of the new and urgent task of human brotherhood on an environmental and cosmic scale,* which arises from the very fact that we are redeemed.

Whoever excludes from hope and from Christian commitment earthly realities — cultural and social structures, the technological world, international relations and so on — is not living according to the meaning of the sacraments and the grace received. A true liturgical spirituality stirs our most authentic energies for the redemption of the world. [10] Those who do not give attention to the proper environment aspect of the sacramental graces cannot bear fruit fully even in other fields. [11]

The cosmic aspect of eschatology demands that every liturgical celebration be prepared by a living, active solidarity with the world of today and in everyday life, in such a way that the transforming, redemptive, consecrating impulse which is passed on to every one of us, will become evident.

[10] Cf. Vagaggini, *Op cit.,* pp. 237-244.
[11] CS 38-39.

4. *The individual sacraments and hope*

The seven sacraments are, altogether, exalted eschatological signs of the pilgrim Church, but each one of them has its particular signification, its specific grace, and thus communicates a particular task.

St Thomas explains how each of the seven sacraments is necessary for the people of God to arrive at individual and social wholeness. [12] The meaning of the signs and words of the sacraments reveal, together with the total experience of the people of God in pilgrimage, the inexhaustible riches and the royal mandate which derives from the grace of God. This will be all the more evident as the sacramental life becomes more integrated with a vital experience of the witness of Christian hope. I draw special attention to this point since it was generally neglected in the moral theology of the last centuries.

(a) *Baptism*

Baptism is a celebration of faith and of hope in the community of salvation in Christ. We experience in baptism our personal insertion into the new and eternal covenant, as members of the chosen people. We are united in one hope in view of our common profession and testimony to faith and hope, and in view of a common eschatological struggle (cf. Eph 4:6). Baptism derives all its meaning from the one baptism Christ endured for all. It installs us 'with Jesus Christ ... enthroned with him in the heavenly realms' (Eph 2:6) in so far as it enables us on earth to suffer with Christ, to share his solidarity and his mission to bring the good news to the poor.

Through the living, signified reality of the grace and task of baptism, we have a share in that kingdom which Christ has revealed as the servant of all, if we in turn learn how to serve and to carry the burdens of others (Gal 6:12).

Baptism makes us conscious of the common battle that must

[12] *Summa Theol.* 3:65:1:4.

be waged against the forces of darkness, sin and all threatening evil powers (this is the meaning of the exorcisms and of the baptismal pledges). Only by accepting that solidarity, brother-hood and concern for the freedom of all, can we overcome solidarity in evil.

The saints, who live according to the grace of baptism, always conscious of its meaning, give everywhere a living testimony to the hope of glory, which in no way allows an alienation from proper aspirations in the social realm.

Those who in Jesus Christ have become 'a new creation' announce 'the new heaven and the new earth' in which the power of all idols will be broken. Sealed with the blood of the new and everlasting covenant they 'do not worship the beast and its image and do not bear its mark on forehead and hand' (Rev 20:4); they are no longer slaves of a self-centred world that passes away. It is true, the baptized have still, again and again, to cross the Red Sea and the desert, but they have left behind the old slavery and know that the promised land is theirs.

The 'already' of faith and baptism points forward to the end, but it does so by drawing grateful attention to the decisive events of the past — Incarnation, passion, death and resurrection, and the outpouring of the Spirit; the past, the present and the future are closely bound together in the eschatological 'already'. The perspective draws, however, more dynamically towards the future as the believer receives with an open mind and heart the gift of the Spirit, and thus is incorporated into the Body of Christ (cf. 1 Cor 12:13).[13] The sometimes painful experience of the 'not yet' in healthy tension with the 'already' has a decisive ethical influence on the life of believers to the extent that it intensifies their consciousness of being fellow-workers in Christ carrying out the saving plan in history. This is what characterizes our ethical decisions if we live according to the dynamics of baptism. [14]

[13] O. Cullmann, *Op. cit.*, p. 260.
[14] *Op. cit.*, p. 338.

(b) *Confirmation*

The very name 'Christ' (the Anointed) is linked to the out-pouring of the Spirit which manifests the coming of the messianic age. John the Baptist is aware of this: 'When you see the Spirit coming down upon someone and resting upon him you will know that this is he who is to baptize in the Holy Spirit' (Jn 1:33). The pouring out of the Spirit at Pentecost is for Peter the proof that the hoped-for messianic age has come: 'God says, "this will happen in the last days: I will pour out upon everyone a portion of my Spirit; and your sons and daughters shall prophesy.... Yes, I will endue even my slaves, both men and women, with a portion of my Spirit, and they shall prophesy" ' (Acts 2:17; cf. Joel 2:28). We should, in this context, not forget that the charism of the prophets is integration between life and faith, a holistic vision of the love of God and of our neighbour, maturity and discernment.

Those baptized by the Spirit who let themselves be led by the Spirit can 'exult in hope' in the midst of suffering and trial. 'Such hope is no mockery, because God's love has flooded our inmost heart through the Holy Spirit he has given us' (Rom 5:5). Since the Spirit is their life, they experience the inner freedom to use present opportunities and to look forward to the final fulfilment of their life; the Spirit is indeed their life and their guide. 'For he has sent down the Spirit upon us plentifully through Jesus Christ our Saviour, so that, justified by grace, we might in hope become heirs to eternal life' (Tit 3:6-8).

It is through the Spirit that the believer can live according to the eschatological virtues and realize the profound meaning of events in his daily life together with 'the signs of the times', seeing everything in the light of the eschatological mysteries of the death, resurrection, ascension and *parousia* of Christ. This is at the very heart of the history of liberation. 'In Christ Jesus the life-giving law of the Spirit has set you free from the law of sin and the snares of death' (Rom 8:2). This freedom makes the believer attentive to the groaning of creation to have a share in it (Rom 8:19-22); the spiritual person lives in full solidarity with the hopes and struggles of all people and of the whole created universe. He is a witness to the liberating power and creativity of a life under the guidance of the Holy Spirit.

(c) *The Eucharist*

In Christ's discourse on the Eucharist and on faith (Jn 6), it becomes strikingly clear that faith in the Eucharist and its hope-inspiring dynamics are thoroughly linked to the pouring out of the Spirit. 'And they shall all be taught by God' (Jn 6:45). 'What if you see the Son of Man ascending to the place where he was before? The Spirit alone gives life; the flesh is of no avail; the words I have spoken to you are both spirit and life' (Jn 6:62-64).

The Eucharist has to be seen in the light of the theology of the covenant which already in the great messianic prophecies points to the Spirit (cf. Jer 31:31; Ex 37:1-14) and which is the heart of the Pauline gospel. The celebration of the new and everlasting covenant in the Eucharist is a prophetic event through the Spirit, filled with hope. The covenant is sealed in the death and resurrection of Christ 'who came in water and blood. He came, not by water alone, but by water and blood; and there is the Spirit to bear witness, because the Spirit is truth' (1 Jn 5: 6-8). It is through the Spirit that Christ, the Covenant, has lived even to his death the truth of love and solidarity. It is through the same Spirit that bread and wine become for us the body and blood of Christ so that we become one body and one Spirit and can fully enter in the prophetic event and covenant of Christ's sacrificial death and resurrection. [15]

It is in this light that we should evaluate the great emphasis that the Orthodox Churches have always put on the *Epiclesis;* it is through this active presence of the Holy Spirit that the Eucharist can bring a final breakthrough of that freedom in

---

[15] Cf. Joseph Ratzinger, 'Is the Eucharist a Sacrifice', *Concilium,* 24, ('*The Sacraments: an Ecumenical Dilemma*'), (New York: Paulist Press, 1967), pp. 66-77.

which believers entrust themselves to the Lord of history and look forward to his final coming. 'Where the Spirit of the Lord is there is freedom' (2 Cor 3:17). Thus 'the Church is precisely the place where the free acceptance of God's grace by man becomes possible'. [16]

It is through the power of the Spirit that Christ's death frees us from the fear of death (Rom 8:2). Through him the Eucharist is the great event and experience of hope and vigilance: 'for every time you eat this bread and drink this cup, you proclaim the death of the Lord until he comes' (2 Cor 11:26). Since the Eucharist is the work of the Holy Spirit, only spiritual persons, guided by the Spirit and thus filled with hope for the banquet of eternal life', are prepared for 'the resurrection on the last day' (Jn 6:54-58), which, again, is the work of the Spirit. 'Eternal life' in the Johannine vision, as life already present in believers and life to be fully manifest only in the future, is promised as the fruit of baptism and the Eucharist for those who believe. By receiving the body and the blood of the risen Lord we grow in consciousness of his presence; he is with us on the road that leads to his final coming.

The Eucharistic celebration in the earthly pilgrim Church, on whose faith and prayer we rely, though her imperfections make us often suffer, unites us with the celestial liturgy of the Lamb standing before the throne (cf. Heb 12:22-24) and strengthens in us the hope for 'the new Jerusalem, coming down from God out of heaven, as beautiful as a bride dressed for her husband' (Rev 21:2).

In some Oriental liturgies, after the commemoration of the passion, death, resurrection and ascension of the Lord, is added 'and of the *parousia*'. In the Ambrosian rite, immediately after the consecration, it was always remembered explicitly: 'So we expect the coming of the Lord, when he will return from heaven'. It was only with the liturgical renewal of the Second Vatican Council that this perspective was brought home into the Roman

---

[16] John Meyendorff, 'The Orthodox Understanding of the Eucharist', *Concilium*, 24 (1967), p. 54.

liturgy: for example through the acclamations by the faithful: 'We proclaim your death, Lord Jesus, until you come in glory'. In the third Eucharistic prayer, offering in thanksgiving the holy and living sacrifice, the community looks forward: 'ready to greet him when he comes again'. In the fourth, the celebrant prays: 'looking forward to his coming in glory, we offer you his body and blood'. The fact that the Church understands herself much more than in the past centuries as a pilgrim Church is thus reflected in the Eucharistic celebrations. This leads naturally to a stronger experience that in the liturgy we celebrate our Christian hope and that, as a consequence, the whole of moral theology and pedagogy should also give more attention to hope.

The form of *festive banquet* proper to the Eucharist obviously reminds us of the value of the prognostic sign of 'the supper of eternal life' (at the heavenly table). It comes through clearly in various biblical texts. For the institution of the Eucharist, Christ chose 'a large room upstairs, set out in readiness' (Mk 14:15). The parables of the wedding banquet, in which many from the east and from the west will participate, (Mt 8:11; Mt 25:10-13; Lk 14-15) begin to be realized in the Eucharistic banquet as prefiguring and preparing for the eternal banquet of the Lamb with his bride (Rev 19:6-9).

However, in these parables that illustrate the festive character of the Eucharist, there is never lacking the aspect of *mysterium tremendum*. Only those who are ready and alert, who recognize the Lord in the poor, who are wearing the wedding garment and have in hand the lighted lamps, will be admitted to the banquet of eternal life. The eschatological separation, already going on, is hope-inspiring only for those who fear the Lord with that holy fear which bears fruit in love and justice for the life of the world.

(d) *The sacrament of reconciliation*

The eschatological significance of this sacrament is to be seen in its intimate connection with baptism and the Eucharist.

The Church and each individual Christian are in constant need of further purification and conversion. A life in the tension between the old eon and the age of the new creation can be lived only through God's patient and pressing love in a constant process of reconciliation. Through the ministry of the Church, and through those of her members who generously live a life of continuous renewal, 'it is as if God were appealing to us (you): in Christ's name we implore you be reconciled to God!' (2 Cor 5:20).

The Church herself is meant to be in constant process of purification and reconciliation. The more she is conscious of this need and humbly confesses her shortcomings, the more she will carry out a task similar to that of John the Baptist: 'to reconcile father and child, to convert the rebellious to the way of the righteous, to prepare a people that will be fit for the Lord' (Lk 1:17). The polarizations and tensions within the Church and society, and even within each family and community, should be brought into the full light and healing power of Christ's patience. Then they can inspire genuine hope and a common striving towards the fulfilment of the great eschatological command: 'Be compassionate as your Father is compassionate' (Lk 6:36); 'Let your goodness have no limits as the goodness of your heavenly Father knows no bounds' (Mt 5:48).

The sacrament of reconciliation gives new strength to those who are wounded and weakened in the eschatological battle. Its aim is to transform all into instruments of peace and non-violence, and it cures the sick members of the Church. By its healing word, the sacrament of penance reconciles those who were harmful and contagious members, and re-admits them to the Eucharistic banquet, thus strengthening all in the hope for the heavenly banquet.

The frequent reception of the sacrament of reconciliation can sharpen awareness that one's whole life has to carry out the baptismal mandate, 'If by the Spirit you put to death all the base pursuits of the selfish self, then you will live' (Rom 8:13).

(e) *Matrimony*

To promise before God and before men faithful conjugal love 'for better and for worse' is a great venture that demands superhuman courage and trust in young people, especially in this testing age. Those who enter into a total covenant 'until death separates them' can do so by putting their faith and trust in the gospel. If a healthy trust in each other is an expression of that redeemed and redeeming love, that 'has no limits to its hope' (1 Cor 13:7), then it is fundamentally hope in the Lord, who comes into the marriage and abides with husband and wife as their companion on the earthly pilgrimage.

A marriage is about to reveal its definitive sacramental witness when husband and wife have conquered the trials, overcome the illusions and integrated the partial failures and frustrations into that faithful love which is supported by God's own promise and fidelity. Since matrimony is a sacred sign of the covenant of love between Christ and the Church which was witnessed on the cross, it also reflects the final victory of love which has become manifest in the resurrection and will be manifest for all with the second coming of Christ. Matrimony is for Christians a prognostic sign of the final fulfilment of the covenant between God and redeemed mankind in the heavenly Jerusalem.

The sacrament of marriage is a *transient* sign; that is, through its present but not yet perfected love, it points to that perfect union with God in the communion of his saints where all genuine earthly love, patience, justice will come to its completion. The human joys and sorrows shared in love gradually build up a deeply felt idea of the hoped-for bliss and beatitude, while making it impossible to look upon these earthly realities as if they were the final fulfilment of human existence. In this respect marriage participates in the eschatological meaning of the Eucharist and of consecrated virginity. They are celebrations of joy only in hope. And from that hope and joy arise the strength and readiness of the persons involved to use present opportunities fully. The loss of this dynamism of hope in solidarity is catastrophic. So many marriages fail in our cultures because of excessive expectations for immediate fulfilment, sometimes in a very narrow way, looking almost exclusively to sexual fulfilment.

With its present opportunities and its dynamic calling to walk together with Christ, the sacrament of matrimony gives the spouses the grace and the task to strive untiringly for the goal of all human love so that, like the virgins, they will ever be mindful that the *kairos* (the present compact and pressing time) is 'short' and that 'the whole frame of the world is passing away', and that, therefore, married people just as much as virgins should live in the fullest freedom to meet the Lord when he comes (cf. 1 Cor 7-29-31). Christian spouses will be grateful for the mutual love which, growingly, becomes a sign and symbol of the love which God shows us; they will also gradually come to the vital experience that their limitations and partial failures serve a great goal: they will never make an idol of each other.

Because the structure of the Christian marriage is one of hope, the spouses are warned that conjugal love and happiness are certainly not the ultimate reality, but that, nevertheless, fidelity to the marriage till death conditions their participation in the nuptials of the heavenly Jerusalem.

In the perspective of 'the sacraments as privileged signs of hope', it also becomes clear that conjugal love, like that of the Church for Christ, needs an ongoing purification. A sacramental vision of hope allows no illusion. Conjugal life is necessarily involved in the eschatological combat, in the final and sometimes most demanding decision for the Lord.

Through faith in Christ's death and resurrection, through the presence of his redeeming love, the sacrament of marriage can become an important sign of liberation, freeing the spouses from the false and ugly forms of passion yielded to selfish and exploitive 'love' of the other. The patient striving of husband and wife for a more and more tender, generous and forbearing love, in reverence for each other and for the unique dignity of each of their children, and the education of themselves and of their children in Christian maturity and inner freedom are all efficacious signs of hope not only for the family itself but also for the world around it.

(f) *Holy orders*

The priest is distinguished by that consecration through the Spirit which enables him to carry out his unique mission to proclaim, in the Eucharistic celebration and by all his ministry and life, 'the death of the Lord until he comes' (1 Cor 11:26). This task does not allow him in any way to feel superior to other Christians or to be isolated from them; it is a mandate to be a channel of peace and a sign of union with God and of unity among men. The priest is meant to pray, to labour and to suffer that believers 'may all be one' in Christ and thus to proclaim to the world their hope for final unity. He should be a leader both in humility and in the striving towards that maturity, discernment and vigilance that sense, in all events and in all the needs of people, the coming of the Lord.

The priest, in a very particular way, is enlisted in the service of reconciliation (cf. 2 Cor 5:14-6:3) which must not, however, de-activate those wholesome tensions in the pilgrim Church which are characteristic of the age between the 'already' and the 'not yet'. If he lives in Christ, he can inspire that love and mutual acceptance which make many tensions and polarizations fruitful. The priest is a man for all, never a part of a party. His role is that of an ambassador of reconciliation, calling all to be fully reconciled with God and with each other. He will speak with courage in favour of just causes and against injustice and seduction, but never against persons.

The priesthood does not signify social status or an overall set of privileges but a service of the Spirit in absolute freedom for the Lord, *in parresia* (in frankness), in serenity and in joy that spring from trust in God and from hope of eternal life (cf. 2 Cor 3:4).

Although celibacy is not necessarily connected with the priesthood as an absolute and although Christian matrimony is also a strong eschatological sign, nevertheless the celibacy of priests, if lived with conviction, freedom, maturity and joy, has a privileged eschatological significance: a life totally dedicated to the proclamation of the kingdom of God, a witness of hope for everlasting life, and an encouragement for those who against their will have to live a celibate life.

(g) *The anointing of the sick*

Our Redeemer 'has fortified, with the sacrament of extreme unction, the end of life as with the most valid defences' in a way that can overcome the final and most violent assaults of the evil one. [17]

The present pastoral approach of the Church emphasizes more the assistance to the sick in general. All serious ailments should be brought home into the death-resurrection reality of faith and hope. The Second Vatican Council prefers us to use the name 'anointing of the sick' rather than 'extreme unction', since it is not a sacrament only for those who are at the point of death. [18]

'By the sacred anointing of the sick and the prayer of her priests, the whole Church commends those who are ill to the suffering and glorified Lord, asking that he may lighten their suffering and save them (cf. Jas 5:14-16). She exhorts them, moreover, to contribute to the welfare of the whole people of God by associating themselves freely with the passion and death of Christ.' [19]

The anointing of the sick signifies the dynamic presence of the Holy Spirit who works in such a way that the faithful can accept the critical hours of illness and of death in the light of the 'final hour', with peace, without spiritual discomfort or weakening. The anointing of the sick is linked to the sacraments of baptism and of confirmation. The work which the Spirit began

[17] The Council of Trent, Session XIV, Denzinger N. 1694.
[18] SC 73.
[19] LG 11.

in these sacraments becomes, by the same Spirit, perfected at
the time of sickness and at the hour of death, if the person truly
embraces the law of the Spirit (Rom 8 : 1), the law of grace which
freed us from fear of death. Sickness and death itself, thus
united to the passion and death of Christ — in which baptism
has already inserted the faithful — are transformed into signs
of hope. They receive a new significance in the light of the
death and resurrection of the Lord. Those who give to their
sufferings and especially to their death this meaning of faith
are giving an outstanding witness of Christian hope.

*   *   *

All the sacraments, then, together and individually, teach us
how to live under the law of grace in this 'time-in-between'.
'The grace of God has dawned upon the world with healing for
all mankind; it teaches us to live a life of temperance, honesty
and godliness in the present age, looking forward to the happy
fulfilment of our hope when the splendour of our great God
and Saviour Christ Jesus will appear' (Tit 2 : 12-13).

He who rightly celebrates and receives the sacraments of
faith and of hope, and lives according to their meaning and
their grace, looks forward gladly to the coming of Christ (cf.
2 Tim 4 : 8) and is vigilant for all the ways in which the Lord
meets and challenges us in this intermediate time.

Celebrating the sacraments of the new and eternal covenant
we give implicitly or explicitly voice to the exclamation,
'Marana tha', 'Come, O Lord!' (1 Cor 16 : 22). In this way,
the expectation of the Lord, who comes and will come, frees
the faithful from selfish desires and, altogether, renders them
vigilant, because they avail themselves of all the opportunities
to serve their brethren, to be of service to all those who have
initially met the Lord. They challenge the alienation of those
who have directed all their hopes towards things which are
passing away.

5. *The sacraments teach the law of growth*

From the manifold meaning and treasures of the sacraments flow important consequences for the moral life. As visible signs of hope, they reveal to the faithful that law of growth that reaches us through the very gifts manifested in the celebration. The eschatological meaning which we have tried to grasp in these pages strengthens above all a specifically dynamic vision of the whole Christian life. One cannot be a disciple of Christ without steadily advancing in a better knowledge of him and of his love for all mankind. With Christ's own love, the sacraments urge us to grow in love of God and our neighbour, and to distinguish better and better true love from its counterfeits.

We are all together in need of constant striving, constant conversion and purification. Christian hope, as an attractive and saving sign of redemption and liberation for the world, cannot be lived unless we who are believers are united in our striving for a more thorough conversion and an on-going renewal of our life, of the Church and of society.

The tensions of the eschatological times between the present and what is yet to come are experienced by Christians who humbly accept the still existing need of prohibitive laws, of fraternal correction and humble confession of sins. However, without ever allowing Christians to become self-satisfied as if they were perfected, the 'already' of Christian hope should shine through even more in a trustful and generous commitment to those norms and commandments of the New Testament which evidence such an abundant outpouring of the Spirit. [20] We should look upon the on-going revelation in history, in our life, and particularly in the liturgy, in the light of what is said about the scriptures: 'They are recorded for our benefit as a warning. For upon us the fulfilment of the ages has come' (1 Cor 10:11).

The New Testament commandment, 'Be perfect' (Mt 5:48), is not a selective mandate which would distinguish a higher

---

[20] Cf. my article, 'The Normative Value of the Sermon on the Mount', *Catholic Biblical Quarterly*, 29 (1967), pp. 376-385.

class of priests and religious from the simple faithful who could abide only by the prohibitive commandments. It is the *normative invitation to all the disciples* of Christ 'according to the measure of the gift' granted to each person in these final ages.

Christian holiness is a *firm commitment* to strive with all one's powers towards the goal defined by the fullness of the times. To the rich young man (Mt 19:21) it is not said: to enter into eternal life, you may make a choice either to keep the old commandments, or if you prefer, to be perfect; rather, it is said: to make the necessary transition from the old economy to the fullness of the times, you must free yourself completely and follow me.

In the letter to the Philippians the apostle refutes any static concept of Christian perfection. No one is perfect. Those are Christians who untiringly 'press on, reaching out for what is ahead' (Phil 3:12-14).

The sacraments instruct us in the law of continuous growth. They tell us that we must strive constantly, 'hoping to take hold of that for which Christ took hold of us'. Thus we live in faith according to that justice by which God graciously justifies us. With Paul we long to know Christ, to experience the power of his resurrection, and to share his sufferings in growing conformity with his death, 'if only I may finally arrive at the resurrection from the dead' (Phil 3:10-12).

It is evident therefore that the energetic orientation of Christian life comes not from goals man sets up for himself according to his own desires, but rather, it is itself an end-goal which the gifts he receives inscribe in him who was created anew by Christ as 'a new creature'.

Thus the *true and effective end* stems from the law of grace which reveals the meaning of the history of salvation. From the same law of grace arises also the dynamic tone of the whole of moral theology and pedagogy.

Chapter 4

THE SIGNS OF ADORATION
IN SPIRIT AND IN TRUTH

In my book *The Law of Christ* I treat of the sacraments particularly, if not exclusively, in the context of the virtue of religion. This choice was determined by the tragic situation of many Christians and Christian communities who had forgotten that not only the Eucharist but all the sacraments are worship, and a school of 'adoration of God in spirit and in truth'. In the more or less recent past, the evaluation of the sacraments was by far too limited. They were presented almost exclusively as means for fulfilling laws and prescripts, and for obtaining grace to perform various duties imposed independently of the signs of God's gracious love.

The liturgical reform promoted by the Second Vatican Council and carried forward in the post-conciliar period has shed light anew on the *cultic aspect* of the sacraments. All the sacraments are primarily worship.

The communal celebration of the sacrament of reconciliation, especially when it flows into a final act of thanksgiving and praise for divine mercy, returns to this sacrament the cultic dimension which it had lost even more than the others. However, much yet remains to be done to integrate this vision of worship into moral doctrine and all moral catechesis. The main concern of this book, and particularly of this chapter, is that our understanding of Christian vocation should be such that it will encourage the integration of the whole Christian life.

1. *Adoration in spirit and in truth*

When Jesus, speaking with the Samaritan woman, comes to the critical subject of how her life would and should be transformed, she escapes into a formalistic question typical of an age of sacralization: 'Our fathers worshipped on this mountain but you Jews say that the temple where God should be worshipped is in Jerusalem' (Jn 4:20). The response of the Lord explains how, in the new era determined by his coming, the whole of life, in all its dimensions, ought to become true worship of the living God: 'Believe me, the time is coming when you will worship the Father neither on this mountain nor in Jerusalem. . . . But the time approaches, indeed it is already here, when the real worshippers will worship the Father in spirit and in truth. Such are the worshippers the Father wants. God is spirit, and those who worship him must worship him in spirit and in truth' (Jn 4:21-24).

These words of the Lord are certainly not intended to confirm a spiritualism that scorns the visible world and visible signs; however, they do exclude any monopoly of worship on behalf of sacred places or of specific liturgical celebrations. They decisively surpass a ritualism and formalism which trust only in an exact repetition of rites and formulas.

Central to true worship is the *conversion to God, the one Father of all men* and to Christ, his *Anointed,* in whom he has willed to show the full splendour of his love and his justice, and by whom he has been truly adored and glorified in a love that returns all men to him.

While the sacraments of the Church express in a privileged and unique way the fact that it is God himself who glorifies his mercy and his name as Father and thus enables and teaches us how to honour him in all our life, they are not the only signs he uses to reveal his glory and to invite men to adoration.

The adoration of God in spirit and in truth is *based on the synthesis between individual conversion and social renewal, the reform of Church, society and culture; it is the integration of prayer and life.* It is fully realized only in Christ, whom the Holy Spirit has anointed for the final revelation of the plentitude of goodness, justice and mercy of the Father and for the response of true worship, the worship of a whole life, even to the shedding of his blood in the service of all men.

The follower of Christ will have a watchful eye and an attentive heart to sense everywhere the way in which God glorifies his name and thus invites men to render him honour and thanks.

The temple of Jerusalem was the privileged place in which God revealed his fidelity and his mercy and invited his people to be gathered as the people of the covenant, to honour him with unity in worship. The people, however, often gave a monopolistic significance to the temple, placing a kind of mechanistic trust in the material fact.

On the other hand, the whole history of prophetism was a continuous call to the adoration of God through one's whole life. 'This place is the temple of the Lord, the temple of the Lord, the temple of the Lord. This catchword of yours is a lie; put no trust in it. Mend your ways and your doings; deal fairly with one another; do not oppress the alien, the orphan or the widow; shed no innocent blood in this place; do not run after other gods to your own ruin. Then will I let you live in this place, in the land which I gave long ago to your forefathers for all time' (Jer 7: 4-7).

The sacraments of 'the new law' *forbid all sterile ritualism* which exhausts, in a scrupulous uniformity of formulas and rubrics, almost all the energies of a person. On the contrary, the sacraments are privileged signs through which God gives to persons and communities the ability to render him honour and thanks, not only in the celebration itself but in a whole life of fidelity to the great realities communicated in the sacraments, a life that can be truly offered as worship of the Father in union with Christ and as harvest of the Spirit.

From here we can draw the main lines for a pastoral approach to the sacraments. We should so celebrate *baptism* that all believers experience their unity in the one baptism in which Christ has honoured the Father by manifesting his total solidarity with all men, drawing all into unity. Baptism will thus generate children of God who become one in Christ, that the world may believe in one God and Father and honour him by becoming more humane, more just, more united in concern for the rights of all men.

The sacrament of *reconciliation* should so bring to our experience the encounter with Christ, our Peace and Reconciliation, that we all become more and more channels of peace and ambassadors of reconciliation on all levels of our private and social life, in praise of God who has reconciled the world to himself in Jesus Christ.

The preparation for *priesthood* and the election or nomination of bishops and popes should all be orientated to their main mission: to be persons who in an outstanding way have reached the integration of faith and life, of prayer and fraternal love so that they can help the other faithful to learn what it means to adore God in spirit and truth.

Participation in the *Eucharist* and in all the liturgical life of the Church should give us such a vital and deep experience of worship, praise and thanksgiving in community that at all times we have at our disposal the most illuminating motives and criteria for our moral choices. Can I offer this thought, desire, action to God as praise and thanksgiving with Christ? Can I unite what I want to do now with the sacrifice of Christ?

The sacrament of *confirmation* especially should be oriented to the formation of mature Christians, who in solidarity, discernment, generosity, creative liberty and fidelity can manifest to the world what a true adorer of God is meant to be.

The sacrament of *marriage,* too, receives this new dimension. The spouses accept each other as the gift of the Father and will offer each other and their children that love, patience, forbearance, respect that can truly render thanks to the Giver of all good gifts. The Christian family will pray, reflect on God's word, on daily events in such a way that their lives become praise of God. 'Be filled with the Spirit, addressing one another in psalms, hymns and inspired songs. Sing praise to the Lord with all your hearts. Give thanks to the Father always and for everything. Defer to one another out of reverence for Christ' (Eph 5 : 18-21).

The *anointment of the sick* should be understood and celebrated in such a way that Christians become able to offer their suffering, ailments, and especially their death with Christ to the praise of the Father and for the salvation of all mankind.

2. *The virtue of religion in relation to the theological and moral virtues*

In the preceding discussion, I spoke of the sacraments as privileged signs and schools of faith, hope and love. We shall now try to consider them as a starting point for understanding more clearly the organic unity of the theological virtues and the virtue of religion.

The 'old peasant of the Garonne', Jacques Maritain, in his book *Liturgie et Contemplation* [1] made himself the champion of the opposition against liturgical reform and against what he considered an undue emphasis on the liturgy in Christian life. He reduces the three theological virtues almost completely to a contemplation without words or signs, seemingly in the hidden soul. He considers the whole liturgy as a typical expression of the virtue of religion which, in his opinion, is only a subdivision of the virtue of justice. Furthermore, he insists that liturgy and

---

[1] J. and R. Maritain, *Liturgie et Contemplation* (Bruges: Desclée, 1960). See the review by L. Bouyer, in *La Vie Spirituelle,* 102 (1960), p. 406, and B. Häring, *This Time of Salvation* (New York: Herder and Herder, 1966), pp. 147-159. This criticism does not, however, intend to diminish the high veneration and gratitude which Maritain deserves for his contribution to the *aggiornamento* of philosophy and theology.

the virtue of religion are very imperfect in comparison with
wordless and signless contemplation.

As I see it, he should have preferred an opposite theological
vision which considers the virtue of religion not as a virtue
added to the theological ones, or as a moral virtue among many
others subordinated to the virtue of justice, but rather *as an
essential and integral part and perspective of the theological
virtues themselves*.

The reason is that when God reveals his majesty, his love
and his saving truth, he does it by means of tangible visible
works and, above all, through his Word Incarnate. By the grace
of the Holy Spirit, this revelation in which God glorifies his
name visibly becomes a dynamic force to which man responds
in a faith that is at the same time adoration, with a hope that
glorifies the fidelity and mercy of God, and with a fraternal love
rooted in adoring love, to the glory of the one Creator and
Father of all men.

A sacramental spirituality emphasizes the cultic aspect of
the sacraments of faith, hope and charity. They properly serve
as a unique dynamism of a life inspired by the same faith, hope
and charity, for the glory of the Father who is glorified when
he sanctifies man and renders him capable of a life fully united
to Christ, Redeemer, High Priest, Prophet and Universal Sacrament of brotherly love. If we say 'glory' we can never under-
value the quality of *visibility* in our life.

The sacraments point to the initiative of God. We place
ourselves on a road strewn with all kind of difficulties and
neuroses when we take as a starting point self-perfection, which
stresses man's own work and concern for his self-fulfilment,
forgetting almost entirely God's initiative and his being the
origin, centre and goal of all life. 'Adoration of God in spirit
and truth' is the most indispensable and saving *criticism of a
too anthropocentric concept of virtue*. The human virtues need
redemption by being integrated into true adoration of God.

In the scriptures, 'adoration of God in spirit and truth' has,
as its point of departure, the glory of God (*kabod Yahweh, doxa*

theôu). When God manifests the splendour and the glory of his saving love, and when man encounters his fascinating and tremendous mystery, the very presence of God urges man to a glad and humble adoration.

The revelation of the *holiness* of God is dynamic. It is the effective presence of the holy God who purifies man and invites him to the glad concelebration of the mystery of his holiness. Holy fear and joy in the Lord give significance and direction to the whole of life for the glory of God. This, however, is possible only through the experience, though imperfect, of the mystery of the holiness of God in his revelation and in history.

'The law of sanctity' is the power of grace which emanates from the dynamic revelation of God's holiness and is inscribed in us as law: 'You shall be holy because I, the Lord your God, am holy' (Lev 19:1). As we see especially in Leviticus 19, already the priestly law of holiness of the Old Testament embraces at the same time explicit worship and all fraternal relations, not only with the chosen people but also and above all with migrants and aliens, so that they may recognize the one God in their lives. Those who, in being chosen as his people, experience the revelation of God's holiness also receive a consecration to a mission to glorify God before all nations. The law of holiness calls for *a life in brotherhood*. 'You shall not nurse hatred against your brother. You shall reprove your fellow-countryman frankly and so you will have no share in his guilt. You shall not seek revenge or cherish anger towards your kinsfolk; you shall love your neighbour as a man like yourself. I am the Lord' (Lev 19:17-18).

In revealing his name *Yahweh* and finally his name *Father*, God turns his countenance to man so that man, in turn, can direct to him the whole of his life, praising his goodness and his justice.

All these biblical expressions reveal the dynamism of revelation and the *character of response and of worship appropriate to the whole life of the people of God*. One cannot understand the virtue of religion without starting from the primacy of grace and the dynamic nature of faith, hope and charity, through which man responds to the pressing and liberating revelation of the glory, salvific truth, fidelity and goodness of God in a visible way.

At first, the approach of St Thomas would seem very different. We ought however, to distinguish the starting point which, for him, is kerygmatic and psychological and the special intention of his treatise. St Thomas considers the virtue of religion as the queen and soul of the moral virtues. In his theology we find a classic example of the concern (which ought always to be predominant) to bring religion and life together again in intimate union.

The virtue of religion 'commands all other virtues'. [2] It has two modes of expression. First there are acts which are specific; attention is directly and immediately given to worship. These acts order directly the person's relationship to God; for instance sacrifice, adoration and other similar manifestations. 'Expressions of other virtues, on the other hand, are fostered indirectly by the same virtue, ordering them to the honour of God; the virtue of religion, in fact, which has as direct object the goal of the honour of God, gives direction to all the other virtues that have as object the means to attain it'. [3]

In view of the vitality and capacity of the virtue of religion to transform the whole life into adoring praise of God, St Thomas can conclude that it is 'superior to all the moral virtues'. [4]

If, in his systematization, St Thomas presents religion as a virtue attributed to justice (*'virtus justitiae adnexa'*), it does not flow from this that, for him, religion in its dynamism would be a virtue subordinated to human justice or that it is conceived on the model of justice that rules juridical structures or commercial exchanges. While St Thomas takes the human experience of justice as point of departure, he transcends it in his concept of the virtue of religion.

[2] *Summa Theol.* 2-2:81:4:1.
[3] *Summa Theol.* 2-2:81:1:1.
[4] *Summa Theol.* 2-2:81:6.

The statement of St Thomas that *the virtue of religion 'is not perfect regarding justice'* is not a very happy one. However, we ought to note immediately the truly theological explanation which the saint gives us: 'Whatever man can offer to God belongs to God and is due to him but it can never be something adequate for what is due; it is written, in fact "What shall I render to the Lord for all that he has given me?" (Ps 115:3)'. [5]

If then, in the external systematization of the virtue of religion, St Thomas follows Aristotle, nevertheless, with regard to its interior dynamism, he emphasizes the initiative of God. Therefore, we can assert that St Thomas has a truly sacramental vision of it in the perspective of the biblical concept of justice (*dikaiosyne*). The position of St Thomas concerning the sacraments is explicit: 'The sacraments are ordered to perfecting man in what belongs to the worship of God according to the religion of Christian life'. [6] In this formula the angelic doctor succeeds in expressing well the dynamism of the sacraments for a life which, in its totality, is worship of God. In his thought, the whole of liturgy and of prayer are explicit and direct expressions of the virtue of religion ('*actus eliciti virtutis religionis*') dynamically tending to make of the whole Christian life an expression guided and shaped by adoration ('*actus imperatus virtutis religionis*'). [7]

The sacraments are more than a school of worship; they are, above all, *acts of Christ* that, by means of the Holy Spirit, enable man to be united to his worship in spirit and truth. 'That is properly called sacrament which is a sign of a sacred reality, in so far as it sanctifies man'. [8] Man, poor creature and sinner, ought always to be conscious that he is unable to render to God a pleasing or adequate worship. Therefore, with St Thomas, we conceive the sacraments first of all as effectual signs of grace in which God himself calls us and makes us

---

[5] *Summa Theol.* 2-2:80.
[6] *Summa Theol.* 3:65:1.
[7] *Summa Theol.* 2-2:81:1.
[8] *Summa Theol.* 3:60:2.

capable of true worship. This does not exclude but rather includes the other aspect of *school*, in which God through the Church instructs us in the true nature of worship. 'The signs appropriately are given to man for him to arrive specifically at things unknown through the known things.' [9]

What Paul, in his letter to Titus, attributes in the first place to the grace made visible in the Word Incarnate can also be applied to the sacraments in their intimate relation to Christ. 'For the grace of God has dawned upon the world with healing for all mankind; and by it we are disciplined to renounce godless ways and worldly desires, and to live a life of temperance, honesty and godliness in the present age, looking forward to the happy fulfilment of our hope when the splendour of our great God and Saviour Jesus Christ will appear' (Tit 2:11-13).

Man, instructed and formed by the grace of the sacraments, sees in all the gifts of God, in all the signs of his goodness, an appeal and an invitation to adore him in spirit and truth.

The sacraments stand at the centre of all the expressions of the virtue of religion. This, however, is not intended to imply that they are the only school of adoration in spirit and truth. Normally they are a necessary gift and experience which gives significance and direction to personal prayer and to all devotions. The Christian ought to give to liturgical celebrations and other explicit expressions of religion as much love and time as is necessary to become capable of giving to his whole life the meaning and purpose of worship in spirit and in truth.

3. *The sacraments as worship and mandate to worship*

All the sacraments are gift and ordinance to worship in spirit and truth. St Thomas distinguishes two aspects: first, the direct ordinance to worship and second, the overcoming of sin which is the chief obstacle to true worship. 'The sacraments

[9] *Summa Theol.* 3:60:2.

have a double purpose: to perfect man in that which concerns the cult of God according to the religion of Christian life and, in the second place, to be a remedy for the deficiencies caused by sin'. [10]

The traditional expression 'sanctifying grace', as much as the traditional doctrine on the *sacramental character*, have set a permanent cultic direction to Christian life. We can synthesize the cultic purpose of the sacraments in the following manner. (a) The sacraments *insert us into the community of worship*, the Church, who, in Christ and through his Spirit, is a sacrament of salvation for the whole of mankind because she is called to be the sacrament of adoration in spirit and truth. (b) By means of the Church which is the sacrament of encounter with Christ, the Christian enters into intimate friendship with him and *participates in the consecrating power of his passion and resurrection* by which the whole of human history becomes an economy of salvation and gives glory to God the Father in the unity of the Holy Spirit. Inserted into Christ, High Priest and Victim, the believer becomes a participant in the cultic gift of himself which the beloved Son offers to the Father in the Holy Spirit. The sacramental life already unites man initially to the heavenly liturgy. (c) By means of the sacraments received in a spirit of worship, the *believer becomes holy* (that is, consecrated to truthful adoration of God) in his most intimate existence, in all of his relationships with his neighbour and with the world and in all the essential aspects of his life.

The sacraments ordain us to a *social worship* because we have become 'a kingdom of priests, a holy nation' (Ex 19:6; cf. 1 Pet 2:9). Through the grace and mandate of the sacraments, we are instructed in and enabled to carry out the mission of ordaining our whole social life in a way that gives praise to the grace and glory of God.

By charity and social justice, especially towards our enemies, we render a true worship to God and can say in truth, 'Our

[10] *Summa Theol.* 3:65:1.

Father'. (d) The sacraments are means of personal and social salvation inasmuch as they instruct us and give us the ability to live our individual and social life in that spirit of responsibility and commitment which is a truly acceptable offering to the glory of God, the Father of all men.

The sacraments, then, are signs of worship in so far as they sanctify man, help him to reach his goal, making him capable of adoring God in spirit and truth in his whole life. In the intention of Christ, the liturgy is a pre-eminent school which effectively introduces us to a life which can span the gap between religion and life, making of everything an expression of adoration in spirit and truth.

Chapter 5

THE SIGNS OF THE NEW LAW

Christ has promulgated his law — of grace, of faith, of hope and love, and of adoration in spirit and truth — by his life and death, by his example and words, but above all by the outpouring of the grace of the Holy Spirit.

All that Christ has taught on the mount of the beatitudes and on Mount Calvary has effectively touched his disciples only through the Spirit promised to them: 'Your Advocate, the Holy Spirit whom the Father will send in my name, will teach you everything and will call to mind all that I have told you' (Jn 14:26; also 15:26-67 and 16:12-15).

In the sacraments Christ continues to teach us his law with words and signs, through his Church in her testimony of faith, hope and adoring love, and principally through the grace of the Holy Spirit. Thus the sacraments are effective signs of 'the law of the Spirit which gives life in Christ Jesus' (Rom 8:2).

1. *Unity between the law of grace and the written law*

The people of the old covenant saw its sacraments as means to and signs of the realization of *ritual purity*. Although the various liturgical celebrations could often arouse the faith which purifies the heart and makes holy the interior life, nevertheless the dominant perspective in which they had come to be seen was frequently externalistic.

'The people of the new covenant, on the contrary, see their sacraments above all as effective signs of *internal purity, that of the heart,* which is the work of grace and of living faith. Christians, enlightened by the Holy Spirit, discover above all the power of inner grace by means of the external signs. The sacraments of the new law, with all that seems material, are not powerless, since they convey effectively the message of internal grace; thus they are capable of becoming channels of justification.' [1]

What the sacraments (especially confirmation, considered, however, together with all the others) communicate effectively to the morality of the followers of Christ is not observance of a written law or a code but, primarily and essentially, a life guided by the Spirit. Through the sacraments God prompts, in us and through us, his law of charity and justice which characterizes the true members of the people of the new covenant.

In 2 Cor 3:6 St Paul says, 'The qualification we have comes from God; it is he who has qualified us to be ministers of his new covenant — a covenant expressed not in a written document but in a spiritual bond'. St Thomas' comments that this verse 'describes the New Testament. ... It needs to be noted that the expression of the apostle is profound. In fact, in Jeremiah (31:31-33) it is said: "I will make a new covenant with Israel. ... I will set my law within them and write it in their hearts." The Old Testament, then, is written in the book sprinkled with blood, as is said in Hebrews 9:19. ... It thus becomes evident that the Old Testament is the testament of the letter. The New Testament, instead, is the testament of the Holy Spirit through whom the love of God is poured into our hearts, as is read in Romans 5:5. Therefore the Holy Spirit, while bringing forth in us charity which is the fullness of the law, sets the New Testament, not in the letter but in its being written by means of the Spirit which gives life.' [2]

---

[1] Thomas Aquinas, *Commentary on Paul's Epistle to the Galatians,* 2:16, lect. IV.

[2] Thomas Aquinas, *Commentary on the Epistle to the Corinthians,* II 3:6, lect. II.

All this St Thomas applies explicitly to the sacraments of the New Testament in his comment on St Paul's words 'In fact you are not under the regime of law but under that of grace' (Rom 6:14): 'It should be noted that Paul does not speak here of the law only as liturgical rules but also as moral norms. In this respect, there are two ways of being subject. The first is the way of him who voluntarily submits to the observance of the law. Thus Christ was also subjected to the law, as Galatians (4:4) says: "born under the law", because he has observed the law. Christians are certainly still bound in this way to the law in its moral content but not in the ritual content. The other way to become subject to the law is that of him who is coerced by the law. In this way he comes under the law who observes it not voluntarily and through love but through fear. He is deprived of grace which, were it present, would incline the will to the observance of the law in such a way as to accomplish its moral demands in love. Every time, then, that someone is submitted to the law in such a way that he does not carry it out voluntarily, sin rules over him. By means of grace, however, another rule takes over, by which man fulfils the law, not as if he were under the law but as one who is free. "We are no slave-woman's children; our mother is a free woman. Christ set us free to be free men" (Gal 4:31). The legal sacraments do not confer grace for men to carry out the law freely; *this freedom is conferred by the sacraments of Christ.* Those who submitted themselves to the legal rites, in so far as the power of those sacraments is concerned, were not yet under the law of grace by means of faith in Christ. Those, on the contrary, who submit themselves to the sacraments of Christ, receive grace by virtue of them, so that they are not under the law but under grace, unless they fall back into the servitude of sin through their fault.'[3]

The new law is characterized by its intimate relation to the new covenant. The new covenant with the Church, which Christ sealed in his blood on the altar of the cross, is the great and

---

[3] Thomas Aquinas, *Commentary on Romans,* 6:14, lect. III.

fundamental sacrament which is present and operative in a privileged way in the seven sacraments. Therefore, if one wants to penetrate the essential character of the new law, one has to consider it in the light of the new covenant and of the sacraments which signify it.

In this respect, a text of St Thomas is very clear: 'The new law is the law of the new covenant. But the law of the new covenant is poured into our hearts.... Now, that which is principal in the New Testament and which constitutes its virtue is the grace of the Holy Spirit deriving from faith in Christ. Therefore, the new covenant is mainly the grace of the Holy Spirit granted to those who believe in Christ ... "because in Christ Jesus the life-giving law of the Spirit has set you free from the law of sin and death" (Rom 8:2). This is why St Augustine teaches, in his book *De Spiritu et littera*, that "the law of faith is written in the heart of the faithful, as the law of external works was written on tables of stone" (ch. 24). And elsewhere (ch. 21): "What are those divine laws which God himself has written in men's hearts if not the presence of the Holy Spirit?" Nevertheless the new law contains some dogmas and orientation which are like elements to predispose to the grace of the Holy Spirit or to live according to that grace; they however, are a secondary aspect of the new law'. [4]

For St Thomas, as is apparent, there is no opposition between the '*law written interiorly*' and the secondary element which is the formulated law. He brings to the fore, then, the unity of what is essential and what is secondary in the new law. The moral law written in the gospel is also the work of the Spirit. 'The Spirit teaches it. In fact just as the law speaks to man in his inner depth teaching the operations of the virtues, so the Spirit interiorly moves and urges us to put them into practice.' [5]

This unity between the interior law written in the heart and the exterior law expressed in formulations is unfolded in every liturgical celebration. The sacraments are visible signs which

[4] *Summa Theol.* 1-2:206:1.
[5] Thomas Aquinas, *Commentary on Galatians,* 5:23, lect. VII.

manifest the interior grace. In them, then, the signified grace is more important than the sign which signifies it. Nevertheless, man ordinarily does not arrive at the interior grace except by means of external and visible signs, that is, by means of the sacraments especially by the seven privileged signs of God's grace. Through the sacraments and the word of God that speak to him eloquently, man is able to penetrate increasingly the mystery of grace.

An instruction on the exterior law, evangelical or ecclesiastical, is then valid only if it helps the faithful to *discern spirits* more and more clearly and leads them to a greater and greater maturity of conscience. As the sacramental signs manifest and draw our attention directly to the interior grace, a truly Christian educator, while teaching that which is secondary in the new law, will above all strive directly to arouse docility towards the law written in the heart, *by the grace of the Holy Spirit.* Every authentic use of external law stems from the 'law of the Spirit which gives us life in Christ Jesus' and leads us still further into it.

The nature of the sacraments also makes obvious the error of those who want to recognize only the interiority of grace and reject the *external laws* found in the bible itself or proposed authentically by the Church. The sacraments, in fact, are instituted by Christ as sacraments of the Church and as visible signs. Therefore, all of their efficacy derives from the Spirit who, however, works where and when he wants.

2. *The privileged role of the sacramental signs and of the good tidings as 'external supplement' to the new law*

The grace of the Holy Spirit infinitely surpasses all that the sacramental signs or words succeed in expressing. The seven sacraments can never monopolize the activity of the Holy Spirit. However, they are also the *expression and the privileged school* which helps us to understand better all that the Holy Spirit does, not only by the sacraments themselves but by all the signs of the goodness and the power of God. It is an authentic possibility to proceed systematically by starting from the sacraments and then, in the light and organic unity towards which they direct us, to consider all the other forms by which God shows his love and manifests his will. However, the grasp of the meaning of the sacraments is normally the result of the many experiences and signs of love in daily life.

The new law — which is revealed to us by and in view of the sacraments as 'law written in our hearts by the manifest grace, and somehow understood by means of signs — has an external supplement.' This consists not so much of the decalogue as of the evangelical teachings, the beatitudes of the sermon on the mount, the examples and words of Christ, and finally, the visible and perceptible message and witness of the saints.

The sermon on the mount has its *sitz im leben* as a catechetical instruction on Christian life according to the new creation. [6] It explains the loftiness of the Christian vocation as expressed and impressed by the sacraments of initiation. Only in this perspective can instruction on the decalogue, and on natural law also, become truly a part of a Christian and Christocentric outlook.

One and undivided, therefore, is the law of Christ, both internal and external. But its principal part, indeed its quintessence, is the *grace of the Holy Spirit*. Whoever makes of this grace something secondary when it calls for works not imposed by a general law, or encloses it within the bounds of an ascetical theology reserved to a restricted circle of virtuous people or whoever teaches that such grace offered the individual person does not by itself oblige that person 'in conscience', deprives the new law of its specific note. One truly lives as a Christian with a mature conscience when one lives in gratitude and docility to the grace which one receives as intimate and dynamic norm. This represents the freedom of the children of God in

---

[6] Cf. J. Jeremias, *Paroles de Jésus: Le sermon sur la montagne — Le notre Père* (Paris, 1965), pp. 44-52.

complete obedience to 'the law of grace'. In this light is to be seen the vocation to sanctity of all the faithful. [7]

In this vision is cast the *fundamental question* of moral theology: how can I distinguish with sufficient certitude the authentic exigency of grace from the innate desires of the selfish self ('flesh', *sarx*)?

To give an answer we should see the relationships between all of God's gifts and the more urgent needs of people. Through faith active in love all gifts of God enter into the dynamics of grace. Those people are truly 'graced' who render thanks to God by using all their talents and earthly goods as well as their special charism for the benefit of their fellowman. Among the criteria of discernment the first place is reserved to the concern for the common good, the building up of the body of Christ (cf. Eph 4:1, 1 Cor 12), followed by the full harvest of the Spirit: interior peace and commitment to the messianic peace that extends to all levels of human relationships, joy and the capacity to bring joy to others, reverence for the conscience of one's fellowmen, benevolence, gentleness, self-control (cf. Gal 5:22).

For discernment we must also avail ourselves of the written law: in the first place the goal-commandments (cf. Mt 5:2-48), then the prohibitive laws by which the scriptures denounce the manifestations of selfishness that are directly opposed to the kingdom of God (cf. Gal 5:19-21). But we shall not forget that the law of grace engraved in the heart of the believer is richer, stronger and more gentle than the written law, especially that of a prohibitive character.

All criteria of discernment become effective through 'purity of heart', watchfulness about our motives; the trust in God that is acquired through knowledge, personal and shared experience and reflection will be enlivened by wisdom, the most precious gift of the Spirit.

---

[7] Cf. *Lumen gentium,* chapter V, and *Optatam totius,* 16, where the main purpose of moral theology is indicated, 'the loftiness of the vocation of the faithful in Christ'.

3. *Life in Christ Jesus and the following of Christ*

Through the sacraments, Christ, in a live and vivid way, invites us to follow him just as, in his earthly life, he called Peter and John after him. The instruction which the Lord himself gave to his apostles through words and deeds was incomplete before the outpouring of the Holy Spirit. Similarly, the external invitation which is extended to us in the sacramental signs would be fruitless without the internal grace. The sacraments thus reveal to us the true nature of the following of Christ.

(a) By the sacraments, Christ makes us *participants in his prophetic priesthood* and in the fruit of it. The law by which Christ 'annulled the law with its rules and regulations' (Eph 2:15), thus giving us a new heart and new spirit, is a law intimately joined to his priesthood and characterized by it. 'For a change of priesthood must mean a change of law' (Heb 7:12). All our trust and our every norm of conduct depend on the prophetic priesthood and the sacrifice of Christ. 'So now, my friends, the blood of Jesus makes us free to enter boldly into the sanctuary. Let us then make our approach in sincerity of heart and full assurance of faith' (Heb 10:19-22). In the letter to the Hebrews, all that is said of the new law written in men's hearts is constantly placed in relation to the priesthood of Christ in its surprising newness.

The doctrine on the 'sacramental character', worked out by scholastic theology, follows the line of vision of the Epistle to the Hebrews. The sacramental character expresses the design of God to model us on Christ's priesthood forever, so that in all our life we can join him who offered himself, once and forever, for the whole of mankind to the praise of the Father. 'The sacramental characters are no other than participation in Christ's priesthood. They derive totally from him.' [8]

According to the manuals of dogmatic theology, the sacra-

---

[8] *Summa Theol.* 3:63:3.

mental character is *'signum distinctivum, dispositivum, configu-rativum et consecratorium'*, that is, it is a calling that marks man in such a way as to *distinguish* him from those who did not receive such a contact with Christ; it *disposes* to a life and activity which corresponds to the calling; the heart of the matter is *configuration* with Christ, an aspect which is particularly dear to Orthodox theology — the goal of redemption is *transfiguration* of the redeemed which will reflect itself in the whole world around men; and finally, the sacramental character is a *consecration* according to the high-priestly prayer of Christ, 'Consecrate them in truth; thy word is truth. As thou hast sent me into the world, I have sent them into the world, and for their sake I consecrate myself, that they too may be consecrated in truth' (Jn 17: 17-19).

In this vision of the sacramental character as configuration with Christ and as a participation in his total consecration for the redemption of mankind to the glory of the Father, any ritualism or magic concept is excluded. What is meant is adoration in truth, a truthful life in accordance with faith, consecration to the undivided service of God in the service of mankind. Consecration by holy orders is of no avail to him who has it if it is not oriented towards a life totally dedicated to the glory of God and the redemption of mankind in the discipleship of Christ.

(b) *Life in Christ*. Saint John and Saint Paul describe our relation with Christ above all as 'life in Christ'. The sacraments have this great message, 'Christ lives in us and we in him', if we believe in him and entrust ourselves to him, ready to fulfil his commandment to love each other in his love.

The Eucharist points to a most committing blood-brother-hood: 'Whoever eats my flesh and drinks my blood dwells continually in me and I dwell in him. As the living Father sent me, and I live because of the Father, so he who eats me shall live because of me' (Jn 6: 56-57). This is infinitely more than a mere moral challenge; it is a reality that transcends our intelligence.

Faith and the sacraments of faith speak of an undeserved gift and vocation which can be expressed only in symbols, images, 'puzzling reflections in a mirror' (cf. 1 Cor 13:12). Neither rationalism nor moralism will ever understand the word, 'To all who did receive him, to those who have yielded their allegiance, he gave the right to become children of God . . ., the offspring of God himself' (Jn 1:12-13). The relationship to Christ cannot be thought of as the result of moral efforts; it is the work of the Holy Spirit who is grafting our life onto that of Christ. 'No one can enter the kingdom of God without being born from water and Spirit. . . . It is the Spirit that gives birth to the spirit' (Jn 3:5-6; cf. 1 Pet 1:23).

Above all, the prayers which follow the institution of the Eucharist point to the new life of the disciples, renewed by the Spirit and nourished by the body of Christ, as life in a mysterious union with Christ's own life, and thus a life with the Father. The unity and love between Christ and the Father become the source of our life and also the rule for our life. The triune life of God becomes visible in Christ, the great Sacrament, who communicates it to us, and writes it as a life-giving law into our being by the grace of the Holy Spirit. In almost all the contexts in which Paul calls the faithful to a genuine Christian life, he refers to this mystery: 'To be and to live in Christ'. This is the 'mystery' proclaimed by the 'gospel of Paul'.

All that is visible in the sacraments points not only to the internal relationship with Christ but also to the calling to make this relationship visible in our life. The sacraments keep us conscious of the truth that discipleship cannot be reduced to an external imitation of the examples of Christ. To follow Christ means, above all, to be aware first of the undeserved and wonderful life-union with him, and then of an allegiance to him in accordance with the law of grace written in our hearts. For Saint Paul, the 'natural law' that guides the Gentiles is already a 'law inscribed in their hearts' (Rom 2:15). Those who live with Christ will be enabled to internalize the 'law of Christ' and integrate into it all that man can learn through shared experience and co-reflection.

(c) *The imitation of Christ* follows the sacramental configuration to Christ (with the mysteries of the Word Incarnate), but one must not consider so much the single acts of the earthly life of Christ as *the mysteries of Christ*. We ought to imitate the 'virtues' that Christ reveals in the mysteries of the Incarnation, passion, resurrection and ascension. 'Let your bearing towards one another arise out of your life in Christ Jesus. For the divine nature was his from the first.... But he made himself nothing, assuming the nature of a slave.... He humbled himself, and in obedience accepted even death — death on a cross' (Phil 2: 5-11). The exhortations that follow refer us explicitly to these mysteries. 'So you, too, my friends ... show yourselves guileless and above reproach ... and profer the word of life. Thus you will be my pride on the day of Christ' (Phil 2: 12-16). 'For you know how generous our Lord Jesus Christ has been: he was rich, yet for your sake he became poor so that, through his poverty, you might become rich' (2 Cor 8: 9). Those who are in Christ, and follow the inner impulse to imitate Christ's mysteries generously in creative liberty, do not shirk sacrifice since this 'virtue' is apparent in the mysteries of the Incarnation and passion.

One of the most classical texts is the sixth chapter of the letter to the Romans: modelled on the death of Christ through baptism, we are, with Christ, dead to sin, raised to life with Christ; united with Christ we ought to live his life. Formed in the eschatological battle of Christ, we ought, with him and with his energy and decision, to wage war against sin.

God 'brought us to life with Christ ... and in union with him he raised us up and enthroned us with him in the heavenly realms.... For we are God's handiwork, created in Christ Jesus to devote ourselves to the good deeds for which God has designed us' (Eph 2: 5-10). 'Were you not raised to life with Christ? Then aspire to the realm above ... and let your thoughts dwell on that higher realm, not on this earthly life' (Col 3: 1-2).

(d) We can say in general that the Johannine-Pauline idea of life in Christ, founded on sacramental configuration to Christ, *was very much alive in the Fathers of the Church, of the West as well as of the East.* In the West, however, after the patristic age, neither liturgical life nor the scriptures (even the writings of John and Paul) had much success in influencing the formation of mentality and morality. The vision paled, lost its strength and was infrequently recalled.

Eventually the 'imitation' of Christ happily recurred, especially with St Bernard and St Francis (and later in the *devotio moderna*). The emphasis, however, now shifted to the humanity of Christ in his earthly life, according to the reports of the synoptics, and later, unfortunately, more often according to dubious private revelations.

(e)   Today we need to *synthesize* this double ecclesial tradition. The solution, it would seem to me, can already be found in St John. The consideration which John gives to the glorious life of Christ and to his dynamic presence in the mystery of the Church in no way diminishes the memory of the intimate and vital experience with Christ during his earthly life. On the contrary, through the ecclesial-sacramental experience, he appreciates all the more deeply his friendship with the earthly Christ. When death came to the last of those who testified from their personal experience with the earthly Christ, the author of the fourth gospel pledges himself to show how the historical Jesus (described by the synoptics) was the same as the Christ living and operating in the mysteries of the Church, and to 'demonstrate the full identity of the Lord present in the primitive Christian community and the historical Jesus'. [9]

The testimony of John is absolutely valid, even particularly precious, because he grasped the historical truth in greater depth in the light of the mystery of the Church. 'A doctrine so rich presupposes that the teaching of Jesus was long meditated in the light of the life of the Church. That is why this insight thus explains clearly the sacramental character of the fourth

---

[9] Cullmann, *Les sacraments dans l'Evangile Johannique* (Paris, 1951), p. 7.

gospel.' [10] John 'is thus led to see in the sacraments administered by the Church a prolongation of the salvific gestures of Christ'.[11]

The gospel of John centres on the mysteries of the Word Incarnate, his passion and resurrection. By means of baptism and the Eucharist, the faithful become participants in the saving death of Christ and thus unite themselves to the glorious Christ who will come anew.

Why does John unify so intimately the *words and signs* of the earthly life of Christ with the sacraments? 'He seeks to outline the earthly life of Christ according to the revelation of Christ, Lord of the Church . . . to validate the identity between the historical Jesus, Christ present in worship, and the Lord of the Church.' [12]

Therefore, because we live in the mystery of the Church united with Christ, and to the extent that we live through the grace and according to the mandate of the sacraments, we can truly follow him whom the apostles, in their early life, followed so imperfectly and whom they knew and followed more perfectly only after the coming of the Spirit. Our relation to Christ is not realized as much through the historical narrative, be it as precise as possible, as through a *present mystical-real contact* which, in the mystery of the Church, the sacraments signify. The sacraments of faith insert us in the history of salvation as 'actors of the word'.

The complete Christian vision of the following of Christ, as expressed and inspired by the sacraments, embraces the following elements.

(1) *The sacramental configuration to Christ* which, in existential depths, gives us a new mode of life according to the meaning and force of the great mysteries of salvation.

---

[10] A. Feuillet, *Introduction a la Bible*, vol. II (Tournai, 1959), p. 673.

[11] *Op. cit.*, p. 674.

[12] *Op. cit.*, p. 675; cf. J.C. Hoffman, *Le quartième évangile: Le Jésus de l'histoire et le Christ, Seigneur de l'Eglise* (Paris, 1952), p. 32.

(2)   The free configuration of our attitudes and deeds with Christ, performed through a living faith, in the strength and with the inspiration of the internal sacramental configuration. This means an active configuration of our life with the mysteries of Christ (cf. Eph 2: 5-10).

(3)   *The imitation of the virtues of Christ,* according to what is revealed to us of his earthly life and proposed to us by the gospels and by the preaching of the Church; an imitation, however, never purely human but always integrated in the sacramental configuration.

(4)   *Obedience* to all the teaching which Christ gave us in the course of his earthly life. This obedience, however, is integrated in the filial obedience to all the graces which Christ now gives us, especially in the sacraments, or which we can come to understand better in a sacramental perspective.

(5)   An imitation and ecclesial following of Christ as founded on and taught by the sacraments which embraces the following elements.

a.   *Mystical union* with 'the bride of the Lamb' by means of the grace signified by the sacraments, a union with all the saints, of whom Mary is the prototype.

b.   Mature internal and external *obedience* to the dispositions of the Church, integrated in the internal law of grace.

c.   *Imitation of the saints* of the past and of the present, whose lives inform us in a vital way of what the authentic following of Christ is. This aspect can never be wanting in Catholic morality. Already in the scriptures we are often admonished: 'Follow my example as I follow Christ's' (1 Cor 11: 1 and 4: 16; 1 Thess 1: 6). 'You have fared like the congregations in Judaea, God's people in Christ Jesus' (1 Thess 2: 14; Heb 6: 12).

Our relationship to the saints, those in the heavenly Jerusalem and those living before our eyes, is related to a sacramental vision of Christian life. By means of the sacraments we become members one of the other, and consequently have the mission to make visible the love of Christ for one another, as the best of Christ's disciples did. Thus all the believers together can become, as it were, a sacrament of salvation for those who do not yet believe. Through their good deeds, inspired by faith and by the grace of the sacraments, Christians can somehow pave the way that leads many to full participation in the sacraments. 'The sacraments of baptism and the Eucharist are hidden in the Church. But while the sacraments remain hidden to the heathen, your good deeds can be seen by them. What is visible arises from that depth which they cannot perceive, much as from the hidden part of the Cross rises that part which is visible.' [13]

---

[13] Augustine, *Ennarrationes in Psalmum CIII*, Migne PL 37, 1348.

PART THREE

THE SACRAMENTS IN A SECULAR AGE

The reader will surely have understood my intention to oppose as vigorously as possible the dangerous trends of secularism, by giving a constructive response to the challenges of secularization. We meet the needs and legitimate demands of a critical culture by being more eagerly concerned for discern- from life and to seek a vital and historically significant synthesis us and forces us to overcome any form of alienation of religion from life, and to seek a vital and historically significant synthesis between faith and life. Our response to the spirit of our era should be not apologetic but rather sympathetic, as an effort to be more faithful to revelation and therefore more attentive to the Lord of history in trying to interpret the signs of the times in the community of believers and in dialogue with all men.

In this last part I try to illustrate how the broader vision of sacramentality might build a bridge from the sacraments of the Church to the many other signs of God's presence in people's lives. I have chosen the sacrament of matrimony and that of reconciliation mainly for two reasons. First, I have, during the past thirty years, spent a great deal of my energy studying the meaning and the history of these two sacraments, and a pastoral approach that is fully aware of the inter-dependence between religion and culture. The principal reason, however, is that these two sacraments are today particularly open to crisis, and at the same time offer new chances to understand better how all the sacraments are related to the most fundamental human experi- ences. Seen in the light of the broader vision of which I spoke they help us wonderfully to see how all the sacraments are directed towards the human person in community, so that all may truly become 'sacraments' of God's loving presence, created and reborn to be an image and likeness of God.

We, surely, cannot forget for one moment that the Eucharist
is the centre of the sacramental life of the Church. Almost
everything that is said in the second part of this book directly
concerns the Eucharist and thus sheds its light on all the sacraments. Much attention has already been given to the sacrament
of baptism, especially regarding the baptism of infants, and in
connection with it 'the baptism in the Spirit', while drawing
attention to the fact that the New Testament speaks of the
sacraments of faith in view of people who can give a conscious
response. Since it is not the intention of this book to give a
complete or somehow scholastic treatise on the sacraments, but
to help lay-people as well as priests to understand a sacramental
spirituality and to find a new appreciation of the sacraments as
a main source of a truly Christian realization of morality, I can
waive a complete examination of the impact of our vision on
each sacrament.

Chapter 1

THE SACRAMENT OF MATRIMONY

As a point of departure we may look to the values and insights which we find in good humanists, even if they are secularists. But we must also ask ourselves incisively what are the specific Christian values. In a liberating dialogue, both partners are willing to listen to each other and, if necessary, to change their minds, at least on some points. We Christians should be well aware that we have not a kind of monopoly of truth and goodness, since we know that the Lord of history works in all, through all and for all. He is actively present also in those parts of the secular world that do not identify with us, the members of the Church. The most dedicated members of the Church along with all men of good will, being sensitive to the present age, bring to the magisterium and to theologians experience and insights that cannot be neglected.

I recognize marriage, then, first of all as a secular, earthly reality which Christians have in common with the inhabitants of our pluralistic world, even if we have not the same ideas about its origin and its ultimate goal. But, insisting on our identity, I have no intention of hiding our vision of matrimony as a sacrament, which means as a way of salvation and a privileged sign of God's active presence in people's lives. [1]

---

[1] The fruitful tension between secular experience and God's saving message is well presented by Edward Schillebeeckx, *Marriage: Human Reality and Saving Mystery* (New York: Sheed & Ward, 1966). Cf. Franz Böckle (ed.), 'The Future of Marriage as Institution' in

M

If we are to communicate our sacramental vision of marriage to people of other world-views, we are obliged to free ourselves from all alienating sacralizations. The last decades have brought great progress in the dialogue with our Protestant fellow-Christians. Not only have they come to appreciate better the Catholic doctrine on the sacramentality of marriage, but we Catholics also have come to understand better what we mean by this doctrine. However, our separated brethren legitimately ask us whether our canon law and pastoral practice correspond to the theological vision which we have exposed, based on scripture and on the very best traditions of the Christian Churches.

As I have repeatedly acknowledged that religious values have little dynamism if they are severed from common human experience, I look first at what matrimony as a secular reality is, and at what kind of marriage we can recognize as having the dignity of a sacrament. From our understanding of sacramentality, it is clear that many marriages celebrated in the Catholic Church, with all the conditions of canon law, can scarcely be understood as privileged signs of God's presence. On the other hand, there are marriages lacking the canonical form which nevertheless have more substantial elements that could qualify as signs of God's presence than many of those recognized by canon law. We have to make some response to a number of problems arising from this condition. We have also to see whether we could not recognize a sacramental value in good marriages of non-Christians.

1. *Marriage: a living sacrament*

The life of a human person and the life of human persons together are bearers of value of salvation and of glorification of God to the extent that, prevalent in them, are authentic love,

---

Concilium 55 (New York: Herder and Herder, 1970); W. Bassett and P. Huizing (eds.), 'The Future of Christian Marriage' in *Concilium* 7 (Paulist Press, 1973).

the inner freedom to grow in that love, and the capacity to discern genuine love from its counterfeits. As I have stressed in the first part of this book, the human person is in a profound sense a sacrament, a sign of God's presence and the image of God's own love. But only throughout one's whole life, and through healthy relationships with others, do we become more fully a sign for others of God's loving presence with us.

When we speak about the human person as created in the image and likeness of God, then we think about man's capacity to submit the earth to himself in such a way that his works and his environment manifest him as co-creator with God and co-revealer of his love. Not all ways in which people manipulate the environment do make man known as God's image. Only when the human person remains free for the love of God and the love of his neighbour, and manifests this freedom in the way he submits the earth to the good of its people, is he an image of God.

From the book of Genesis it already becomes evident that marriage is a privileged state where man — male and female — can develop the capacity for that love which reveals them as image of God. 'God said, "let us make man in our image to rule the fish in the sea, the birds of heaven, the cattle, all wild animals on earth, reptiles that crawl upon the earth". So God created man in his own image, in the image of God he created him: male and female he created them' (Gen 1: 26-27).

The human person cannot develop his highest nobility — to be the image of God — in isolation, but only in interpersonal relationships. A person living only with the material world and animals would not be able to reflect God as his image. God himself, infinite love, lives his life in communion-communication. He is the triune God. And when God creates the world in his Word, and puts life into it by his Spirit, then all this is com-munication. It is all directed to man, who can admire, understand the message, respond to God and communicate with other people. Only in mutual love and dialogue are we becoming truly co-creators and co-revealers with God. The highest creativity and freedom of human persons is expressed in mutual love, in helping each other to become masterpieces of God, privileged signs of his loving presence.

In this light, human sexuality has not only a biological goal. By God's design, man and woman are drawn together so that, in the community of their life and love, they can come to a deeper understanding that God is love and that he who abides in love abides in God.

Marriage is the place where the love of God becomes visible in the mutual love of the spouses, in the love of the parents for their children and the love of the children for the parents. The most noble fruit of matrimony — not only for Christians but for all men — is the authentic experience of love that creates persons who are more and more able to radiate love, joy and peace, and to foster discernment through all of their lives.

In the design of the Creator, matrimony has always, in all times and all places, had this fundamental sacramental value of freeing the human person from isolation, from imprisonment in selfishness, and committing him or her to the main dynamics of history, which is the growth of love and of discernment.

Matrimony is the most noble school of integrated love. And we should ask the question whether authentic friendship, and the very life of the Church as a community of love and mutual trust, would be possible without the totality of experience of love, fidelity and creativity that results from the life of all families throughout the ages.

In a marriage that fosters and expresses the dimensions of human relationships — respect, kindness, gentleness, dedication, — sexuality comes to its full meaning. Certainly matrimony goes far beyond mere sexuality; but the sexual component is the bearer of a special dynamics and task in an irrevocable community of man and woman, where they unite their experience of life and share their ideals in a solid synthesis of love of God and neighbour, of responsibility for future generations and for the world around them.

This integrated experience is an essential part of the history of creation and redemption. Each marriage has its source and origin in the Word of God, in whom all things are made and who calls man to become more and more an image of God. And each marriage throughout history has an intimate relationship with the life of the Word Incarnate in whom all human experiences reach their summit and are summoned to a new purity and growth.

Therefore our conclusion is that wherever, throughout the history of mankind, two persons are united in an integrated, faithful marital love that helps them and others to become more fully an image of God, there is a privileged sign of God's loving presence. In other words, there we are faced with a true sacramentality. But wherever, in family life, persons exploit each other and treat each other as objects or means, or seek anything less noble than love, they are obscuring and obstructing the creative and redemptive presence of God.

In Israel, God frequently compares with marriage the covenant which liberates the people. This comparison, signifying good news, would not have been possible if there had not existed genuine experiences of good and faithful marriages. When the people breaks the covenant and falls into miserable moral, social and religious alienation, God likens this to adulterous or prostitute relationships. So the whole experience of faith becomes, implicitly and frequently explicitly, a call to live marriage faithfully, in a way that reflects and fosters the covenant of salvation between God and his people.

Not only in Israel but everywhere throughout history, the family that is united by fidelity and solidarity is a privileged sign of God's loving presence. And since we believe that there exists only one order of salvation — the one manifested in Jesus Christ — we have to say that whatever in marriages throughout history is good, honest, just, right, fostering maturity and liberating is a sign of salvation, praise to the one God and Father of all men and to the love of Jesus Christ, and the fruit of the grace of the Holy Spirit.

Since we reject the idea that the Christian marriage has a monopoly of grace and sacramentality we have, at this point, to ask ourselves, 'What, then, beyond that of others, is the privilege of matrimony between Christians'?

If a marriage between two Christians manifests and fosters the love of God, mutual love, helpfulness, growth towards maturity, creative freedom, justice and peace less than a good marriage between two non-Christians, it deserves less the noble title of 'sacrament' than the one between non-Christians. But comparing two good marriages, one between Christian believers and the other between good non-Christians, we can affirm (1) a special grace and calling and opportunity of Christians to an explicit and grateful consciousness of Christ's presence, and an explicit trust in the grace of the Holy Spirit, and (2) a special support that the marriage of Christians receives from the Church and gives to the Church who, in Jesus Christ, is the primordial sacrament of the covenant, a community of faith, hope, love, truthful adoration.

If we speak of what is characteristic in the Christian marriage, we do not mean any title for Christians to boast about, but a special motive for thanksgiving and a special obligation to render witness to the world. Every grace is a call to consciousness, to gratitude and to generous service of one's fellowmen. Christian believers know, through Jesus Christ, the origin, the dignity and the ultimate goal of their marriage. Through the message and testimony of the whole Church, and particularly through holy married people, Christ manifests to all men his design for marriage and family.

Christians who live the vocation meant by the sacrament of matrimony are not only accepting a doctrine about Christ's presence but are becoming more and more gratefully aware of his presence. They give shape to their relationships and their whole life by conscious adherence to Christ who is the Way, the Truth and the Life. Christian spouses turn to the Holy Spirit who gives life, and implore his grace that makes them more and more sharers in the life of Christ Jesus. So they look consciously and gratefully to Christ, the supreme Sacrament, who reveals the genuine nature of creative and redemptive love, and thus they accept their vocation to share as co-creators and co-revealers in Christ's redeeming love.

St Paul's great vision of Christian life applies in a very special way to the sacrament of matrimony: 'The life-giving law of the Spirit in Christ Jesus has freed you from the slavery of solidarity in sin' (Rom 8:2). To the extent that the members of the Christian family are guided by the Spirit, their life manifests to the world that 'the harvest of the Spirit is: love, joy, peace, patience, kindness, goodness, fidelity, gentleness and self-control' (Gal 5:22).

Conjugal chastity is not something besides conjugal love; it is its harvest and its attractive countenance, and fosters the growth of love and fidelity. Christian spouses, strengthened by faith and by the testimony of the Church, and living consciously in the presence of Christ and his Spirit, are victors in the fight against behaviour that belongs to incarnate selfishness: 'fornication, impurity and indecency, idolatry and sorcery, quarrels, a contentious temper, envy, fits of rage, selfish ambitions, dissensions, party intrigues and jealousy, drinking bouts, orgies and the like' (Gal 5:20).

This quotation from the Epistle to the Galatians mentions idolatry among the various signs of incarnate selfishness. Christian spouses who live according to their faith are well aware that they are not the source and ultimate goal of life and love. Therefore they do not cling to each other in a kind of idolatry. Rather, they are very appreciative of the good they find in each other because they live a life of thanksgiving before God. And since they refer all the good that is in them to God, they are also becoming able to accept their finiteness and the partial frustrations in their relationships. So their glad experience of love, as well as its inevitable imperfection and frustrations, turns them more and more to him who is infinite love and absolute graciousness.

Christian spouses who consciously live their vocation to become increasingly a sign of God's loving and saving presence can communicate to the world around them the great song of love: 'Love is patient; love is kind and envies no one; love is never boastful, never conceited nor rude; never selfish, not quick to take offence. Love keeps no score of wrongs; does not gloat over other men's sins, but delights in the truth. There is nothing love cannot face; there is no limit to its faith, its hope and its endurance' (1 Cor 13:4-7).

The partners in a truly Christian marriage know that their earthly abode is not permanent. Their marriage comes not only to an end but also to fulfilment in the hour of their death. United in the love of Christ, they can face death because they know that their 'love will never come to an end' (1 Cor 13:8). All that they have lived together in a redeemed and redeeming love will continue and bear fruit in their children, in their friends, and in future generations, and will have incorruptible value in the new heaven and the new earth.

A Christian marriage is of an unsurpassable nobility. Therefore the spouses will never think that they have loved each other enough. However, the distance between ideal and realization will not cause discouragement or despair because Christ, who calls them who are imperfect people to become more and more signs of his presence in love, is infinitely patient.

The truth expressed by the Second Vatican Council becomes a great motive of trust and energy: 'The Saviour of man and the Spouse of the Church comes into the lives of married Christians through the sacrament of matrimony. He abides with them thereafter, so that, just as he loved the Church and handed himself over on her behalf, the spouses may love each other with perpetual fidelity through mutual bestowal. . . . By virtue of this sacrament, the spouses fulfil their conjugal and familial obligations; they are penetrated with the spirit of Christ. This spirit suffuses their whole life with faith, hope and charity. Thus they increasingly advance their own perfection as well as their mutual sanctification, and hence contribute jointly to the glory of God.' [2]

The normative ideal of Christian marriage is lofty. The world in which the ideal is realized is, however, frequently a confusing and difficult one. The tension can be lived only in patience, mutual forgiveness, on-going reconciliation. The prototype of matrimony as a sacrament is the covenant between God and mankind, between Christ and his Church; and Christians know that this covenant persists and brings salvation only because God is patient and Christ is the Reconciler. Mankind could have little hope, and the Church little chance, if God had not revealed himself in his compassion, in his healing and forgiving love.

The sacraments are promises of God's unfailing fidelity and his call to a free response in humble fidelity on the part of man.

The readiness to forgive, to heal, to help, to bear the burdens of each other, and gently to offer encouragement and correction, are an essential part of a Christian matrimony that reflects the covenant of Christ with the Church and the covenant of God with mankind. If, deep in their hearts, all spouses would know Christ the Reconciler, and would put their trust in him, they would be able to accept each other, to meet each other in forgiveness and with a healing love.

2. *Contract or covenant?*

Recent canon law identified marriage as a contract with the reality of marriage as sacrament. It might seem that this word 'contract' could meet the thinking of the secular world which is full of contracts. Everyone knows what it means to stipulate a contract. A required condition is the freedom of agreement, which must be reciprocal. In this point there is a similarity between contract and marriage. Mutual consensus, given in that

---

[2] *The pastoral constitution on the Church in the modern world* 48.

freedom which is proportionate to such an important step, is essential. Even cultures that frequently ignored or annulled the right of woman to give or withhold her consent have, in our time, become more sensitive to the importance of a freely given mutual consensus.

However, there are two aspects in the idea of contract that do not fit into the understanding of the sacrament of matrimony. (1) A contract is reversible by those who have freely agreed to it, at any time they come to a new agreement to stipulate other conditions or to dissolve the contract wholly. As Christians, we are convinced that marriage, as a God-given vocation, has an essential content and substantial goals which cannot be changed by the two people who enter into it. (2) Contracts are about concrete rights and duties; they are, above all, about things and works. In this spirit, canon law determined that marriage, as a sacrament, is the very contract by which the spouses irrevocably give each other the right to certain acts, namely, the conjugal act in so far as it is ordained to procreation. [3]

People of today, who experience the depersonalizing trend in the world of contracts, work and achievements, do not seek just another contract in marriage; they are promising each other a communion of life, of shared ideals, and above all, a covenant of love.

It is to this experience that the proclamation of the mystery of Christian marriage can relate. Because of the irreversibility of the freely given consensus in Christian marriage, and because of the deeper insights into the nature of the sacrament, and in response to new experiences, the Second Vatican Council has bypassed the word 'contract' in favour of the word 'covenant' when speaking of Christian matrimony. 'The intimate partnership of married life and love has been established by the Creator and qualified by his laws. It is rooted in the conjugal covenant by irrevocable personal consent. Hence, by that human act whereby spouses mutually bestow and accept each other, a

[3] CIC can. 1081.

relationship arises which, by divine will and in the eyes of society too, is a lasting one.' [4]

As a covenant, matrimony means not only a right to certain acts but a mutual gift of two persons, an intimate union. As we have seen, it is in this direction that we seek the sacramental nature of marriage: that is, it can make visible the covenant of love and fidelity between Christ and the Church in so far as the love, fidelity and reconciliation of the spouses become a visible witness to each other, to their children and to the world.

Some two centuries ago, St Alphonsus de Liguori (1696-1781) had already proposed a similar vision of matrimony and its essential constitution and goals. He distinguishes three kinds of goals or ends of matrimony.

First, there are *the intrinsic and essential goals*, those inborn orientations that are indispensable for the consent and the free living of the marriage. These are two: the mutual self-bestowal that gives meaning and norm for the conjugal act, and the insoluble bond, the 'covenant'. Alphonsus insists that these two constitutive elements must be present in the consent by which the spouses enter into the covenant, and must also characterize each conjugal act. That is, it has to be an expression of this intimate union of love and should strengthen and manifest the indissoluble bond.

Secondly, St Alphonsus speaks of *intrinsic, accidental goals*, namely, procreation and a remedy for concupiscence (a remedy for the restless sexual drive). According to St Alphonsus, these two goals arise from within the marital vocation but in a way that they can be dispensable: for instance, in the marital consent of spouses who know that the age of fecundity has passed or who have proportionate reasons to renounce the transmission of life. [5]

---

[4] *The pastoral constitution on the Church in the modern world* 48.
[5] Alphonsus de Liguori, *Theologia Moralis,* book VI, ch. I, doubt 1, n. 882. See my book, *Love is the Response* (Denville: Dimension Books, 1970) where I explain St Alphonsus's important testimony to a tradition and theology that opposes Augustinian pessimism about marriage and sexuality.

Thirdly, St Alphonsus held that there are manifold goals of marriage that do not arise from within but from external circumstances and freely chosen motivations of the persons involved, such as, for instance, friendship and peace between two families, economic success, the furtherance of a career and so on.

It seems to me that the presentation of marriage as a covenant, as it is made by the Second Vatican Council and in the best of our tradition, is very important if we want to speak significantly about marriage as a sacrament in a truly Christian sense, and convincingly to sensitive modern man.

The marriage catechumenate, the pedagogy and the daily living of the marriage will be widely different according to whether one makes the choice in favour of a contract about duties or in favour of a covenant reflecting the covenant between Christ and the Church.

3. *Does infant baptism without subsequent faith give a marriage the special sacramental value and firmness over and above that of unbaptized persons?*

If the understanding of specifically Christian matrimony outlined above is appropriate, then some hard questions follow regarding canon law and pastoral practice.

Marriage tribunals consider marriage as a Christian sacrament and therefore, if consummated, absolutely indissoluble wherever the persons involved are baptized. For those baptized in the Catholic Church, baptism administered to infants meets the criterion for submitting a person to the canon law that states the conditions for a validly expressed consent. This practice is probably the most crucial point in the crisis about infant baptism. The situation would look much better if not infant baptism alone but baptism followed by evangelization and personal commitment of faith to the Church were the basic criterion.

As we have seen earlier, Thomas Aquinas expresses well the doctrine of the Church when he says that salvation comes from faith. Applying this to our concrete question, it would follow that the privileged sacramental nature of Christian matrimony comes, above all, from faith and from baptism in so far as it can be called a sacrament of faith. If two people entering into a marriage have nothing in common with the Catholic Church except infant baptism administered to them, how can we then see anything that distinguishes their marriage from that of unbaptized persons? It can even be much inferior to a marriage of persons not baptized but believing in God and in Jesus Christ.

The firmness and sacredness of the Christian marriage as a covenant lived in view of the covenant between God and humanity, and brought to perfection by the covenant between Christ and the Church, comes from the faith that unites the spouses in the love and fidelity of God, which he made visible in Jesus Christ, the faithful witness, Redeemer and Reconciler. Christian spouses who live their unique vocation in faith, in prayer, supplication and thanksgiving, thus honour God's unfailing promise given in the sacrament, and obtain, day by day, that divine grace that makes their love indestructible or, in other words, enables and motivates them to live the indissoluble covenant of the Christian marriage.

If the practice of canon law and the pastoral approach make the privileged sacramentality of marriage depend only on the ritual performance of infant baptism, then we have no hope whatsoever of giving a convincing testimony to the secular world about the specific nature of a Christian marriage as a sacrament.

We should be grateful to today's critical world that forces us to seek with greater courage our own identity and authenticity. Christian religion must not be confused with ritualism. It is not enough to say this in explanation of Church doctrine; the whole life and practice of the Church must make known that we give our main attention to faith; and faith is the fruit of evangelization and witness.

The conclusion is an appeal to the commission which is preparing the new canon law, not to submit people to the canonical form, under sanction of invalidity, if they are not evangelized by the Church and do not actually believe in the Church's mission. A more important conclusion is that we need a marriage catechumenate that brings home to believers what Christian matrimony means, how they should prepare themselves, and how they can give convincing testimony to the world. The support that Christian spouses can expect from the Church is, above all, a deepening of consciousness: an education in faith that will help them to live their lofty vocation consciously in faith.

4. *The relevance of the celebration of matrimony in the Church*

Before the Council of Trent, the validity of a marriage between Christians was never made dependent on a certain canonical celebration. When the Church evangelized the ancient world, she did not change the customary form of marriage, but she was present with the light, the comfort and the pedagogy of the gospel, and with her prayer and support. It was only because of the need to fight against clandestine marriages that the Council of Trent, after heated debates, declared invalid the marriage of her members who refused to present themselves to the Church: that is, to the priest and two other qualified witnesses.

The motive for this decision is logical because it is contradictory to consider marriage a sacrament — that is, a visible sign — and at the same time attempt to hide its very existence. Because marriage is a visible sign of grace not only for the spouses themselves but also for their children and the world around them, they are expected to give witness and to contribute visibly to the salvation of the world.

But this perspective of the social character of matrimony should also motivate, and did generally motivate, the Church not to sever the form of celebration from the customs of the diverse cultures. Unfortunately, this aspect was forgotten when, in the first decades of our century, the decision of the Council became finally an inflexible law. The chief reason for its existence was forgotten.

The solemn expression of the marital consent before the community of the Church has a profound meaning if everything is done in a serious way. The consent before the qualified witnesses of the Church as a community of faith means a vow, a solemn 'yes' to God who is love and fidelity in the covenant of his grace, and to God who is the giver of all life. The marital vows are the expression of trust in God's unfailing promises and, in response, the promise to manifest him and his covenant with the Church in and through the marriage.

The moment in which spouses express with faith their consent before God and his Church, and also before the secular world, can be compared with the moment of perpetual vows made by religious. It is a moment of grace and of commitment. However, the sacramentality belongs not just to this point in time, which is only the solemn beginning, but to the marriage in all its phases, which is meant to have and to manifest the sacramental quality more and more. Since it is a covenant of love and of life in fidelity, the sacrament of matrimony, just as the sacrament of baptism does, requires growth. Marriage is a sacrament being-in-becoming. 'Through this union they experience the meaning of their oneness and attain to it with growing perfection day by day.' [6]

The serious exchange of the marital vow has high sacramental significance. The promises of the spouses respond to God's promise of unfailing fidelity. They know their weaknesses and therefore entrust themselves to his powerful grace. They honour God if they continue together, and each alone, to implore his grace so that they can keep the promises they have made. We must not reduce the sacramentality of marriage

[6] *The pastoral constitution on the Church in the modern world* 48.

to the celebration in the Church, despite its deep significance. It is the irreversible beginning of a life that should manifest more and more the presence of the Lord and the response of the spouses to him.

It is a great evil if the marriage celebration and the concept of sacrament are reduced to a sentimental rite and/or the idea of a naked contract. The Church must be very much concerned to eliminate, as much as possible, empty rituals and 'sacred lies' where a commitment of faith and trust in God's grace is thoroughly lacking. The celebration of the marriage must be carefully prepared through evangelization and prayer.

A new phenomenon spreading in Japan and some other countries might help us to understand better the significance of the marriage celebration in the Catholic Church. A good number of non-Christians, who know the gospel and appreciate the Church as a community of prayer, desire a religious celebration before the priest. Frequently their request is not refused. The celebration is prepared by a protracted dialogue on God's goodness and fidelity and on the power of trustful, fervent prayer.

These non-Christian couples do not think that the juridical validity of matrimony depends upon the blessing or the assistance of the priest, but by celebrating their matrimony in the Church they do express a great confidence in the grace of God. The celebration of their marriage can be a more significant and truthful event than many celebrations of Catholic marriages where everything is on the level of folklore and sentimental ceremonies, or where the spouses only reluctantly accept as an imposition the necessity to marry in the Church in order to see their marriage recognized as valid among members of their families. Nevertheless, the celebration of this marriage of two non-Christian spouses before a priest of the Church does not have the same profound meaning as the exchange of the marital vows of two believers who are conscious of entering into a new dimension of their already acknowledged relationship to the covenant between Christ and his Church.

5. *Can the Church declare null and void the matrimony of unbelievers on the ground of their baptism?*

Canon law that reflects the Constantinian era of 'the Church of the empire' declares as subjects of Church laws all those who, as infants, were baptized in the Catholic Church. Even now, after substantial improvements in the marriage laws of the Church, people who were baptized in the Catholic Church but have never been evangelized and never believed in the Church cannot, according canon law, enter a valid marriage unless they submit to the canonical form or obtain the Church's dispensation from it. In today's world, this law produces a number of very negative consequences.

Each year, outside the Church, millions of marriages are contracted, where one or both partners were baptized by a Catholic priest but do not believe in the Church. The official law considers these marriages invalid. As a consequence, if later the marriage breaks down, or if one of the spouses maliciously abandons his partner, he as well as the abandoned spouse can contract, validly and solemnly, a new marriage in the Catholic Church. This diminishes, in the eyes of many people, the credibility of the Church's teaching on indissolubility. It must be said however, that not only theologians but also a growing number of canonists would stress the obligation of these people not to take advantage of this regulation of canon law. Especially a Catholic, who intrudes into such a marriage in order to marry one of the spouses whose marriage is canonically invalid, acts immorally. The declaration of invalidity cannot free any person from obligations that arise from moral responsibility inherent in promises.

Others, baptized as infants in the Catholic Church and equally rejecting the Church, do, however, perform their marriage before the priest because they want to be sure that the members of their families and their friends recognize the validity of their marriage. Many priests feel that they cannot refuse their request, in spite of plainly expressed or manifested unbelief, because they

N

have the right not to have their marriage socially weakened because of the existence of this special marriage law.

The Church, who must be concerned for the seriousness and truthfulness of sacramental celebrations that should always be sacraments of faith, and equally concerned for the stability of all marriages whether of believers or unbelievers, should change the present marriage law. The voices that sound this request are multiplying, and there is good hope that they will be accepted by the Church authorities. [7]

Believers should gratefully celebrate their marriage before the Church, after solid preparation and in absolute seriousness. People whose faith is wavering should not be refused the blessing of the Church. But people who do not at all adhere to the Church although they were, as infants or later, baptized, should be advised to celebrate their marriage in a socially approved form. They should also know that the Catholic Church does respect the stability and firmness of their marriage and does not allow any Catholic, who later wants a Church marriage, to interfere with these civil marriages.

6. *When love is lacking?*

The emphasis on matrimony as a visible and efficacious sign of love poses new and complex problems about the criteria of validity. These new problems are disquieting if the main concern is juridical control. They are a fruitful challenge, however, if the main emphasis is on a constructive pastoral and pedagogical approach that helps people in the choice of their mate, in the preparation for marriage, and in their whole effort to live the sacrament of matrimony significantly.

Marriage can be and can become more and more a sacrament reflecting the covenant between Christ and the Church, only

---

[7] Cf. C. Di Mattia, *La Forma Canonica. Revisione Radicale* (Rome: Edizioni Paoline, 1972). The author is a canonist and can refer to a good number of his colleagues in his proposal of a radical change in the canon law.

in so far as the vocation to love and to grow in love is fundamentally accepted. The system of canon law has been rather
'practical' for the marriage tribunals. It was easy to determine
whether one of the two persons was baptized in the Catholic
Church and therefore, under invalidating sanctions, submitted
to the canonical form; and it was almost equally easy to determine whether the people contracting marriage had accepted the
right and duty to concrete acts, to conjugal intercourse in so far
as it is procreative. The change in mentality in the Church,
fostered also by a significant growth in secular society, seems
to be irreversible, and has already greatly influenced the practice
of many marriage tribunals in the United States, Canada and
throughout the world.

Conjugal love is essential for marriage to come into existence,
as it is essential as a condition to bring marriage to fulfilment.
However, if we say 'love', we should know what we mean. It
is not a matter of a sentimental 'falling in love', although it is
normal for young people to be in love also sentimentally when
they marry. But we do not speak only of love or of friendship
but of conjugal love that includes some sexual attraction.

There are various cultural ways and modalities by which
love is accepted as a constitutive element in marriage. In a
number of Asian and African cultures, the two families make all
the stipulations and the choice of the mate. However, the two
families and the two partners do expect to live the marriage in
mutual love. And this is sufficient. In today's western cultures
the partners make their own choice, and the question is whether,
in the motivation of the choice, there is included love and the
intention to grow in love. We do not speak of an extraordinarily
high level of love, but of a basic capacity and/or willingness to
love each other with that love that is constitutive of marriage.

It is my thesis, shared by many other men and women of
the Church, that a marriage cannot be considered as a valid
sacrament and therefore indissoluble if either the capacity to
love in a conjugal way, or the willingness to do so, is radically
excluded by one or both partners. Take the case of a business

man who marries a girl because he needs the dowry for his economic plans, and he wants a housekeeper and helper in his business. He may also be willing to have one or two children to continue his business, but being so thoroughly concerned with business, he does not even dream of giving love to his wife; he is, indeed, as a thoroughly one-dimensional man, unable to live a marriage as a covenant of love.

In cases where there is serious doubt about the initial capacity and willingness of one or both partners to love each other, the marriage should have the favour of the law and the support of the pastoral councillor as long as there is any hope that it can finally, although imperfectly, become a covenant of love. But where a marriage has irretrievably failed and there is sufficient evidence that it never was and, because of the inability or unwillingness of one or both partners, never could become a conjugal communion of love and life, the decision should be for invalidity. And indeed many marriage tribunals do now coherently follow this approach.

7. When love is fading away?

We have to warn against hasty conclusions made from an imperfect understanding of marriage as a covenant of love. Some would think that if one partner no longer loves the other, or if one feels no love any more, the marriage could or should be ended and considered as non-existent any more. We have to contradict this opinion. We should never forget the prototype of a Christian marriage. When Israel was unfaithful and greatly lacking in love of God, the Lord of the covenant still remained faithful and did everything to call Israel back to a renewed love. The same is even more evident in the covenant between Christ and the Church. If the continuation of the covenant were one-sidedly dependent on the faithfulness of the Church and on her love for Christ, there could arise anguishing doubts. Christ always continues to renew the Church and to call her by his grace to a renewed love.

Seeing the Christian marriage in this light, our response will be that where, initially, the marriage was accepted as a covenant of love by two persons who were able to make it an experience of love, the fact that one of the partners is no longer in love, and even does temporarily refuse all expression of love, cannot invalidate the Christian marriage. God's unfailing promise is a call to conversion, a call to prayer and to all possible efforts to renew the mutual love. This especially includes a great readiness to forgive and to heal the wounds. A Christian committed to the covenant of love between Christ and the Church will manifest generosity, patience and endurance in order to win again the affection of the other and to renew and deepen his own conjugal love.

The situation is different if, in spite of all efforts, a marriage has irreparably broken down. In this case the ancient oriental practice, and that of today's Orthodox Churches, speak of 'the moral death of the marriage; and the question arises whether the Church, in this case, must oblige the abandoned spouse to lifelong celibacy. Where the community of faith is strong and gives truly loving support, such celibacy for the kingdom of God is possible. It has a high value as a testimony to faith, and is an encouragement to spouses to do whatever can be done to save a marriage, and also to find the inner freedom to live a full Christian life after a terrible disappointment.

The Orthodox Churches strongly recommend celibacy for the kingdom's sake in such a situation. However, they do not impose it by a general and absolute law; they leave space for *epikeia* or, as they express it, *oikonomia*. They do not grant liturgical solemnity to a second marriage, but they pray and help the spouses to make this second marriage, in which something is lacking, as much a sign of God's loving presence as possible.

There is much reflection in Catholic theology and among the pastors of the Church about whether the practice of the Orthodox Churches could somehow be reintroduced into the life of the Roman Catholic Church. However, to look for easy solutions without deepening the commitment to irrevocable fidelity and generous forgiveness and reconciliation would surely not show the mind of Christ. Yet there must be a clear distinction between the situation of the innocent partner and that of Christians who maliciously or selfishly abandon their spouse in order to marry another. The judgment of Christ about this sin is most severe.

Another question for the Church is how to treat those spouses whose marriages have failed in spite of good will and who now feel unable to live a lonely life. The Church has to pray and to reflect much in order to find solutions which do not weaken the fidelity and stability of marriage. But while being absolutely faithful to the task of promoting fidelity, she must at the same time be a sign of fidelity to God's own economy of compassion and mercy.

8. *The Pauline privilege*

In 1 Corinthians 7:12-16, Paul gives advice for the mixed marriages in which the believer is exposed to intolerance and pressure from the unbeliever. The apostle allows separation in cases where the believer cannot live in peace, and where a marriage is the opposite of a way of salvation. Most probably, Paul allowed not only separation but also remarriage.

Canonists have worked out a simplistic explanation and application of the so-called Pauline privilege. They took as the fundamental criterion infant baptism, with the basic supposition that the marriage of two baptized persons, performed in canonical form, is absolutely indissoluble, whether there is faith in one or both or in neither. This way of thinking does not do justice to the right understanding of the sacraments of faith or to the main concern of Paul, namely, freedom of conscience, and especially the freedom to live one's faith in marriage.

Biblical scholars have given attention to the text, and propose a more profound and historically realistic explanation than that of modern canonists. [8] They suggest that, in the spirit of Paul, the marriage of baptized persons of which one was from the beginning or has become a believer, while the other was or has become an intolerant unbeliever, can no longer be considered as a way of salvation or a sacrament, because the intolerant attitude of the one spouse endangers the integrity and wholeness of the other. Therefore in the eyes of the apostle separation is indicated. He does not just think of the baptismal character lacking in one and being given in the other. He declares the believer to be free for the sake of his salvation. In these cases which are not infrequent today, the word of the gospel, 'what God has joined together, man may not put asunder', would not be contradicted, because these people cannot be considered as 'joined together by God', while such a situation makes married life impossible. Since it is generally accepted that the Pauline privilege, as it is meant originally, allows for a new marriage, it seems to me that, in such a crucial situation, the economy of salvation would suggest a new marriage if, for the believer, celibacy for the kingdom of God does not constitute a realistic choice.

St Paul gave his advice and motivation for the matrimony of believers in a time of enthusiasm that led him and his fellow-Christians to expect the second coming of Christ in the near future. If one thinks that the end of the world is imminent, then the hardships in marriage, and patriarchal structures that demand particular sacrifices from women, can be more easily accepted; yet Paul was realistic enough not to impose on Christians a life in marriage with an intolerant unbeliever. And it seems that, after separation in such a case, he does not try to impose on the people of God a lifelong celibacy, although he does recommend it for those who have the charism. For those who do not have such a special gift, he warns against an unrealistic attempt to live, within marriage, a long-protracted continence (cf. 1 Cor 7: 1-11). To the unmarried and to widows he gives the advice to

---

[8] Cf. Rudolph Pesch, *Freie Treue. Die Christen und die Ehescheidung* (Freiburg: Herder, 1971).

marry if a realistic approach shows that they would not live celibacy without sin or great frustration.

The Church cannot find the solutions of all problems explicitly in scripture. However, she can learn in what spirit to approach old and new questions.

9. *Responsible parenthood*

Throughout three million years, humankind had to struggle for survival. It is one of the most astonishing facts that the human race did not disappear, as did so many species of animals. While the human race as a whole struggled for survival, so did each individual family. Children were most necessary for a family. Only numerous offspring, of which about one-third could be expected to survive, could guarantee some security for the future and assure social influence.

Now we find ourselves in a totally new situation. Infant mortality has been radically reduced, and the average life expectation has been raised from about twenty-five to seventy years. Young people need a much more expensive and protracted education to prepare for life in this scientific and technical age. If there are children, a family has to dedicate a great part of its income to their professional education. Taking it from a material point of view, children are neither necessary nor useful for the ordinary family.

These radical and profound changes in our whole way of life make moral and religious education much more difficult. Along with many other aspects of the world today, they have brought forth a quite different approach to procreation and education.

It was natural in past centuries and millennia that parents would not only desire more children, but generally accepted them as they came. Six hundred years ago, Thomas Aquinas did not have to fear strong contradiction when he determined that the primary content of the natural law for a family was 'that which nature teaches all animals, namely, sexual union between

man and woman, and procreation and education of offspring'. [9]
But today, transmission of life, like so many other things, is a
matter for reflection and conscious deliberation.

While the new situation has seduced many people into making
transmission of life a matter of utilitarian calculation, the Church
and all sensitive and magnanimous people call for responsible
parenthood. For the believer this means making the transmission
of life a response to the Creator, an expression of thanks for the
gift of life and for all his other gifts, and a response of the
spouses to each other, while seeking together the will of God.
It is no longer 'what instinct teaches them as it does animals';
it is one of married people's most decisive moral decisions. The
way they reach the decision and carry it out will manifest the
quality of their relationships.

When almost all economic incentives are falling away, and
a materialistic culture no longer appreciates the family with more
than two children, Christian spouses, by their free decision to
desire as many children as they can educate, will manifest their
faith that God is love and offers us eternal life. More and more,
the depth of their faith and the quality of their mutual relationships will enable them to transcend the egoistic attitudes of a
one-dimensional culture. And their witness will be all the more
convincing and attractive to people of good will when these
parents show themselves to be not only co-operators with God
but co-revealers of his love. This means that, even for the
procreative goal, conjugal love comes first as the basic value
and criterion.

The time is long past for such formulas as: 'It is said in
Genesis 2:18-20 that woman is made for the help of man, but
no other help is meant than that of transmitting life through
sexual relationship; for in any other respect man can be better
helped by a man than by a woman'. [10] It was also thought by
Gregory of Nissa and some other Fathers of the Church that
woman was made only in a 'second creation', that is, in view of

[9] *Summa Theol.* 1-2:94:2:c.
[10] *Summa Theol.* 1:98:2, *sed contra.*

sin, and that in Paradise transmission of life would not have been by sexual intercourse. However, St Thomas Aquinas held that even in the state of innocence woman had been necessary — but only for procreation.

We have to free ourselves from every vestige of this kind of instrumental thinking. We have to see that the quality of the transmission of life, the education of children, and the witness of the Christian family depend on the mutual love of the spouses, which is the source of a guarantee of love for the children.

The basic question of responsible parenthood is not one of methods but of motivation. If, motivated mainly by selfishness or materialistic thinking, or manipulated by the anti-baby trend of their environment, spouses decide not to have more children although they could have them and should desire them, then any method they use is contaminated by the basic fault of their approach. In the debate on contraception there was a distracting one-sided emphasis on methods; but where there is no basic conversion to generosity, to witness of mutual love, or no inner energy to withstand the consumer approach to sex, casuistic or methodological 'solutions' are of little value. We have to withstand a contraceptive culture that leads people to believe in sex idols and to seek satisfaction without commitment or genuine expression of faithful love.

The Church is a powerful protectress of life, not only through her teaching and her absolute rejection of abortion as a means of planned parenthood or responsible parenthood, but above all through those believers who, by all their life, manifest their responsible 'yes' to God who is the giver of life.

We should not be scandalized that, with respect to the use of contraceptive methods such as calculated use of periodical continence and other manipulations of nature, the Church did not have immediate responses, and some dissent continues still in the Church about the many conflict situations where sincere spouses have difficulty in harmonizing the responsible transmission of life with the fundamental exigencies of conjugal love, harmony and stability. The thirty-five years from the encyclical of Pius XI *Casti connubii* (1930) to the chapter on marriage in

The pastoral constitution on the Church in the modern world of the Second Vatican Council (1965) have brought a gigantic step forward. And we are not surprised that even now there are unresolved questions. But mature believers who know the loftiness of their vocation as Christian spouses have enough light to make fitting choices and to give a convincing witness to today's world.

10. *New models of authority*

God manifests his unique authority by revealing, in all his works but especially through Jesus Christ, his love for all people. He, the Son of the Father and the Servant of all, is the great Sacrament of God's authority. If the Christian family wants to be, in a very special way, a sign of God's loving presence to men of this time and age, then the authority structures of marriage and family must reflect the divine love as manifested in Jesus Christ, in a pattern understandable by the man come of age, and be free from antiquated modalities that contradict growth in maturity.

When St Paul preached the liberating gospel for the marriage and family of believers, he had, by necessity, to speak to people who knew only the patriarchal type of family that reflected the authoritarian and male-centred culture of his time. In today's scientific, democratic and critical world of North America and Europe, and gradually in other parts of the world, the patriarchal or matriarchal family has yielded its place to partnership where dialogue, equal dignity, shared ideals, common search for what is true, good and helpful, replace the commands of the one spouse over the other and over the children. In this new context we shall stress less St Paul's word: 'Wives, be subject to your husbands as to the Lord; for the man is the head of the woman just as Christ also is the head of the Church' (Eph 5:22-23), and give more attention to his other word which gives meaning to the whole text: 'Be subject to one another out of reverence for Christ' (Eph 5:21), and 'Husbands, love your wives as Christ also loved the Church and gave himself up for her' (Eph 5:25).

How authority is exercised in marriage and family is very decisive for the growth of a culture. After the fall of the dictators in Germany and Italy, sociologists eagerly studied the family structures in those countries, since they knew the interdependence between the way of life in marriage and family and the total structures of society and culture. Democracy and full development of maturity and liberation in any society are possible only if the familial relationships between husbands and wives, parents and children, are fostering them.

This fact is also very fundamental for a sober theology of liberation in Latin America. Liberty cannot be gained by violent revolutions while a cult of male domination continues in the life of the family. The same is somehow true for the life of the Church. Priests and bishops who come from friendly patriarchal families feel, almost naturally, that in the name of God they have to continue the authority style of their families in the Church. As a result, they tend to consider the people as their 'subjects'.

Marriage is a saving reality for the world of today if the relationships of the spouses are mature and if the parents allow their children to grow in responsibility and maturity. They will not so much impose the authority of their will as motivate, convince and educate their children to discernment.

It depends greatly on the authority-style of the family whether collegiality, subsidiarity, and the co-responsibility of the lay-people will operate in the Church; but it depends also on the total life in Church and society whether family and marriage can develop a style of authority that contributes to the wholeness and salvation of persons and of the community.

For those who have reached a mature understanding of sacramentality, the decisive religious question is whether, and to what degree, all the members of the family make visible to each other and to the world around them the love, the fullness of life, the fidelity, compassion and liberating authority of God who has revealed himself fully in Jesus Christ and continues this revelation in his children.

Chapter 2

THE PRIVILEGED SIGNS OF RECONCILIATION

The sacrament of penance, too, or, as I prefer to call it, the sacrament of reconciliation, can gain much from a broader and deeper vision of sacramental life. A better knowledge of the biblical message and various traditions of the Church can help us to overcome the present crisis of confession. [1]

In this sacrament we stand before Christ, the great Sacrament of the covenant and of the fidelity of the Father, a fidelity that expresses itself above all in his readiness to reconcile humanity with himself. God the Father has sent Jesus Christ as the great Sacrament of salvation, liberation, forgiveness, peace and reconciliation. He, the Good Shepherd, the Divine Physician, makes us know the Father. These names of the Lord enrich our knowledge of God's design to make the Church the primordial sacrament of salvation, forgiveness and reconciliation for all who seek God with a contrite heart.

[1] Cf. A.B. Come, *Agents of Reconciliation* (Philadelphia: Westminster Press, 1964); O. Betz (ed.), *Making Sense of Confession, A New Approach for Parents, Teachers and Clergy* (Chicago: Franciscan Herald, 1969); B. Häring, *Shalom: Peace, Sacrament of Reconciliation, the Function of the Church* (New York: Sheed and Ward, 1969); E. Schillebeeckx (ed.), 'Sacramental Reconciliation', *Concilium* (New York: Herder and Herder, 1971); F. Buckley, *The Sacrament of Penance Today* (Notre Dame, Ind: Ave Maria Press, 1972); W. Freburger (ed.), *Repent and Believe, The Celebration of the Sacrament of Penance* (Notre Dame, Ind.: Ave Maria Press, 1972); B. Basset, S.J., *Guilty, O Lord. Yes, I Still Go to Confession,* (Garden City, N.Y.: Doubleday, 1974).

Nothing helps us more to understand the mission of the Church than to turn our eyes totally to Christ and to see how he receives sinners, all those who, by the power of the Spirit, know that they are in need of God, those who are emarginated and written off by the self-righteous; and to see, conversely, how Jesus tries to shake the conscience of the hard-boiled and the self-righteous.

The Church can fulfil her privileged role as the primordial sacrament of reconciliation by honouring God in constant thanksgiving for the gift of reconciliation that has come to us in Jesus Christ and that he continues in his Church. But the first task of the Church is not to celebrate a concrete rite of reconciliation; rather it is to live gratefully, in all times and in all dimensions of her mission, according to the gift she has received: to proclaim everywhere the gospel of reconciliation, and to be thoroughly committed to promoting forgiveness, reconciliation, commitment to peace among all men, so that all may understand what it means to receive the gift of reconciliation and respond by reconciling actions. The Church cannot authentically celebrate the sacraments of reconciliation unless she is, in all her life, a visible and effective sign of forgiveness, peace, conversion and renewal in the new justice that comes from God and leads to him.

All the reconciling actions and endeavours of the Church, the testimony of her life as a community of reconciled and reconciling people, the sacramental celebration and commitment to reconciliation, have their source of strength in the gift of the Holy Spirit. Jesus baptizes the Church in the Holy Spirit. 'He breathed on them saying, "Receive the Holy Spirit. If you forgive any man's sins, they stand forgiven; if you pronounce them unforgiven, unforgiven they remain"' (Jn 20:22-23).

Baptism in the Holy Spirit does not primarily mean a special sacrament. It means that the whole messianic era and the life of the Church, in so far as the pentecostal event of the abundant outpouring of the Holy Spirit continues in her, renew the hearts of men and the face of the earth, especially by bringing forth the fruits of the Spirit: forgiveness, peace, healing, reconciliation.

1. *The divine message and human experience* [2]

If we want to know the meaning of the sacramental mission of the Church, then we must start with that revelation wrought in Jesus Christ: that Jesus himself takes, as basis, human experience. We do not understand the sacraments if we forget the human experience that should be brought into the light of faith. Jesus reveals himself as liberator from sin, bringer of peace, reconciler, according to the concrete situation in which he finds people. He accepts the humble avowal of sinners according to their temperament and condition.

The paralyzed man who is aware, according to Jewish tradition, of a connection between sin and ailment, comes to Jesus seeking healing, and receives it as a sign of forgiveness and reconciliation (cf. Mk 2: 6-12). Mary of Magdala humbles herself under the eyes of the self-righteous, washing the feet of Jesus with her tears of repentance. Jesus receives her. Her tears and expression of trust are visible signs of the grace of forgiveness and of hope for a new life. There is no need for a materially complete confession of all her past sins. The woman caught in adultery remains silent before the Lord when her self-righteous accusers have left. Jesus accepts her humility and grants her peace, while warning her not to turn back to sin. The most moving experience is that of the father welcoming his youngest son who has squandered his heritage but has come home because he knows that he has a forgiving father. The celebration of the homecoming transcends all the expectations the repentant son could dream of. Reconciliation proclaimed and communicated by Jesus Christ is an even greater experience.

Again and again Jesus makes clear that unless men learn from the heavenly Father to be forgiving and to become instru-

---

[2] Cf. J.D. Crichton, *The Ministry of Reconciliation* (London: Chapman, 1974); Ch. Ducquoc, 'Real and Sacramental Reconciliation', *Concilium* 61, (New York: Herder and Herder, 1971), pp. 26-37; F. Funke, 'Survey of Published Writings on Confession during the past ten years', *Concilium* 61 (1971), pp. 120-132.

ments of peace, they cannot receive and keep the gift of divine reconciliation. The human experience of the unfaithful steward for whom his master has cancelled a debt of millions and who nevertheless mistreats his fellowman who owes him a few pounds (cf. Mt 18:23ff) is used by Jesus as a stern warning to unforgiving persons.

The preaching and the reconciling action of Jesus do not take as starting point the rituals of the Jews but rather the most vital human experiences of daily life. He who is THE Prophet joins the fight of the prophets against ritualism, but he does not at all discard the cult. All his healing and forgiving action turns to the praise of the Father. The gift of Jesus is truly accepted at the moment when those who are healed and forgiven begin to render thanks and to praise the Lord, and all the people join them. In the life of forgiving and healing people, this becomes adoration in spirit and truth.

Here we come to a very crucial point. Many people of our critical age find it difficult to understand why the Church should fulfil her reconciling role also in liturgy, in the celebration of special sacraments. If we free ourselves from all tendency towards ritualism and follow the simplicity of the gospel stories, then we have a good chance to explain the necessity and blessing of the sacrament of reconciliation.

Again and again I stress the point that the Church has to be and to become more and more a sacrament of peace and reconciliation in all her life and the life of all her people. But since reconciliation with God and among people is an undeserved gift coming from the Father in Jesus Christ and through the Holy Spirit, it cannot be truly received where thanksgiving and praise are lacking.

Our experience of reconciliation and our commitment to it are a part of the history of salvation and should consciously enter into its dimensions. The sacrament gives us the awareness, in faith, that we enter into contact with Christ who is our peace and our reconciliation, and in contact with all history in so far as it is transfigured, and is to be more and more transfigured, by Christ the Reconciler and his disciples. The more the acceptance of the gift becomes cult, praise and thanksgiving for God's mercy, the more sincerely and effectively we shall accept our mission to be messengers of peace and ministers of reconciliation.

The sacraments are an experience of faith, a light and strength that come from the Holy Spirit. They are effective signs of the unfailing promise of God who is merciful and faithful. This experience of peace, healing, forgiveness, reconciliation, will be the more truthful and inspiring of action, the more we allow the Spirit in us to praise the Father. We shall then understand the sacraments as good tidings proclaimed in the Church and through the Church, the reality of the gospel received in order to carry it out in all our life.

2. *The sacrament of penance in a critical age*

In this age of powerful currents of diverse thoughts and world-views, the age of mass media and manipulation, whoever wants to live his own life and to find his unique name has to be critical. Yet criticism can be superficial, vicious and destructive. The believer, too, can be contaminated or manipulated. The remedy against bitter criticism, however, cannot be conformism and traditionalism; it can only be that virtue of criticism which traditionally is called discernment. The truly religious person is more critical than his unbelieving neighbour; for he has received the word of God and the grace of the Holy Spirit; and the community of faith is a unique help. He discerns the various currents of thought and the meaning of events in the light of the gospel, and therefore with love for all men.

If we ask ourselves how to approach the sacrament of penance and the undeniable crisis in which we find it, we shall try to respond with discernment, not as isolated critical people but in an open dialogue of faith with our fellow Christians. The only purpose of our effort to discern is fidelity to the gospel,

o

vigilance, openness to the present opportunity, and awareness of the dangers.

We believe firmly that the Church has received from Christ the gift of the Holy Spirit and the mission to continue his own ministry of healing, forgiveness, peace and reconciliation. But because of the present crisis, and because of a better knowledge of Church history and biblical theology, we are more critically aware than the theologians of the last centuries that Christ has not taught his disciples the particular form in which the sacrament of penance has been celebrated during the past centuries and as we have known it from our childhood.

We know more now about the great diversity of the concrete forms and conditions under which the Church has given liturgical and sacramental expression to her mission to be a sign of the reconciliation of sinners. The sociology of religion and of culture has given us new insights into the inter-dependence between concrete forms of culture, society, and their structures, and the various expressions of faith, including the forms of the sacraments. This does not cause us serious difficulties if we consider the data of history in the light of the Incarnation. However, we can also see that not all historical forms of sacramental life were the best possible incarnations of the gospel message in the diverse situations.

We are aware that even the Church is not free from the temptation either to yield unconsciously to social and cultural pressure or to cling scrupulously to forms of liturgical expression that belong to the past. We know about the temptation of the scholastic theology of the last four centuries to absolutize and sacralize the latest form of 'tradition'. This happened chiefly because theologians did not always understand that Christian religion is the history of God with mankind.

Papal and conciliar decrees are not infallible when they speak about past history in so far as facts and data are concerned. There is no doubt today in the minds of competent researchers that the Fourth Lateran Council (1225) and the Council of Trent, and other synods that were important for the development of the sacrament of penance, had insufficient knowledge about the previous history of this sacrament. [3]

As Pope John XXIII has frequently stressed, the magisterium of the Church is essentially pastoral, and a decision or doctrine can be pastorally the right one even if it is conditioned by and explained with imperfect knowledge about the past. However, we should also see that a better understanding of the historical, cultural context of various parts of the Bible and concrete liturgical practices gives the Church a greater degree of freedom when faced with new needs and opportunities. People — ordinary people as well as theologians — who appreciate the Church's present effort to find more appropriate forms for the celebration of the sacrament of penance and a better legislation, and who express frankly their convictions and wishes in favour of a more courageous adaptation, are manifesting their loyalty to the pilgrim Church and their trust in the Lord of history.

Our discernment is challenged especially in relation to the following points: the laws concerning the individual auricular confession; the extension of the obligation to confess all grave sins, and the whole problematic about what 'grave' sins meant throughout history and in Church legislation; the role of the priest as it is meant by Christ, but also as it is partially conditioned by the authority structures of a particular culture; and the liturgical forms in so far as they should guarantee that the sacrament becomes truly a visible sign that speaks to the heart and mind of Christians in diverse cultures.

The first question asked about religious practices by the critical minds of our time, and especially by Christians formed by the prophetic tradition of the Old and New Testaments, is whether they contribute to the integration between faith and life. Everything regarding the sacraments of reconciliation must be tested as to whether or not it helps to present as gladdening

[3] Cf. Bernhard Poschmann, *Penance and Anointment of the Sick* (New York: Herder and Herder, 1964); A. Nocent, *Le sacrement de la reconciliation dans l'Eglise d'Occident* (Rome: Sant'Anselmo, 1972).

news the gift and obligation of conversion and renewal, and an impelling invitation to believers to become, themselves, peacemakers, committed workers for reconciliation.

3. *Penitential celebrations in the light of history*

A great number of qualified theologians and historians have explored the history of the sacrament of penance and have confirmed some of the main truths regarding the sacrament, while offering also clearer insights into the Church's freedom for adaptation.

It is clear that there is a special role for the ministerial priesthood concerning the reconciliation of Christians who, after baptism, have gravely sinned. However, we have also become more sharply aware that the understanding of what is meant by 'grave sins' has varied throughout the ages and in the various parts of Christianity.

For a long time historians have concentrated their research mainly on the institution of the canonical penance during the first centuries. There, the bishop is obliged to intervene for the sake of the Church's credibility, wherever the members of the Church commit sins that cause enormous public scandal. It was not a question of distinguishing between mortal and venial sins; rather, the gravity of the sin was measured according to the scandal it caused and which had to be repaired. In all parts of the ancient Church, at least the following sins were submitted to the canonical penance: apostasy, homicide, abortion, and adultery if it had caused public scandal. Local Churches could add one or another sin which, under the concrete circumstances, had to be considered as gravely scandalous. We should realize that the canonical penance was only one form among many practices in the Church that later flowed together in the sacrament of penance as it was practised in the West from the seventh century onwards and solemnly regulated by the Fourth Lateran Council and the Council of Trent.

Presuming that the reader is well acquainted with the history and meaning of the canonical penance, I want to draw attention to other forms in which the Church exercised her ministry of reconciliation.

(a) *Fraternal correction*

'Fraternal correction', as taught by the Old and the New Testaments, has probably contributed most to the development of the spontaneous confession to a priest without the penitents' being submitted to canonical penance. It seems to me important to know that, in this form, the aspect of judgment is either thoroughly excluded or, rather, reduced to that loving discernment that allows appropriate expression of fraternal charity. We are not speaking here of fraternal corrections about minor or meticulous matters but about serious sins where, however, the aspect of a particular scandal is lacking, and it is a matter of helping a brother in Christ on the road to salvation.

I want to give special attention to fraternal correction in this context also because it seems to me that here we easily find the bridge between the experience of life and sacramentality. A classical text is in the Epistle to the Galatians, and a deeper understanding of it might give us the key to the interpretation of other important texts and a great part of the history of the practice. 'If the Spirit is the source of our life, let the Spirit also direct our course. We must not be conceited, challenging one another to rivalry, jealous of one another. If a man is caught doing something wrong, my brothers, you who are endowed with the Spirit must set him right again, very gently. Look to yourself, each one of you; you may be tempted too. Help one another to carry these heavy loads, and in this way you will fulfil the law of Christ' (Gal 5: 26-62).

Fraternal correction, as taught here, is a work prompted by the Spirit. All the attitudes that betray incarnate selfishness, such as jealousy and grumbling against others, must be thoroughly excluded. Surely all Christians are obliged to offer this important fraternal help, but they can do so only if they are 'endowed with the Spirit' and bear the harvest of the Spirit, as Paul has just explained in Galatians 5:19-25. The emphasis is therefore on gentleness, with the reminder that the one who offers correction could also be tempted and in need of the same kind of help.

Fraternal correction is a most significant expression of 'the law of Christ'. It emphasizes, above all, the solidarity of salvation, and is not possible without self-denial, some suffering and risk.

Another not less important text is in the letter of St James. James excludes, as much as Paul does, any attitude of judgment. 'Be patient, my brothers, until the Lord comes. You too must be patient and stouthearted, for the coming of the Lord is near. My brothers, do not blame one another for your troubles or you will fall under judgment, and there stands the judge at the door' (Jas 5:7-9).

When we offer each other the help of fraternal correction and encouragement, then we must particularly honour the prerogative of God who alone knows the deepest thoughts of the heart and alone can judge men. We do not act in the name of God as judge but in the name of Jesus Christ, the Reconciler, the Divine Physician, the Good Shepherd.

The text of James speaks first and directly of the prayer for forgiveness offered for sick members of the Church. When James then speaks of confessing one's sins, he repeats once more the insistence on prayer: 'The prayer offered in faith will save the sick man, the Lord will raise him, and any sins he may have committed will be forgiven. Therefore, confess your sins to one another and pray for one another, and then you will be healed. A good person's prayer is powerful and effective' (Jas 5:15-16).

Here we may think directly of a kind of liturgical confession which was always understood as *confessio laudis* (confession of sin to the praise of God's mercy). However, it also means a mutual fraternal correction, or a fraternal correction for one who is troubled in situations where there is no case of scandalous sins reserved to the bishop or the priest. While St Paul, in the Epistle to the Galatians quoted above, speaks emphatically of the role of the Spirit, James insists on the necessity of prayer. The meaning is the same: we can help each other on the way of salvation, on the road to conversion and reconciliation only when relying on God's grace.

For an understanding of fraternal correction and the historical development of sacramental penance, the eighteenth chapter of Matthew is very important. Here Jesus first warns against scandals that would endanger the salvation of the weak ones. The gospel then offers us the picture of the good shepherd who is seeking the lost sheep, and Christ invites his disciples to act in the same way, never letting down a brother or sister who may be in great danger. 'If your brother commits a sin, go and take the matter up with him strictly between yourselves. If he listens to you, you have won your brother over. If he will not listen, take one or two others with you, so that all the facts may be established on the evidence of two or three witnesses. If he refuses to listen to them, report the matter to the congregation; and if he will not listen even to the congregation, you must then treat him as you would a pagan or a tax-gatherer' (Mt 18:15-17). However, this expression 'treat him as you would a pagan or a tax-gatherer' must be understood in the context of Matthew. Matthew himself was a tax-gatherer and is won over by Jesus, who constantly associated with people of the same kind in order to save them. So the text means, if the first methods fail altogether, we still must follow the good shepherd.

A few manuscripts read, 'If your brother commits a sin against you'. We should remind ourselves that every sin does harm to each member of mankind. However, we should not think about fraternal correction only or mainly in cases where a brother has directly wronged us. The whole context of Matthew 18 speaks about solidarity in salvation, of which fraternal correction is a most important expression.

The text makes clear that concern for the salvation of others is not a matter only for priests. Only if the efforts of those who live in closest relationship with the sinner have failed, should the matter be brought to the congregation and its office-holders.

Immediately following the quotation above comes the important word of the Lord: 'I tell you this: whatever you bind on earth shall be bound in heaven, and whatever you loose on earth shall be loosed in heaven' (Mt 18:18). The same words are said to Peter in Matthew 16:19. Frequently it is argued that here the power to bind and to free is extended to the twelve apostles and their successors. However, it seems to many scholars that the word applies also to all efforts of the faithful, guided by the Spirit and trusting in the power of the Spirit, when it is to save the brother through fraternal correction. The more authoritative intervention of the office-holder in the congregation is not excluded but included in the text. Since all share somehow in the active solidarity of salvation, to all is given the guarantee that their efforts, prompted by the Spirit, will have value in heaven.

As in James, so here too is a clear reminder that our efforts must be supported by prayer: 'If two of you agree on earth about any request you have to make, that request will be granted by my heavenly Father. For where two or three have met together in my name, I am there among them' (Mt 18: 19-20). Where we meet with our brothers and sisters in the urgent matter of salvation, there we truly meet in the name of the Lord. But this sacramental mission can be fulfilled only if the one who offers reconciliation and the one who receives it become one, united in the presence of the Lord and with trust in the Holy Spirit.

As the Lord teaches us in the 'Our Father' that we can be forgiven only if we ourselves forgive, so here too he insists emphatically on this essential perspective. When Peter asks whether one should forgive as many as seven times, Jesus responds, 'I do not say seven times; I say seventy times seven'

(Mt 18:22). And that means without limit, just as the heavenly Father knows no bounds to his mercy. This teaching is underlined by the parable of the scoundrel who was forgiven a huge debt and yet would be harsh to his fellow-servant who owed him a pittance.

What the Lord tells us about saving solidarity, expressed in fraternal correction and in wholehearted readiness to forgive, excludes any kind of ritualism; yet the religious dimension is of enormous importance. With the tradition that was unbroken until the thirteenth century, we can say that fraternal correction is a kind of sacrament when it is carried out in a spiritual way with gentleness and humility, with everything brought before God in humble and trustful prayer, and the sinner acknowledges his wrong-doing and is repentant. The prayer of the just man is powerful before God, and if the one who has accepted the correction unites his prayer with him, then they are gathered in the name of Jesus and are sure that they will be heard by the Father.

What the Bible says about the salvific value of fraternal correction makes us understand how believers in the Church of the first centuries came to spontaneous confession of their sins, made to a spiritual person. Those who understood the fullness of grace offered by the Lord would confess spontaneously to people 'endowed by the Spirit' those sins which legalists would not consider as serious. And since priests were chosen for their ministry in view of the harvest of the Spirit, and the grace of the Holy Spirit was called upon them in ordination, people confessed their sins most of all to the priests but without excluding confession to others in daily life.

Normally, lay-people were never authorized to hear confessions in the liturgical setting; this is reserved to the priests. However, in the Orthodox Churches the spontaneous way of opening one's conscience to a spiritual lay person in order to obtain his advice and fervent prayer is even now appreciated as a sacramental event.

Since, historically and psychologically, the fraternal correction carried out in common conditions of life is the bridge to the confession of those sins not submitted to a special disciplinary institution, the point has to be stressed that it does not suffice to confess one's sins to the priest unless we are willing to acknowledge our wrongs also before those whom we have wronged and before all to whom we have given a bad example.

A personal experience may illustrate this point. One of the first times I exercised my ministry as confessor, a German gentleman confessed, 'I disobeyed my wife'. I asked the favour of an explanation, since we had been taught that it was the wife who was to obey the husband. He answered graciously, 'Father, it is easy to explain: I knew my wife was right and I was wrong'. However, when I asked him whether, as penance, he would like to tell his wife this, he responded, 'No, these things are to be confessed here, not there!' This is a classical example of the alienation of liturgy from life.

(b) *The Cup of Salvation for the forgiveness of sins*

At the centre of the whole life of the Church, including her ministry of reconciliation, is the Eucharist, which we celebrate always for the forgiveness of sins. 'This is the cup of my blood, the blood of the new and everlasting covenant, shed for you, that sins may be forgiven.' [4]

Baptism is the fundamental sign of our being reconciled and integrated into the Eucharistic community. But what baptism has begun, the Eucharist will continue and bring to completion.

When we underline the dimension of the Eucharist, bringing forgiveness of sins, purification and wholehearted reconciliation, we are not thinking only of the penitential rite at the beginning of the Mass. Rather, it is the whole Eucharist that manifests this dimension.

[4] Cf. Jean Marie Tillard, 'The Bread and Cup of Reconciliation', *Concilium* 61 (1971), pp. 38-54; F. Nikolasch, 'The Sacrament of Penance: Learning from the East', *Concilium* 61 (1971), pp. 65-75; D.A. Tanghe, 'L'Eucharistie pour la Remission des péchés', *Irenikon* 34 (1961), pp. 65-181.

Bibliography

(Page numbers printed in bold at the end of an entry denote references in the text of this book.)

*ABERCROMBIE, M. L. JOHNSON. *The Anatomy of Judgement*, Penguin Books, 1969. **81.**

— *Aims and Techniques of Group Teaching*, (in the press. Monograph of the Society for Research into Higher Education). **81.**

ADORNO, T. W., FRENKEL-BRUNSWIK, ELSE, LEVINSON, D. J. and SANFORD, R. N. *The Authoritarian Personality*, N.Y., Harper Bros., 1950, **111.**

ALLEN, THOMAS W. and WHITELEY, JOHN M. *Dimensions of Effective Counselling*, Charles E. Merrill Publishing Co., Columbus, Ohio, 1968. **124.**

ARBUCKLE, D. S. '*Five Philosophical Issues in Counselling*', Journal of Counselling Psychology, 1958. Reprinted in *Counselling Readings in Theory and Practice*, McGowan and Schmidt (eds.), Holt, Rinehart & Winston Inc., 1962. **23.**

*ARGYLE, MICHAEL. *The Psychology of Interpersonal Behaviour*, Penguin Books, 1967. **41, 51, 54, 81.**

— *Social Interaction*, Methuen, 1969. **54.**

BEECH, H. R. *Changing Man's Behaviour*, Penguin Books, 1969. **40.**

BERNE, ERIC. *Games People Play. The Psychology of Human Relationships*. First published 1966. Penguin Books, 1970. **50.**

BION, W. R. *The Leaderless Group Project*, Bull. Menninger Clinic 10, 1946. **84.**

BION, W. R. and RICKMAN, J. '*Intra-Group Tensions in Therapy*', Lancet, November 27th 1943. Reprinted in *Experiences in Groups and other papers*, W. R. Bion, Tavistock, 1961. (Social Science Paperback, 1968). **65.**

BRITISH INSTITUTE OF MANAGEMENT. Report on European Productivity Agency Project No. 399 on Group Dynamics, 1956. **83.**

*BROWN, J. A. C. *Freud and the Post-Freudians*, Penguin Books, 1961. **18, 80.**

CHOMSKY. See LYONS, JOHN. **46.**

CONCH, A. and KEMSTON, K. 'Yeasayers and Naysayers', Journal Abnormal Soc. Psychol. 60, 1960. **112.**

CRONBACH and GLESER. *Psychological Tests and Personnel Decisions*, University of Illinois Press, 1957. **96.**

EDWARDS, A. L. *Social Desirability and Personality Test Construction*. Reprinted in *Personality Assessment*, B. Semeonoff (ed.), q.v. **111.**

— *Techniques of Attitude Scale Construction*, Appleton-Century-Crofts, 1957. **111.**

EYSENCK, H. J. and RACHMAN, S. *Dimensions of Personality*. Reprinted in *Personality Assessment*, B. Semeonoff (ed.), q.v. **111.**

FOULKES, S. H. *On Group Analysis*, International Journal Psychoanalysis, Vol. 27, 1946. **65.**

FOULKES, S. H. and ANTHONY, E. J. *Group Psychotherapy*, Penguin Books, 1965. **77.**

FLUGEL, J. C. *Man, Morals and Society*, Duckworth, 1945. **79.**

FREUD, SIGMUND. *The Interpretation of Dreams*, authorised translation by A. A. Burell, Allen & Unwin. First published 1913. **18.**

— *The Psychopathology of Everyday Life*, translated by Alan Tyson, paperback edition, Ernest Benn, 1966. **57.**

FROMM, ERIC. *The Fear of Freedom*, Routledge & Kegan Paul, 1942. **17.**

GESELL, ARNOLD. *The First Five Years of Life*, Harper & Row, 1940. **15.**

*GOFFMAN, ERVING. *Asylums*, Penguin Books, 1968. **9.**

— *Behaviour in Public Places*, The Free Press, N.Y., 1963. **50, 51.**

GORER, G. and RICKMAN, J. *The People of Great Russia: A Psychological Study*, Cresset Press, 1949. **47.**

GOSLING, R., MILLER, D. H., TURQUET, P. M. and WOODHOUSE, D. I. *The Use of Small Groups in Training*. The Tavistock Institute of Medical Psychology, 1967 **107, 109.**

GRUMMON, DONALD L. 'Client-Centred Theory', Chapter 2 in *Theories of Counselling*, B. Stefflre, (ed.), q.v. **26.**

*HALMOS, P. *The Faith of the Counsellors*, Constable, 1965, **5.**

— *The Personal Service Society*, Inaugural Address, Cardiff, University of Wales Press, 1966. **12.**

— *The Personal Service Society*, Constable, 1970.

HOMANS, G. C. *The Human Group*, Routledge & Kegan Paul, London, 1950. **82.**

HORNEY, KAREN. *New Ways in Psychoanalysis*, Norton & Co., N.Y., 1939. **23.**

HUXLEY, A. *The Doors of Perception* and *Heaven and Hell*, Penguin Books, 1959. **29.**

ISAACS, SUSAN. *Intellectual Growth in Young Children*, Routledge & Kegan Paul. **78.**

JAQUES, E. *The Changing Culture of a Factory*, Tavistock, 1951. **81.**

*KLEIN, JOSEPHINE. *The Study of Groups*, Routledge Paperback, 1967. **67, 68, 76.**

KLEIN, MELANIE. *The Psychoanalysis of Children*, Hogarth Press, 1932. **77.**

KNIGHT, MARGARET. *William James*, Penguin Books, 1950. **14.**

KÖHLER, W. *The Mentality of Apes*, translated by Ella Winter, N.Y., Harcourt, Brace, 1925. Reissued Penguin Books, 1957. **37, 38.**

LEWIN, K. *Principles of Topological Psychology*, translated by F. Heider and G. M. Heider, McGraw-Hill, 1936. **69, 70.**

— 'Field Theory and Learning', Chapter 4 in *The Psychology of Learning*, Nat. Soc. Stud. Educ., 41st yearbook, Part II. N.Y., McGraw-Hill, 1936. **69.**

LIPPITT, R. *Training in Community Relations*, N.Y., Harper Bros., 1949. **83.**

LIPTON, WALTER M. *Working with Groups: Group Process and Individual Growth*, Wiley, N.Y., 1966. **117.**

LYONS, JOHN. *Chomsky*, Fontana Modern Masters Paperback, 1970. **46.**

MEAD, G. H. *Mind, Self and Society—from the Standpoint of a Social Behaviourist*, University of Chicago Press, 1934. **49.**

MEDAWAR, SIR PETER. *The Art of the Soluble*, Methuen, 1967. **2.**

*MILLER, GEORGE. *Psychology—the Science of Mental Life*, Penguin Books, 1966. **110.**

OESER, O. A. *Teacher, Pupil and Task*, Tavistock, 1955. **81.**

OTTAWAY, A. K. C. *Learning through Group Experience*, Routledge & Kegan Paul, 1965. **81.**

RICHARDSON, ELIZABETH. *Group Study for Teachers*, Routledge Paperback, 1967. **81.**

ROGERS, C. R. *Counselling and Psychotherapy*, Houghton Mifflin Co., 1942. **23, 24.**

— *Client Centred Therapy*, 1951. **25.**

— *On Becoming a Person*, 1961. **25.**

— *The Actualizing Tendency in Relation to Motives and Consciousness*, Nebraska Symposium on Motivation. University of Nebraska Press, 1963. **25.**

RUSSELL, B. *History of Western Philosophy*, Allen & Unwin, 1946. **38.**

*RYCROFT, C. (ed.) *Psychoanalysis Observed*, Constable paperback, London, 1966. **58, 59.**

SCHEIN, E. H. and BENNIS, W. G. *Personal and Organizational Change through Group Methods*, John Wiley & Sons, N.Y., 1965. **73.**

SCHULTZ, WILLIAM C. *Joy: Expanding Human Awareness*, Grove Press Inc. N.Y., 1967. **119.**

SEEBOHM, F. (Chairman). Report of the Committee on Local Authority and Allied Personal Social Services, HMSO, 1968. **7.**

SEMEONOFF, B. (ed.) *Personality Assessment*, Penguin Modern Psychology Readings, 1966. **97, 111.**

SKINNER, B. F. *Science and Human Behaviour*, Macmillan, 1953. **56.**

— *Walden Two*. **56.**

STEFFLRE, B. (ed.) *Theories of Counselling*, McGraw-Hill, 1965. **13.**

SZASZ, THOMAS S. *The Myth of Mental Illness: Foundation of a Theory of Personal Conduct*, Secker & Warburg, 1961. **49.**

THORNDIKE, E. L. *Animal Intelligence*, N.Y., Macmillan, 1911. **28.**

— *The Psychology of Learning*, N.Y. Teachers' College, 1913. **28.**

TRUAX, C. B. *Elements of Psychotherapy*. Discussion Papers, Wisconsin Psychiatric Institute No. 38, University of Wisconsin, 1961. **26.**

TRUAX, C. B. and CARKHUFF, R n, *Towards Effective Counselling and Psychotherapy*, Chicago, Aldine, 1967. **26.**

*VERNON, M. D. *The Psychology of Perception*, Penguin Books, 1962. **53, 69.**

VERNON, P. E. *Personality Assessment*, Methuen, 1963.

— 'The Concept of Validity in Personality Study' in *Personality Assessment*, B. Semeonoff (ed.) q.v. **110, 111.**

VERNON, P. E. and PARRY, J. B. *Personnel Selection in the British Forces*, University of London Press, 1949. **97.**

WALLIS, J. H. *Someone to Turn To*, Routledge & Kegan Paul, 1961, **6.**

WATSON, J. B. *Psychology from the Standpoint of a Behaviourist*, Philadelphia, Lippincott, 1919. **28.**

*WHYTE, L. L. *The Unconscious before Freud*, Tavistock, 1962. **19, 20.**

WHYTE, W. H., JNR. *The Organization Man*, Penguin Books, 1957. **100.**

WILLIAMS, JAMES. *The Marital Relationship as a Focus for Casework*, Report of a Conference on the Implications of Marital Interaction for the Social Services. Codicote Press, 1962. **107.**

WINNICOTT, D. W. *Collected Papers*, London, Tavistock, 1958. **78.**

WISEMAN, S. '*The Marking of English Composition in Grammar School Selection*', British Journal Educational Psychology, 1949. **97.**

RECOMMENDED READING

Books marked with an asterisk together with the following:

1. BORGER, R. and SEABORNE, A. E. M. *The Psychology of Learning*, Penguin Books, 1966.
2. FOSS, BRIAN M. (ed.) *New Horizons in Psychology*, Penguin Books, 1966, especially pp. 152–166 on Psycholinguistics.
3. GOFFMAN, ERVING. *Stigma*, Penguin Books, 1968.
4. LYTTON, HUGH. *School Counselling and Counsellor Education in the United States*, Nat. Foundation for Educational Research, 1968.

REFERENCES

Penguin Books publish several excellent series dealing with psychological topics. They are:—

Modern Psychology Readings which contain a selection of original papers on each particular subject;

The Science of Behaviour series and *Pelican Books on Psychology* edited by C. A. Mace.

Wherever feasible these or other paperbacks have been chosen for reference rather than more expensive hardbacks.

Index

The Eucharistic celebration should be a peak experience of the contrast-harmony between the mystery of God's holiness and the attractive power of his graciousness. It is grace and appeal to holy fear and to absolute trust in God's healing love. We should also not forget the purifying power of the word of God proclaimed in the Eucharist. Those who eagerly open themselves to the word of the Lord are told, 'You have already been cleansed by the word that I spoke to you. Dwell in me, as I in you' (Jn 15:3).

The proclamation of the word of God includes also the homily. In medieval times it was frequently followed by a general confession of sins and by general absolution. Here again, I would not want to speak of that general absolution as a sacrament in itself but rather as a part of the liturgy which produces its grace by the totality of its meaning, of its signs and words.

The Eucharistic celebrations of ancient times were masterpieces of the proclamation of the good news that conversion is possible and urgent. Even the incensing of the bishop, the main celebrants, the priests and the lay-people, had at the beginning the meaning of a call to humble confession and awareness that we are in need of this sacrifice. The Eucharist in all its dimensions is grace and call to conversion. It fosters our relationships with God and with the community of our fellowmen. Our active participation in it is a renewed commitment to fight against individual and collective egoism, against everything that is an obstacle to the kingdom of God.

As in the ancient Church of East and West, still today in the Orthodox Churches, all Christians except those submitted to the canonical penance because of grave scandal can receive Communion without previous individual confession if they are sure about their contrition and good intention to fight constantly against all those attitudes opposed to the kingdom of God. The celebration has therefore to do everything to dispose the participants to a profound sense of sorrow, to great trust and firm purpose. To all those who have not made their thorough-going conversion, the warning is loudly announced, 'The Holy One to the holy'.

(c) *Communal celebrations outside the Eucharist*

The Church has always believed that forgiveness of sins that
are not submitted to canonical penance and involve no particular
scandal can be obtained in various ways; but in all times there
has been the strongest emphasis on the absolute need of conversion on both the individual and social level. The gospel that
conversion is possible and urgent was particularly stressed at
important moments of the liturgical year, during Advent, during
Lent, and on the vigils of the great feasts. All these efforts
entered into the broad scope of the Church's own sacramentality,
her being and becoming more and more a sacrament of reconciliation. There was a firm conviction that, in all her efforts to
bring people closer to salvation through profound contrition,
trust in the Lord, and renewed purpose, the Church acted as an
effective and visible sign of God's mercy. The diversity of forms
such as Bible vigils, Lenten services, general absolutions, also
encouraged the readiness of believers to confess their sins
humbly before a priest.

Until the eleventh century there was no absolution in the
form of a declaration, 'I absolve you'; the absolution was just
the Church's fervent prayer, expressed by the minister of the
Church, that the Lord might grant forgiveness, liberation from
sin, and peace. There were many forms of this prayer. Always,
however, there was an awareness that those grave sins which
were called *criminalia* should be confessed individually to gain
the explicit sign and word of reconciliation, although there are
uncertainties and considerable diversities about how the line
was drawn between serious sins that could be forgiven in
various ways and those grave sins (*criminalia*) that had to be
submitted to the keys of the Church.

(d) *The combination of various traditions and practices*

During the past seven hundred years, many theologians and
canonists have been seeking the origin of the present form of the
sacrament of penance in the institution of the canonical penance

of the first centuries. One of the negative consequences was that the judicial aspect proper to the canonical penance was then applied to confession as it developed in the Irish-Scottish Church from the sixth century onwards.

For the future of the Church's reconciling ministry it seems to me important to distinguish the diverse rivers that flowed together into the one great stream of our sacrament of penance. The great contribution of the Irish-Scottish monks to the sacramental preaching of conversion and penance should not be under-estimated. They broke the ancient rule that absolution for the gravely scandalous sins could be given only once during a lifetime. Although they put great emphasis on doing penance, they were less rigoristic than the other parts of the western Church. They greatly encouraged people's readiness to confess all their sins to priests and to accept spiritual guidance. We should not blame these great missionaries and promoters of humble confession for the present crisis of the sacrament of penance. It is our own fault if we perpetuate the paternalistic and rather authoritarian style in which the clergy at that time exercised the ministry of reconciliation. It followed the style of that society.

Since the Irish-Scottish monks had been influenced by the monasteries of the oriental Churches, it is even more urgent for us to learn from the eastern traditions. There, a sharper distinction exists between the role of the bishop or his delegate when it is a matter of absolving from gravely scandalous sins and, on the other hand, the recognition that in the average confession the priest acts not so much as a judge but rather as a representative of Christ, the Divine Physician, the Good Shepherd.

The combining of the canonical penance with other forms of confession and penance brought some confusion into the concept of 'grave sins' that must be confessed. In studying the tradition, we have to give the greatest attention to the context in which 'grave' sin is spoken of. It can mean the gravely scandalous sins (*criminalia*); it can mean mortal sin (the refusal of God's friendship); or it can mean grave, even very grave, venial sins (attitudes and sinful acts that expose the Christian increasingly ro the danger of losing God's friendship).

Even in today's vocabulary and way of speaking about the sacrament of penance, this combination is a cause of confusion. For instance, we speak sometimes, without distinction, about reconciliation with God through the Church, when it is a matter of sins that broke neither the friendship with God nor solidarity with the Church. We thereby perpetuate that vocabulary which was most appropriate to the canonical penance, although it can be applied only in an analogous way to the confession of those who live in peace with the Church and pursue generously an ongoing conversion towards greater holiness.

4 The crisis in the concept of sin [5]

During the last seven centuries, Church discipline regarding the obligation to confess to the priest has been based on the distinction between venial and mortal sins. Following the Council of Trent, canon law determined that all mortal sins committed after baptism must be submitted to the keys of the Church by an individual confession that had to indicate the number and species of these sins.

There were always people in the Church who realized that there is an enormous problem on how to determine the qualitative difference between mortal and venial sin. The greatest and most dangerous over-simplification simply equated all serious sins with mortal sins, and regarded all sins that are not mortal as slight or not serious. This, however, contradicts the major currents of our tradition. In a culture in which underdevelopment of the great masses was accepted, it seemed almost normal that the few specialists on morals should determine what had to be confessed as mortal sin and what was to be considered as

[5] Cf. my book, *Sin in the Secular Age* (Slough: St Paul Publications, 1974).

only venial sin. It was forgotten that men like St Augustine had praised God that he had hidden from us these borderlines so that nobody could become arrogant.

Widespread atheism and a better knowledge of history show us how much the concept of grave and mortal sin has varied. The behavioural sciences, especially depth psychology, discourage priests and moralists from judging other peoples' consciences as whether they have committed a mortal or a venial sin. There are no such things as general borderlines that could assure a person that, up to this or that point, God would not take seriously his command and the gifts through which he calls man to respond. Criteria that help us personally to evaluate our situation as to whether it spells growth or decline do not allow us to judge the subjective gravity of others' faults. How can we know the measure of grace, of insight, of freedom and liberation from all the manipulative influences of the environment? In a world so greatly tempted by organized and unorganized atheism, how do we speak about the proportion between sins of human frailty, partial malice, and eternal exile from God? We know the devastating influence of rigorism and Jansenism that drove so many people into scrupulosity and others into rejection of the sacrament of penance and even rejection of faith in God, when only rigorism should have been rejected.

A renewed sense of responsibility and co-responsibility, and new insights into the tremendous influence of public opinion and oppressive or liberating conditions of life, have caused and are causing a more and more significant shift regarding the sense and concept of sin. We have to return to a biblical vision where sin is spoken of more in the perspective of conversion, both individual and social, than of a detailed individual confession. This also leads to a better understanding of a humble confession.

One aspect may best illustrate the whole problematic. The catechisms which we used in our youth stressed, besides the 'grave matter' as condition for the possibility of mortal sin, full deliberation and liberty. Today we know from biblical studies and better knowledge of our best traditions, and from depth psychology, that each sin that is not counteracted by contrition and renewed purpose, gradually desensitizes the conscience, diminishes freedom and blocks genuine deliberation. We should realize the absurdity of the conclusion to which the catechism's statement leads: that mortal sin is not possible if, by repeated venial sins and lack of contrition, one has gradually lost one's freedom and one's sensitivity to sin.

My own conclusion is that neither of those who equate all grave sins with mortal sins nor of those who react within the vicious circle and assert that mortal sin is not at all possible or scarcely possible. I see, rather, two possibilities of falling into the state of mortal sin. The first is that a person who is not yet immersed in the darkness of a hardened conscience becomes sufficiently aware that a certain way of acting is totally opposed to the friendship of God, and yet commits the sin although he has sufficient freedom to resist the temptation. The second and probably more common way is by a gradual sinful loss of freedom and of the sense of sin, as well as of the sense of God. Then the spiritual death is the result of the many occasions when the person has resisted the grace of God, has acted in various degrees against his conscience, and has frequently delayed or refused contrition and renewed effort. The more important assessment is therefore whether one is on a path of decline and decay or, in spite of weakness and serious falls, is really on a way of growth and continuous conversion. Every Christian should realize that he exposes himself to the danger of mortal sin and final alienation if he does not accept the fundamental law of growth and ongoing conversion.

I think that in this perspective the sacrament of penance could be understood and highly appreciated. It should be clear that one does not go to the doctor only when one is sure one is dead. We turn to the Divine Physician with our maladies and let him who is the light shine upon us. We open ourselves in humble confession in order not to plunge ever more deeply into darkness.

While this vision diminishes legal pressure and the danger of scrupulosity, it can make the sacrament of penance more attractive. Christians should see it not so much as a law imposed but as a grace offered by the Lord.

5. *Diverse forms of celebration*

The official liturgical renewal of the sacrament of penance, which is now coming into practice everywhere, is the result of new awareness and the effort to respond to new needs, although this is done with a careful gradualness. Whoever has seen the broad vision of the sacramentality of the Church, and her total ministry of reconciliation, will surely not be scandalized by the present change. The more we see the full picture, and the more we are concerned not to allow any gap between religion and life, the better we shall profit from the new opportunities.

It seems to me that we have to give particular attention to fraternal correction as an expression of co-responsibility and solidarity in salvation. I am thinking particularly about the examination of conscience in Christian families. It is a moment of grace if, after a serious tension or after a hurt unjustly caused, the members of a family are united in the name of the Lord, pray together, and assure each other of their wholehearted forgiveness. In this reconciling event, thanksgiving should never be forgotten. The revision of life has a similar role in religious communities and in groups of lay-people particularly committed and sensitive to the solidarity of salvation.

The Church has re-evaluated communal celebrations. Everyone should be aware that they have a great tradition behind them in all parts of Christianity. Not only are they a good preparation for individual confession — an aspect that should not be under-estimated — but they are also a privileged moment of grace for the community. They help us to see the social aspect of sin and salvation. They are not so much in competition with the individual confession as a complementary experience.

The communal celebrations of penance, not followed by general absolution or by individual confession and individual absolution, are not yet recognized as a sacrament in the specific sense; but this might be the case in the future, at least under certain conditions.

Pope Paul VI has given to the episcopal conferences great freedom to allow general absolution on the occasion of communal celebration of penance. However, those who are aware of having turned away from God in mortal sin are still obliged to make later, if possible, an individual confession to a priest. This should not be seen as an arbitrary imposition. Jesus, too, has forgiven people on the Easter day when he appeared and shared his peace with them. Peter, however, had also his individual encounter with the Lord, who three times asks him whether he truly loves him. Although Peter was grieved on that occasion, it became a source of great peace and joy for him. Further, we should not forget that those who have reasonable doubts about their serious sins being mortal sins are, by Church law, not obliged to make an individual confession. It is sufficient, and at the same time very necessary, that they are sure about contrition and firm purpose of renewal.

It should never be forgotten, either, that a Christian is not just under law but responds to the offer of grace. The humble personal confession before the priest, as well as the spontaneous prayers for forgiveness during the revision of life or at communal celebrations, can bring us to greater appreciation of God's mercy and healing forgiveness, and to a profound gratitude that gives new energies to our life. It is my conviction that communal celebration and the penance rite during Mass could be exposed to various dangers of superficiality, escapism and alienation if we refused humble confession because of a lack of humility. If we are willing to open ourselves to a spiritual adviser, we come to a deeper knowledge of ourselves and to greater gratitude towards God.

The new *Ordo Poenitentiae* promulgated by Pope Paul in 1974 is a great step forward, in which we should gratefully co-operate. The individual confession is understood as shared prayer between priest and penitent, a respectful dialogue and praise of God's mercy. There is a great richness in the use of scripture and in prayers by which we are also explicitly reminded that it is the power of the Holy Spirit that cleanses us from our sins and gives us peace.

It becomes more and more evident that the sacrament of reconciliation requires a great diversity of expression according to the diversity of cultures and situations. For an innocent child of seven years, a mature grandmother, and a person who after many years turns back to God and the sacraments of Christ, the sacrament cannot be expressed with the same formula. The routine, and the repetition of always the same expressions can greatly damage the significance and effect of the sacrament of reconciliation.

6. *The sacrament of liberation* [6]

Both scripture and tradition teach us that there is an intimate relation between salvation and liberation. It is not enough to say that the sacrament of penance frees us from the slavery of sin or from punishment deserved by sin. This is true, but we should not overlook the positive aspect that the sacrament frees us for the love of God and restores or increases in us the liberty of the children of God who are sensitive to the longing of all creation to have a share in the freedom which Christ has brought. Freedom and liberation are the essential concern of the most sensitive people of our age. It is therefore necessary to explore all the dimensions of the sacrament of reconciliation in this respect.

Sin is a blinding and enslaving power. The person who does not repent in order to receive freedom again and again as a new gift from God gradually loses his inner freedom and his capacity

---

[6] Cf. J.B. Sherin, *The Sacrament of Freedom. A Book on Confession* (Milwaukee: Bruce Publishing Co., 1961).

to distinguish between true freedom and its counterfeits. Thus
he jeopardizes discernment and can no longer join others in the
growth of freedom. We should realize that unrepented sins cause
not only a gradual loss of one's own individual freedom but also
an increasing obstacle to the salvation and freedom of all people.

The celebration of the gospel of redemption and liberation
in the sacrament of reconciliation not only unmasks our partial
lack of freedom but makes us aware that we can be much
freer, much more illumined, much more able to know God and
his design for the liberation of the whole world, if we respond
to all the opportunities God offers us. It is therefore most
important that after each sin — that is, after not giving the
appropriate response to God's grace — we awaken in ourselves
a profound sorrow and a lively trust in God's restoring and
liberating power. If all this is brought into the light of Christ
in this great sacrament, then we can resist sin and its blinding
action and all false concepts of freedom. Whoever experiences
the liberating power of repentance and confession will never
deny moral freedom.

To face humbly our situation as sinners before God and
before the community is an act of courage and of true freedom
that opens to us new horizons. Modern psychotherapy has given
us clearer insight into the blinding and disturbing power of the
repression of guilt, and the liberation that can break through
from a trustful dialogue with our fellowman, especially if we
have confidence that the other will understand us and can
encourage us on the road towards more light.

The celebration of the reconciliation which is God's gift,
speaks to us about freedom, which is both God's gift and man's
task. If we have understood the social dimension of the sacrament and of the gift of reconciliation, then we shall become
more and more committed to common efforts to increase the
chances of freedom for all people, and to promote the structures
of life that favour it.

The communal celebration of penance and reconciliation
greatly helps us to discover the social dimensions of freedom.

Commitment to conversion and renewal leads to the investment of the spirit of freedom in the world around us. It is not just a matter of self-defence against manipulation and exploitation, but a shared effort to foster genuine freedom in human relationships in the economic, cultural, social and political fields, and above all, in the life of the Church.

We have seen, now, that every sin, and especially every unrepented sin, is an obstacle on the road to liberty, not only for the individual but also for the whole of mankind. But we should not forget that there are sins that directly oppose the growth of liberty and therefore are a grave injustice against Christ, the Liberator.

Not only in communal celebrations but also in the individual confession, we should give the greatest attention to those sins that jeopardize our vocation to be witnesses to and promoters of true liberty. I think, above all, about the dangers of the manipulation of persons and groups through misguided public opinion; and in this respect we should not forget the sins of omission. We should prepare ourselves and help others to promote intelligently, and in a liberating way, sound public opinion.

The sacrament of reconciliation makes us aware that not only forgiveness of sins but the restoration and growth of freedom is a gift of the Father of all and of the Redeemer of all of mankind, given in the Holy Spirit who is the source of unity. When we celebrate gratefully the name of Christ the Reconciler and Liberator, we commit ourselves more and more to that saving solidarity that creates a world in which our brothers and sisters can grow in freedom and resist all the powers of perdition.

The celebration of the sacrament is always and essentially praise and thanksgiving. Whoever understands the greatness of the gift of reconciliation and renewed freedom will become an apostle of freedom, with that joy and gentleness that are its main energy. Thus the social apostolate of believers will reach its depth and fullness of meaning.

The celebration is a profound experience that God accepts us with all our shadows and weaknesses, and sustains us if we seek him who is the Way. This experience of faith, by assuring us that we are on the road with Christ who is the light, the truth, the freedom, gives us renewed freedom not only to accept ourselves but also to accept our fellowmen with their shadows and their troubles, and to grow together in authentic freedom, responding together to the yearning of all creation to have a share in the freedom of the children of God.

Since this aspect of growth in liberty and commitment to liberty is essential to the sacrament of reconciliation, both the confessor and the penitent must take special care not to contradict this grace and the mission that comes from it. Any kind of authoritarian imposition of one's own opinion, and even of the Church's doctrine, must be excluded. Christ does not want to have slavish subjects. 'I call you slaves no longer; I call you friends, for I have shared with you what I have received from the Father' (Jn 15:15).

Only a formation of conscience that leads to sincere convictions and the readiness to act according to one's own conscience and to seek more and more light, is on the wavelength of the sacrament of penance. We honour this sacrament only if we celebrate it in such a way that the obligation arises from the very perception of the gifts of God, and if we are led to understand better and better what the perfect law of liberty, the law of grace, the law of faith means.

Whoever has understood this dimension will never try to force anyone to make his confession or to use manipulative means to obtain a materially complete confession. Attempts to bring pressure to bear on parents and children in order to obtain individual confessions from the whole class in preparation for first Communion are not only obstacles to a grateful appreciation of the sacrament but also contradict its very essence.

The penitent should not try to get clearcut recipes from the confessor but rather the necessary insights and criteria for discernment, so that he will really make his own decision and form his own conscience in the light of Christ. The confessor will respect the conscience of the penitent even if he thinks that it is erroneous. He will never try to impose something, but only to help the penitent to search sincerely and to act according to his own conscience. Especially in matters in which there is a diversity of opinions in the Church and in situations where there is conflict between various values and duties, the confessor will be most careful to refrain from any tendency to impose his opinions.

It can happen, and sometimes has happened, that the confessor creates something like a schizophrenic conscience. On the one hand, the penitent has sincere convictions; on the other hand, the confessor creates a super-ego by imposing a law, or an arbitrary interpretation or explanation of law that contradicts the penitent's conscience. This can become a major obstacle on the road towards freedom.

A sad (and true) example may illustrate the problem. A couple has five children, two of whom are most gravely retarded and handicapped. They are loving spouses and also very affectionate parents, as they keep their two retarded children at home with them. They have fairly decided not to risk having a third retarded child. However, they feel that, in their difficult situation, they have special need of the reciprocal expression of their tender conjugal love. The husband, who tends towards scrupulosity, makes his confession to a well-known priest who is considered a saint. He confesses that sometimes, during the expression of his affection, he has lost the seed, although this was not his intention. The confessor reacts most severely with the question, 'So you, too, want to go to hell? Now go and say the rosary and make up your mind; then come back to me'. Frightened, the penitent, after having said three rosaries, returns to the confessional and accepts the imposition made by the confessor, to have only normal and complete conjugal relationships. The result is the third gravely handicapped child. The wife develops not only a profound neurosis of anguish but also disaffection with the husband who, one-sidedly with the confessor, made the decision to have marital relations open to procreation. A Catholic marriage counsellor suggests the need for psychotherapy and a sterilization which he considers, under these circumstances, as an essential part of therapy. Both spouses are convinced that this is the right solution; but this time the pious wife seeks the approval of the confessor. The priest, whose principle is to be short in his responses in order to be effective, says only, 'You have to make up your mind whether you want to continue to receive the sacraments or to commit such a great crime against human nature'. The point here is not whether the priest's opinions were appropriate, but the lack of respect for the consciences of the penitents.

St Paul gives us the most liberating instruction on how we should respect the conscience of our fellow Christians. And if there is any place where there must be the greatest effort to do so, then it is in the sacrament of reconciliation: 'Everyone should reach conviction in his own mind' (Rom 14:5) and 'Anything which does not arise from conviction is sin' (Rom 14:23).

St Alphonsus, in his book *The Practice of the Confessor*, is most emphatic, warning the confessor against any temptation to impose something on the penitent against a sincere conviction, whenever it is a case of 'invincible ignorance'. That means whenever the penitent is existentially unable to interiorize what the confessor considers as the objective truth. St Alphonsus does not speak only in relation to cases where there is a diversity of opinions in the Church but even in matters of a clear doctrine of the Church about natural law.

In the life and the writings of Cardinal Newman, this absolute respect for the sincere conscience is one of the main concerns. The Second Vatican Council follows and confirms this Catholic tradition: 'Conscience frequently errs from invincible ignorance without losing its dignity'. But the Council also warns immediately: 'The same cannot be said about a man who cares but little for truth and goodness, or of a conscience which by degrees grows practically lifeless because of habitual sin' (*The Church in the modern world,* 16).

7. The sacrament of healing [7]

Along with the ministry of reconciliation, the Lord has entrusted to the Church the mission to heal. In the public ministry of Christ we find a surprising synthesis between healing and forgiveness of sins. Christ does not accept the widespread conviction of the Semitic world of his time, which looked down upon the sick person as a sinner; yet, to the paralyzed man who is seeking healing, he says, 'My son, your sins are forgiven'. There are ailments that are to the glory of God but there are others that are deeply linked with sin.

The best of psychotherapy can help us to see more clearly the connection between reconciliation and healing, especially in those ailments that are typical cases of psychogenic or noogenic disorders. Great therapists and humanists like Karl Menninger, Erich Fromm, Erik Erikson and Viktor Frankl, define genuine human health, above all, in view of healthy relationships and the capacity to relate healthily to one's fellowmen, to one's self and to the whole of creation. Man, as an embodied spirit, is essentially on the way to healing if he finds liberating relationships with God, with his fellowmen, the community, himself and his environment.

In the sacraments, the divine Physician helps us to rediscover our essential 'We-You-I' relationships and to live them. Man cannot find his true self unless he is seeking the ultimate goal and meaning of his life, transcending the selfish self, and finding joy in loving and serving his fellowmen.

In the sacrament of reconciliation we come to a deeper and deeper experience that God accepts us and is calling us to be at home with him. We do not feel worthy. But if the Father accepts the prodigal son, he is kind also to the older son who always stayed with him although he did not always appreciate fully the gratuitousness of this gift.

[7] Cf. A. Snoeck, *Confession and Psychoanalysis* (Westminster: Newman Press, 1964).

Q

God seeks and accepts man where he is, in order to direct him to better self-realization, to openness and gratitude towards him who is the source of our life, and to loving acceptance of his fellowmen. As our gratitude grows for God's patience and healing love, we learn how to accept ourselves with all our shadows and limitations, and at the same time we learn to accept wholly our fellow-travellers on the way to the final union with God.

If we rightly understand and celebrate the sacraments, and especially the sacrament of reconciliation, we live in healthier relationships with our neighbour and our community. Because we are grateful that Jesus was willing to bear our burdens, we learn to be grateful to others who forbear with us and accept our common vocation to bear the burdens of each other and thus to fulfil the law of Christ.

In the first chapter of the Epistle to the Romans, Paul warns that the chief source of perversion and misery in human relations is the lack of gratitude to God. 'Knowing God, they have refused to honour him as God and to render him thanks. And all their thinking has ended in futility, and their misguided minds are plunged in darkness' (Rom 1: 21-22). The new liturgy of the sacrament of penance helps to lead the whole celebration to thanksgiving and praise, which then should mark our life and create a divine *milieu* in which prevail peace, joy, gratitude and reciprocal trust. In such an environment, thoroughly alive and marked by these healthy relationships, we continue to carry on the healing power of the sacrament of penance.

To reap from the sacrament of reconciliation this harvest of healing, it is evident that we do not look upon the confessor as one who is seated on the judgment seat but as a brother in Christ who proclaims peace and, in fervent prayer, leads us to greater trust in the Lord. The Church shows us in the new rite that penitent and confessor join in the dialogue of faith, in humble prayer of supplication, and in praise of the Lord's goodness.

I think that the numerous healings obtained in prayer meetings of the charismatic renewal [8] can, at least partially, be explained through the deep experience of faith, of trust, of fervent prayer, and above all, of the spirit of praise and thanksgiving. The fact that many or most of these events of healing can be explained by psycho-somatic medicine and by the findings of logotherapy does not at all diminish their value as faith healings. On the contrary, it shows that through a divine *milieu* of faith, goodness and praise of God, man can receive in the best way the wholeness and health that always point towards salvation.

---

[8] Cf. J.C. Haughey, 'Healed and Healing Priests', *America,* Aug. 7, 1975, pp. 46-48.

CONCLUSION

In all areas, but especially in that of sacramental life, dialogue with secular thinkers and with people of other religious beliefs is above all a call to identity. It helps us to open our mind to the riches of our own tradition. If I say 'our own' I include that of the eastern Orthodox and of the Reformed Churches; for all have preserved and partially developed the common heritage.

What unites us as Christians is Christ. So we have asked ourselves whether our understanding of moral life and of the sacraments make him known to our fellowmen. He is the sign that pierces the hearts of men and lays bare the thoughts of many (cf. Lk 2:35). For those who believe in him and are united in his love everything takes its full significance, becomes radiant in his light.

To adhere to Christ the Sacrament of salvation for all the world commits us to the service of all people. We discover their dignity and all the good in them. And when we gather around Christ to listen to his word and to receive the signs of his graciousness our eyes and our hearts turn to each human person since we believe that they are created in the image and likeness of God, and that all things, and particularly the sacraments, are offered us to grow together as living signs, as it were, as sacraments of God's creative and redemptive presence. 'As believers succeed in finding appropriate external forms by which to express their commitment to God in Christ, they become living symbols and beacons of hope in the world.' [1]

[1] A. Dulles, *Models of the Church* (Garden City, N.Y.: Doubleday, 1974), p. 67.

By welcoming Christ as the visible image of the invisible
God and thus discovering the lofty vocation to become in
Christ more and more configured with God's own goodness,
mercy, gentleness, creativity, and generosity we are set free from
the slavery to idols. Thus, living under the eyes of Jesus Christ
the visible image of the invisible God, we honour all men and
observe truly the commandment: 'You shall have no other
god to set against me. You shall not make a carved image for
yourself nor the likeness of anything in the heavens, or on earth
below, or in the waters under the earth. You shall not bow
down to them or worship them' (Ex 20:3-5). The sacramental
economy of the new covenant turns our hearts and minds to
Christ in whom the Father has given us everything and revealed
himself fully. And united in Christ's love we discover together,
in mutual respect and in co-responsibility, our lofty vocation
to be and to become a truer and truer image, a living sign of
God our Father. This is the focal point of Christian morality.
And I shall set no other image against it.

The Christian sacraments teach us effectively that there is
no other way to the invisible God than that fraternal love in
which the love of the heavenly Father and of his Son Jesus
Christ and the power of the Holy Spirit shine forth. When, in
and through Jesus Christ, we become for each other co-revealers
of God's goodness and holiness then we realize that true
adoration reflects and expresses itself above all in our shared
effort to bring the work of God in us to completion. When we
join hands on our road to full life we discover that the Lord is
in our midst. And we offer to God the honour and love which
we give to our fellowmen.

Each time when, in the sacraments, we commit and re-
commit ourselves to God's kingdom, we accept gratefully our
mission to create together that divine *milieu* of goodness, justice
and peace in which everyone can grow and become a masterpiece
of God, his true image on earth.

BIBLIOGRAPHY

Eliade, Mircea, *Images and Symbols. Studies in Religious Symbolism* (New York: Sheed & Ward, 1961).

Gustafson, James M., *Treasure in Earthen Vessels. The Church as Human Community* (New York: Harper & Row, 1961).

Bouyer, Louis, *The Word, Church, and Sacraments in Protestantism and Catholicism* (New York: Desclée, 1961).

Fransen, Piet, 'Sacraments: Signs of Faith', *Worship* 37 (Dec. 1962), pp. 31-50.

Jeremias, Joachim, *Infant Baptism in the First Four Centuries* (London: SCM Press, 1960).

—, *The Origins of Infant Baptism: A Further Study in Reply to Kurt Aland* (A.R. Allenson, 1963).

Schillebeeckx, Edward, *Christ, the Sacrament of Encounter with God* (New York and London: Sheed and Ward, 1963).

Martimort, Aimé George, *The Signs of the New Covenant* (Collegeville/Minn.: Liturgical Press, 1963).

Rahner, Karl, *The Church and the Sacraments* (New York: Herder and Herder, 1963).

—, *Nature and Grace* (New York: Sheed & Ward, 1964).

McCabe, Herbert, *The New Creation. Studies on Living in the Church* (London and New York: Sheed and Ward, 1964).

O'Callahan, Denis (ed.), *Sacraments, the Gestures of Christ* (New York: Sheed and Ward, 1964).

O'Neil, Colman E., *Meeting Christ in the Sacraments* (Staten Island, N.Y.: Alba House, 1964).

Schnackenburg, Rudolf, *Baptism in the Thought of Saint Paul* (New York: Herder and Herder, 1964).

—, *The Church in the New Testament* (New York: Herder and Herder, 1965).

Cooke, Bernard, *Christian Sacraments and Christian Personality* (New York: Rinehart and Winston, 1965)

Schmemann, Alexander, *Sacraments and Orthodoxy* (New York: Herder and Herder, 1965).

Semmelroth, Otto, *Church and Sacrament* (Notre Dame: Fides Publishers, 1965).

Häring, Bernard, *A Sacramental Spirituality* (New York: Sheed & Ward, 1965; London: Burns & Oates, 1966, under the title: *A New Covenant*).

Richards, J. Hubert and Peter de Rosa, *Christ in the World. A Study in Baptism, Eucharist, Penance and Marriage* (Milwaukee: Bruce, 1966).

246

Dillenschneider, Clement, *The Dynamic Power of the Sacraments* (St Louis: Herder, 1966).

Moody, Dale, *Baptism: Foundation for Christian Unity* (Philadelphia: Westminster Press, 1967).

White, James, *The Wordliness of Worship* (New York: Oxford Press, 1967).

Küng, Hans (ed.), 'The Sacraments, an Ecumenical Dilemma' in *Concilium* 24 (New York: 1967).

Nocke, Franz Josef, *Sakrament und personaler Vollzug bei Albertus Magnus* (Münster: Aschendorff, 1967).

Bro, Bernard, *The Spirituality of the Sacraments. Doctrine and Practice for Today* (New York: Sheed & Ward, 1968).

Jansen, G.M.A., *The Sacramental We: An Existential Approach to Sacramental Life* (Milwaukee: Bruce, 1968).

Moeller, Charles, *Modern Mentality and Evangelization* (Staten Island: Alba House, 1968).

McCauly, George, *Sacraments for Secular Man* (Denville: Dimension Books, 1969).

McCormack, Arthur, *Christian Initiation* (New York: Hawthorn Books, 1969).

Berkower, Gerrit Cornelis, *The Sacraments* (Grand Rapids: Erdmans, 1969).

O'Shea, Kevin, *The Christian Life, its Idealism and its Realism* (Staten Island: Alba House, 1969).

Häring, Bernard, *Shalom: Peace — The Sacrament of Reconciliation* (New York: Doubleday, Image Book, 1970).

Henri, Denis, *Les sacrements ont-ils un avenir?* (Paris: du Cerf, 1971).

Schillebeeckx, Edward (ed.), 'Sacramental Reconciliation', in *Concilium* 61, 'Religion in the Seventies' (New York: Herder and Herder, 1971).

Schmidt, Herman (ed.), 'Liturgy: Self-expression of the Church' in *Concilium* 72 (New York: Herder and Herder, 1972).

Hellwig, Monica, *The Meaning of the Sacraments* (Dayton: Pflaum-Standard, 1972).

Schmidt, Herman and D. Power (eds.), 'Liturgical Experience of Faith' in *Concilium,* new series, vol. 2, n. 9 (New York, 1973).

Segundo, Juan Luis, *The Sacraments Today* (Maryknoll, N.Y.: Orbis Books, 1974).

Margerie, Bertrand de, *The Sacraments and Social Progress* (Chicago: Franciscan Herald, 1974).

Dulles, Avery Robert, *Models of the Church* (Garden City, N.Y.: Doubleday, 1974).

INDEX

253